Design and Deploy Azure VMware Solutions

Build and Run VMware Workloads Natively on Microsoft Azure

Puthiyavan Udayakumar

Apress®

Design and Deploy Azure VMware Solutions: Build and Run VMware Workloads Natively on Microsoft Azure

Puthiyavan Udayakumar
Abu Dhabi, United Arab Emirates

ISBN-13 (pbk): 978-1-4842-8311-0 ISBN-13 (electronic): 978-1-4842-8312-7
https://doi.org/10.1007/978-1-4842-8312-7

Managing Director, Apress Media LLC: Welmoed Spahr
Acquisitions Editor: Smriti Srivastava
Development Editor: Laura Berendson
Coordinating Editor: Shrikant Vishwakarma
Copy Editor: Mary Behr

Cover designed by eStudioCalamar

Cover image designed by Pexels

Distributed to the book trade worldwide by Springer Science+Business Media New York, 1 New York Plaza, Suite 4600, New York, NY 10004-1562, USA. Phone 1-800-SPRINGER, fax (201) 348-4505, e-mail orders-ny@ springer-sbm.com, or visit www.springeronline.com. Apress Media, LLC is a California LLC and the sole member (owner) is Springer Science + Business Media Finance Inc (SSBM Finance Inc). SSBM Finance Inc is a **Delaware** corporation.

For information on translations, please e-mail booktranslations@springernature.com; for reprint, paperback, or audio rights, please e-mail bookpermissions@springernature.com.

Apress titles may be purchased in bulk for academic, corporate, or promotional use. eBook versions and licenses are also available for most titles. For more information, reference our Print and eBook Bulk Sales web page at www.apress.com/bulk-sales.

Any source code or other supplementary material referenced by the author in this book is available to readers on GitHub via the book's product page, located at www.apress.com/978-1-4842-8311-0. For more detailed information, please visit www.apress.com/source-code.

Printed on acid-free paper

*To my mother and father, who taught me everything
from delinquency to conquest,*

and

*to my beloved better half, thanks for everything you do
for me in thriving in our life journey,*

and

to my dearest brother

Table of Contents

About the Author

Puthiyavan Udayakumar is a cloud infrastructure architect/senior infrastructure consultant with more than 14 years of experience in the information technology industry. He is a Microsoft Certified Azure Solutions Architect Expert, VMware Certified Professional, and VMware vExpert. He has worked as an infrastructure solution architect/senior engineer in designing, deploying, and rolling out complex virtual and cloud infrastructures. He has extensive hands-on experience with products such as Citrix, VMware, Microsoft Virtualization, and cloud technologies. He has a strong knowledge of cloud solution design and deployment, managed cloud services, cloud migration, and multi-cloud infrastructure management services.

About the Technical Reviewer

Doug Scobie's career has spanned three decades, from high school network administration to enterprise IT with global companies. He has spent the last 10 years working for IT vendors specializing in datacenter technologies, cloud computing, and software solutions for transforming customers.

Outside of work, he leads a busy outdoor-focused lifestyle with his wife and two daughters. He has a strong affinity for the ocean, bush, and nature.

Acknowledgments

Great thanks to Smriti Srivastava, Acquisitions Editor at Apress, for continuously shaping this book proposal from day 1. Special thanks to Shrikant Vishwakarma for tirelessly helping to materialize the book. Special thanks to Silembarasan Panneerselvam. Finally, thanks to all of the Apress production team members.

Introduction

VMware workloads can be run natively on Azure with the Azure VMware Solution. Organizations can migrate VMware workloads seamlessly from their data center to Azure and integrate their VMware environment with Azure. While you modernize your applications with Azure native services, you can continue to manage your existing environments with VMware tools. This book provides a 360-degree view of the AVS solution.

In this book, I will explain each essential skill for performing the design and deployment.

This book offers IT professionals the following:

- Helps the Azure VMware administrator and Azure cloud architect upskill with a broader understanding of Azure VMware Solution with real-world case studies and best practices

- The standard AVS framework and design methodology to be applied in the design workshops in the Microsoft AVS solution

- The right blend of knowledge and skills to plan, prepare, and run Microsoft AVS workloads

- A method to analyze and assess end-user needs, define requirements, and define migration methodologies for a well-defined AVS service

- A comprehensive practical guide to managing and securing an AVS environment via site reliability engineering practices along with real examples to automate AVS tasks using Azure PowerShell, Azure CLI, Azure resource templates, and Terraform

CHAPTER 1

Getting Started with AVS

Azure Cloud for VMware Solutions simplifies the process of harnessing the enormous potential of the cloud for an organization. You can migrate VMware workloads to the Azure Cloud using tools, technologies, and skills currently used in cloud consumer environments on-premises.

VMware Cloud Foundation is used to design and deploy Azure VMware Solution. Its software-defined compute, storage, networking, and management provide an end-to-end solution for Infrastructure as a Service (IaaS). Integrated into Microsoft Azure, it provides a hosted platform for the VMware Software Define Datacenter with end support by Microsoft. VMware skills and tools can be leveraged within the global Microsoft Azure infrastructure. VMware workloads can be seamlessly migrated to Azure from on-premises environments without the need to rearchitect applications or retool operations using Azure VMware Solution.

This chapter provides the fundamentals on getting started with AVS, key terminologies, and the foundation needed for Azure VMware Solution. By the end of this chapter, you should be able to understand the following:

- Fundamentals of cloud computing and Microsoft Azure

- The foundation of Azure VMware Solution

- Key Microsoft AVS terminologies

- The inner engineering of AVS

Fundamentals of Cloud Computing and Microsoft Azure

In this section, you'll learn what cloud computing is. A cloud computing service delivers IT resources and applications via the Internet with pay-per-use pricing on a pay-as-you-go basis. Suppose cloud consumers need to share photos with millions of mobile users

1

© Puthiyavan Udayakumar 2022
P. Udayakumar, *Design and Deploy Azure VMware Solutions*, https://doi.org/10.1007/978-1-4842-8312-7_1

or provide services that help enterprises run effectively and efficiently. In that case, the cloud offers rapid access to flexible and low-cost IT resources.

Cloud computing delivers computing functions like compute, network, storage, databases, software, analytics, artificial intelligence, and other IT functions to businesses and consumers through a secured network, thus achieving economies of scale.

The concept of cloud computing has evolved enormously from a confusing and highly insecure concept to one that IT consumers widely embrace. Many cloud consumers, regardless of size, adopt cloud computing to provide services and as crucial part of achieving their IT strategy.

Providers such as Microsoft Azure, Amazon Web Services, Google Cloud, and others own the network-connected devices required for cloud services and implement and allow consumers to utilize cloud services as needed. An illustration of cloud computing's key characteristics is shown in Figure 1-1.

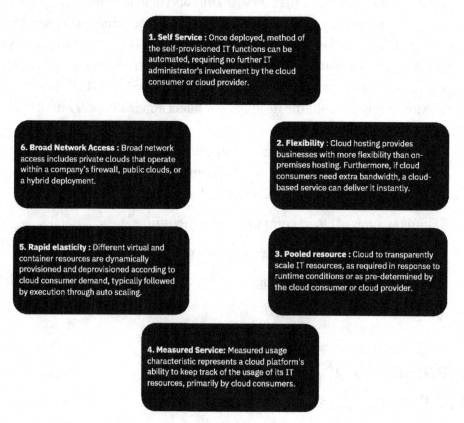

Figure 1-1. *Characteristics of cloud computing*

Consumers of cloud computing don't have to make significant up-front investments in hardware or spend a great deal of time managing it. In contrast, cloud consumers can select the exact type and size of computing resources they need. The cloud consumer IT department needs to run the newest bright idea. Using cloud computing, cloud consumers can access as many resources as they need almost instantly.

In simple terms, cloud computing allows you to access servers, storage, databases, and a wide range of application services over the Internet. Cloud computing service providers such as Azure own and maintain the network-connected hardware necessary for these application services while also providing and using the computing resources required by cloud consumers.

Cloud computing introduces a paradigm shift in how businesses obtain, use, and manage their technology and how they budget and pay for technology services. Adapting the computing environment quickly to changing business requirements enables organizations to optimize spending. As usage patterns fluctuate, capacity can be automatically scaled up or down, and services can be temporarily taken down or shut down permanently as needed. In addition, Azure Cloud services become operational rather than capital expenses with pay-per-use billing.

Top Six Benefits of Cloud Computing

Both small and large organizations use cloud computing technology to store information in the cloud and access it from anywhere using an Internet connection.

Moving to the cloud varies based on the organization, but six advantages are illustrated in Figure 1-2.

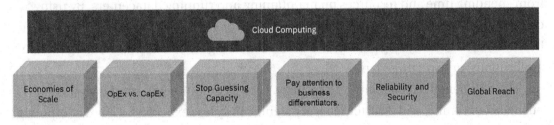

Figure 1-2. *Benefits of cloud computing*

The first benefit is economies of scale: cloud computing is available in both global or local availability to meet security, regulation, and compliance requirements.

Enterprises can lower their variable costs compared to private cloud consumers. Azure, for example, can achieve economies of scale by aggregating usage from hundreds of thousands of customers, which translates into lower prices.

The second benefit is OpEx vs. CapEx: cloud computing eliminates the need for capital expenditures such as hardware and software running in on-premises datacenters, power and cooling, and staffing such as subject matter experts managing complex components 24/7.

Cloud service providers run on a consumption-based model, meaning no upfront cost or no CapEx and only OpEx. Thus, cloud service providers can offer the ability to pay for additional resources only when needed and the ability to stop paying when no longer needed.

The third benefit is forecasting capacity: cloud computing runs in dedicating datacenters connected globally on a worldwide network. The systems are very highly secured and are frequently patched and upgraded to the latest and greatest computing systems. Cloud computing offers excellent benefits compared with on-premises traditional datacenters.

Organizations often end up with expensive idle resources or limited capacity requiring a capacity allocation or procurement decision before deploying applications. Cloud computing allows organizations to stop guessing about their infrastructure requirements for meeting their business needs. With a few minutes' notice, cloud consumers can scale up or down as necessary.

The fourth benefit is focusing attention on business differentiators. Instead of spending time racking, stacking, and powering servers, organizations can focus on their business priorities with cloud computing. This paradigm shift can free organizations from spending time and resources on maintaining and running datacenters. By using cloud computing, businesses can concentrate on projects that differentiate their specific business, such as analyzing petabytes of data, delivering video content, creating mobile applications, or exploring Mars.

The fifth benefit is reliability and security. Cloud computing makes data backup, business continuity, and disaster recovery significantly less expensive. Cloud computing has site-level redundancy. Application and data are replicated and mirrored across the redundant sites or availability zones simply via the subscription.

Modern-day cloud service providers offer security components, controls, policies, compliance needs, and regulations standards which, when utilized correctly, heavily improve the security posture end to end. As a result, the application infrastructure can be highly data secure and can manage potential vulnerabilities and threats.

The sixth benefit is global reach. Cloud computing also provides the advantage of going global in minutes. Organizations can deploy their applications globally in just a few clicks. Organizations can use this technology to provide redundancy across the globe and provide lower latency and better experiences to their customers at a minimal cost. Cloud computing makes it possible for any organization to go global, which was previously only available to the most prominent corporations.

Three Delivery Models of Cloud Computing

Organizations can encounter abnormal freight on their IT infrastructure to meet growing client expectations for speedy, secure, and stable services. As they strive to develop their IT systems' processing compute and storage abilities, these organizations often find that improving and managing a hardy, scalable, and secure IT foundation is prohibitively high-priced.

Cloud computing equips DevOps, DevSecOp, and SRE engineers with the ability to converge on what matters most and withdraw undifferentiated trade such as procurement, support, and retention planning. As cloud computing has increased in prevalence, numerous distinct models and deployment strategies have emerged to fit the specific needs of other users. Each cloud service and deployment organization provides consumers with diverse control, flexibility, and management levels.

Cloud-native and hybrid cloud deployment models are the two available cloud computing deployment models that enterprises focus on. Understanding how each strategy applies to architectural decisions and options is crucial. Figure 1-3 depicts the delivery model of cloud computing.

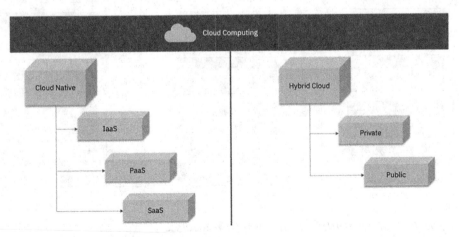

Figure 1-3. *Cloud computing deployment types*

Cloud native refers to when all application components are running on the cloud and the cloud-based application is fully deployed in the cloud. Applications in the cloud have either been developed using cloud technology or migrated from conventional infrastructure to take advantage of the cloud's benefits. In cloud-based applications, low-level infrastructure pieces or higher-level services can be used, abstracting away the management, scalability, and architecture requirements of core infrastructure.

Cloud hybridization refers to workloads run on an on-premises or co-located infrastructure, while also having infrastructure hosted in the cloud. A hybrid cloud environment enables cloud consumers to maximize the agility and flexibility of a public cloud environment while taking advantage of their existing investments.

Imagine using the same tools cloud consumers have used for years to manage all these resources. Cloud consumers can extend the VMware infrastructure on-premises to the Azure Cloud, thereby creating a hybrid cloud. The hybrid cloud enables quick and secure expansion of resources, consolidation of datacenters, building disaster recovery environments, and moving traditional workloads close to cloud-native toolsets to facilitate modernizing applications. The cloud native delivery models is defined by specific elements of IT resources offered by a cloud provider. Cloud computing has three distinct delivery models called Infrastructure as a Service, Platform as a Service (PaaS), and Software as a Service (SaaS), depicted in Figure 1-4.

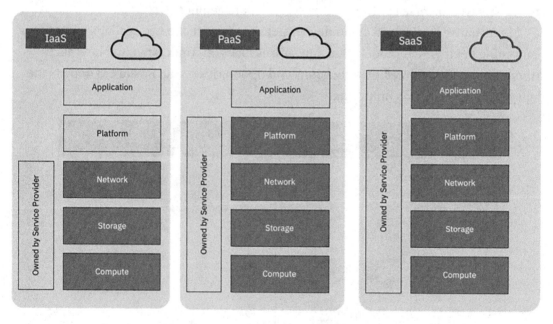

Figure 1-4. *Cloud computing deployment models*

Infrastructure as a Service is about delivering compute, network, storage, and backup as a service that can be consumed on a yearly, monthly, or hourly basis. Resource units and their prices are provided via a catalogue.

Platform as a Service is all about IaaS with an integrated set of middleware functions. Software development and deployment tools mean you have a constant way to create, modify, update, and deploy an application in the cloud environment.

Software as a Service is when the application is hosted on top of PaaS or IaaS, either dedicated or shared. In this deployment model, cloud consumers only pay per the app's consumption. The cloud service provider fully manages the underlying infrastructure and platform.

Now let's explore the Azure Cloud.

Microsoft Azure Overview

Azure is Microsoft's hyperscaler cloud offering. Azure offers 200 or more IT services online and enables businesses to accomplish almost all their needs in modern digital environments. The services are sets of integrated tools, prebuilt templates, and managed services to make building and operating enterprise, mobile, web, and IoT apps easier. Many of the products in Azure leverage the tooling skills cloud consumers already have and the technology they already understand.

Azure supports the broadest range of Microsoft operating systems, programming languages, frameworks, tools, databases, and devices. With Docker integration, cloud consumers can run Linux containers; build apps with JavaScript, Python, .NET, PHP, Java, and Node.js; and create back ends for any device. Millions of users trust the Azure service.

Azure has features such as networking with secure private connections, hybrid databases, storage solutions, and data residency and encryption to integrate with existing IT environments. With Azure Stack, cloud consumers can bring the Azure model of app development and deployment into their datacenters.

Microsoft provides industry-leading protection and privacy to cloud consumers. The EU's data protection authorities have recognized Azure for its commitment to strict EU privacy laws. At the time of writing this book, Microsoft is also the first global cloud provider to adopt the new ISO 27018 international privacy standard.

Cloud consumers only pay for what they use with Azure's pay-as-you-go services. At the time of writing this book, Microsoft manages Azure's worldwide network of datacenters in 26 regions (more than Amazon Web Services and Google Cloud combined). With this fast-growing global footprint, cloud consumers can run apps and expect excellent performance. Moreover, Azure is the country's first multinational cloud service.

Azure's predictive analytics services redefine business intelligence, including machine learning, Cortana Analytics, and stream analytics. By analyzing cloud consumers' structured, unstructured, and streaming IoT data, these analytics can improve customer service and uncover new business opportunities.

No workload is too big or too small for Azure. At the time of writing this book, Azure is used by more than 66% of Fortune 500 companies because it offers enterprise-grade service level agreements, 24/7 tech support, and round-the-clock service monitoring.

Generally, large businesses integrate Azure into their existing environment by migrating from a lower one. Cloud computing is not just about moving workloads to the cloud. With constant improvements and new features, it is much more.

Cloud consumers access Azure services via a web-based unified console that replaces command-line tools. The Azure portal can be used by businesses to manage Azure tenant subscriptions, and IT can deploy, manage, and monitor all subscribed IT services. Customized IT dashboards can be created in the Azure portal so that cloud consumers can see structured views of IT services they consume. Azure portal users can also customize accessibility options for a better experience.

The first key concept to start with is to broadly understand the foundation of Azure Cloud. Azure Cloud mainly offers cloud high availability, scalability, reliability, elasticity, agility, geo-distribution, resiliency, security, and Edge to provide the end users maximum uptime. Figure 1-5 depicts the Azure foundation.

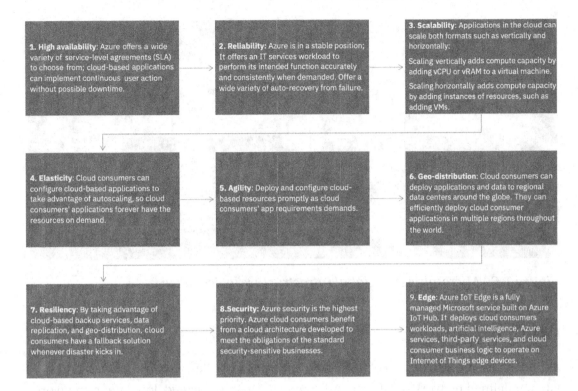

Figure 1-5. *Microsoft Azure's foundation*

The second concept to understand in the Azure global infrastructure is that it is developed with two key elements. The first is the physical infrastructure, and the second is the connective network components. The physical infrastructure comprises 200+ physical datacenters organized into regions and connected by one of the most extensive interconnected networks.

The Azure global infrastructure is classified into the following: Azure regions, Azure geography, Azure availability zones, and sets. Figure 1-6 depicts the Azure logical building blocks.

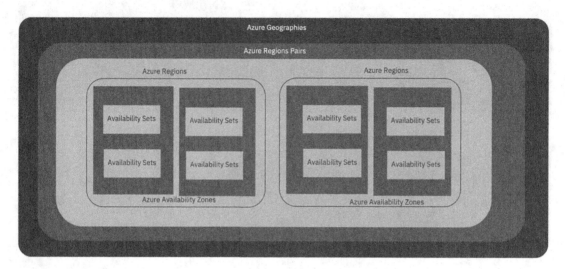

Figure 1-6. Microsoft Azure global infrastructure logical view

Azure Region

Azure regions are a collection of physical datacenters installed within a security and latency-defined network perimeter and connected via a dedicated, low-latency network.

Dedicated regional low-latency networks connect each region's datacenters within a latency-defined perimeter. Azure's design ensures optimal performance and security for all regions.

With Microsoft Azure, cloud consumers have the freedom to install and configure applications on demand. The Azure region is equipped with a variety of IT services and pricing.

A pair of regions is what Azure calls a logical boundary, and regional teams contain two geographically defined regions.

Azure regions are defined by a specific geographical boundary, typically hundreds of miles apart. Figure 1-7 depicts the Azure region.

Figure 1-7. *Microsoft Azure geography*

There are more Azure regions globally than any other cloud provider. Because of the global presence, Azure architects can bring cloud consumer applications close by putting them in these regions no matter where cloud consumer end users are located. The global regions provide better scalability and redundancy, and cloud consumers can also maintain data residency.

Azure Geography

Azure geography is composed of regions that meet various compliance and data residency requirements. As much as possible, Azure geography enables cloud consumers to keep their apps and data close to their business. Azure geography is fault-tolerant to withstand region failure via the dedicated high-capacity networking elements of Azure.

By utilizing dedicated high-capacity networking elements, Azure geography is fault-tolerant to withstand region failures. There are at least two regions separated by a considerable physical distance in each geography, which is vital to Azure Cloud. This pattern allows Azure to achieve disaster recovery in the region.

Microsoft encourages customers to replicate their data across multiple Azure regions. Microsoft promises network performance between regions of 2 milliseconds or less.

Azure Availability Zones

Microsoft Azure developed a cloud pattern named availability zones to achieve maximum availability for IT services that demand maximum uptime. Locations are unique to a region. Datacenters in each zone/region are equipped with independent power, cooling, and networking. Microsoft Azure mandates a minimum of three availability zones enabled within each region wherever they exist.

In Azure, availability zones are physically separate locations within a region that can withstand local failures. There can be a variety of failures, including software and hardware failures, earthquakes, floods, and fires. Due to Azure's redundancy and logical isolation, it has a high degree of fault tolerance. Each availability zone-enabled region has a minimum of three availability zones for resiliency.

Availability zones apply only to the available services and not all services offered by Azure.

By deploying IT services to two or more availability zones, the business achieves maximum availability. Microsoft Azure offers a service-level agreement of 99.99% uptime for virtual machines provided if two or more VMs are deployed into two or more zones.

For the first-time learner, it isn't easy to differentiate between availability zones and availability sets. Availability sets allow IT service to create two or more virtual machines in different physical server racks in an Azure DC. Microsoft Azure offers a service level agreement of 99.95% with an availability set whereas it provides a service level agreement of a 99.99% with availability zones. Figure 1-8 depicts the Azure availability zones.

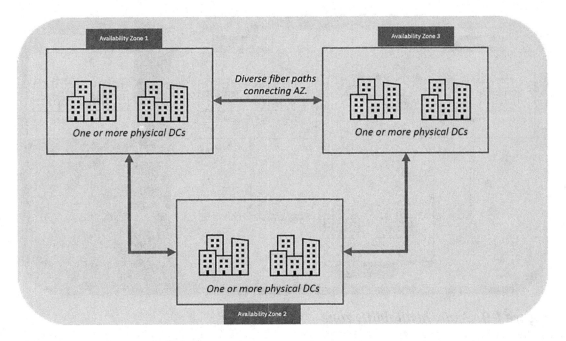

Figure 1-8. *Azure availability zone*

Microsoft Azure offers three types of availability zones: zonal services, zone-redundant services, and zone non-regional services.

Microsoft Azure zonal services are IT services such as virtual machines (VMs), managed disks used in VMs, and public IP addresses used in VMs. To achieve the HA design pattern, the IT function must explicitly install zonal services into two or more zones.

Microsoft Azure zone-redundant services are services such as zone-redundant storage and SQL databases. To use the availability zones with ZRS and SQL DB services, you must specify the option to make them zone-redundant during deployment.

Microsoft Azure Non-Regional Services

Azure services are constantly ready from Azure geographies and are resilient to zone-wide blackouts and region-wide blackouts.

Azure services enabled by availability zones are designed to offer the right reliability and flexibility. There are two ways this can be configured. Depending on the configuration, they can be zone-redundant, with automatic replication across zones, or zonal, with instances pinned to specific zones. Clients can combine these patterns. Figure 1-9 depicts the zone-redundant setup.

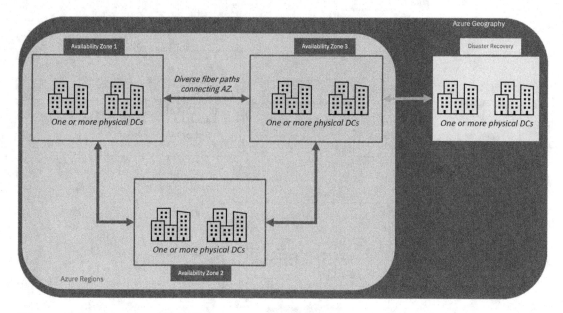

Figure 1-9. *Azure availability zone*

High availability zones and protection from large-scale phenomena and regional disasters are essential to some organizations. Azure regions are designed to protect against localized disasters by utilizing availability zones and protection from regional or large geographic disasters by using disaster recovery by utilizing another region.

The third key concept is to understand FinTech management, a choice offered by Azure. By grouping your Azure subscriptions, you can take bulk actions on them. You can manage your subscriptions and resources efficiently by creating an Azure management group hierarchy tailored to your business needs. You can apply governance conditions to any Azure service, such as policies, access controls, or full-fledged blueprints using the full platform integration. You can manage resources better and get visibility into all your resources. Via a single dashboard, you can monitor costs and usage.

Microsoft Azure requires you to assign virtual machines to Azure resource groups when you create them. Even though this grouping structure may seem like just another form of administration, you can use it for better infrastructure governance and cost management. Figure 1-10 depicts the Azure infrastructure governance and cost management.

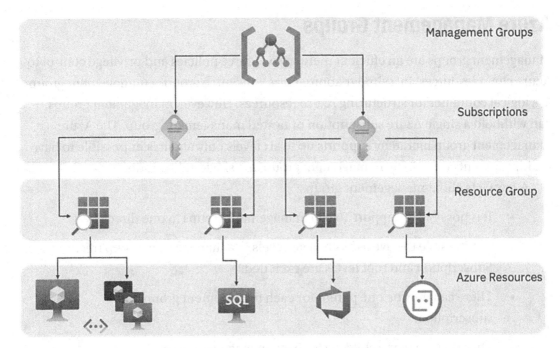

Figure 1-10. *Azure infrastructure governance and cost management*

Let's walk through each level of organization from the bottom up after looking at the top-down hierarchy:

- A resource is an instance of a service cloud that consumers create, such as a virtual machine, storage, or SQL database.

- Resource groups act as logical containers that Azure uses to deploy and manage resources, such as web apps, databases, and storage accounts.

- An account subscription is a grouping of user accounts and the resources they create. A certain number of resources can be created and used per subscription. Organizations can use subscriptions to manage costs and the resources that users, teams, and projects create.

- You can manage access, policies, and compliance across multiple subscriptions with management groups. All subscriptions inherit the conditions applied to the management group in a management group.

Let's get started with the Azure resource group.

Azure Management Groups

Management groups are an efficient method to enforce policies and privilege control to Azure cloud resources. In a similar approach as a resource group, a management group is a logical container for structuring Azure resources. However, management groups can withhold a single Azure subscription or nested management group. The Azure management group hierarchy supports up to six levels only and it is impossible to have multiple parents on a single management group or a single subscription.

A few facts about management groups:

- It is possible to support 10,000 management groups in one directory.

- It is possible to have a depth of six levels in a management group tree. Subscription and root levels are excluded.

- There can only be one parent for each management group and subscription.

- There can be many children for each management group.

- All subscriptions and management groups are grouped into a single hierarchy in each directory.

Azure Subscriptions

An Azure subscription is automatically initiated as soon as a user signs up for Azure Cloud Kick Start and all the resources created within the subscription. However, enterprises or businesses can create additional subscriptions that are tied to an Azure account. Other subscriptions use cases are applicable whenever companies want to have logical groupings for Azure resources, especially for reports on resources consumed by departments.

Microsoft Azure subscriptions are offered in the following three categories:

- Free Trial: Completely free access for a limited time per account for limited resources. Expired accounts cannot be reused.

- Pay-As-You-Go: Pay only for resources consumed in Azure. No CapEx involved and cancellation is possible at any time.

- Pay-As-You-Go Dev/Test: A subscription for Visual Studio that can be used for dev and testing. No production usage.

For a Microsoft Azure subscription, each one has a unique identifier called a subscription ID. Microsoft recommends using the subscription ID to recognize the subscription.

Azure Resource Group

A resource group is a logical collection of virtual machines, containers, storage accounts, virtual networks, web apps, databases, and dedicated servers. Users typically group related resources for an application, divided into production and non-production, but you may decide to further subdivide on demand.

There is a logical group for all Azure services subscribed to a resource group. Azure admins can deploy and run all services integrated with a specific app by grouping them. Maintaining an enterprise array of services within a silo is now unnecessary.

It is impossible to attach an Azure resource to more than one resource group. You can move resources from one group to another whenever you delete a resource group. All resources associated with a resource group are deleted when the resource group is deleted.

Azure Resource Manager

Azure Resource Manager (ARM) is a crucial component for managing underlying IT resources. To avoid operational overhead in managing all Azure services separately and to quickly deploy and manage Azure services, Microsoft developed a solution named Azure Resource Manager.

Azure Resource Manager is a deployment and management service that runs in Azure, and it interacts with most Azure services.

Both the Azure portal and the Azure command-line tools work by using Azure Resource Manager, which permits cloud consumers to deploy multiple Azure resources on the go quickly.

Azure Resource Manager makes it possible to reproduce any redeployment with the consistent outcome if there is a failure of the existing build.

The following are the most popular Azure resources and services:

- Azure virtual machines are an IaaS from Microsoft, and Microsoft manages the underlying physical compute, network, and storage. Cloud consumers manage the operating system, apps, and data run on top of the VM.

- Availability sets protect VMs with fault domains. Fault domains protect VMs from a hardware failure in a hardware rack.

- Scale sets allow the business to set up auto-scale rules to scale horizontally when needed.

- Azure App Service makes it easy to host web apps in the cloud because it's a PaaS service that removes the management burden from the user.

- App Service apps run inside an App Service plan that specifies the number of VMs and the configuration of those VMs.

- Containers allow cloud consumers to create an image of an application and everything needed to run it.

- Azure Container Instances (ACIs) allow cloud consumers to run containers for minimal cost.

- Azure Kubernetes Service (AKS) is a managed service that makes it easy to host Kubernetes clusters in the cloud.

- Azure Cosmos DB is a NoSQL database for unstructured data.

- Azure SQL Database is a Microsoft-managed relational database.

- Azure Database is a Microsoft-managed MySQL database.

- An Azure virtual network provides Azure services to communicate with several others and the Internet.

- Azure Load Balancer can distribute traffic from the Internet across various VMs in a dedicated vNet.

- ExpressRoute allows cloud consumers to have a high-bandwidth connection to Azure of up to 10 Gbps by attaching to a Microsoft Enterprise Edge router.

- Azure DNS accommodates fast DNS responses and high domain availability.

- Azure Disk Storage is virtual disk storage specific to Azure VMs. It manages disks, which removes the operation burden of disks.

- Azure Files allows cloud consumers to have disk space in the cloud to map to a drive on-premises.

- Azure Blob Storage offers Hot, Cool, and Archive storage tiers based on how long cloud consumers intend to store data.

- Azure DevOps uses development collaboration tools such as pipelines, Kanban boards, Git repositories, and comprehensive automated and cloud-based non-functional testing.

- Azure Virtual Desktop makes apps and desktops readily available to multiple users from almost any device from anywhere.

Azure Management Offerings

Management in Azure is the foundation building block for deployment and operation support of the resources in Azure. Management tools can be divided into visual (graphical user interface, GUI) and code-based tools at a high level. Figure 1-11 depicts the Azure management tools classification.

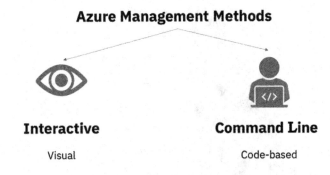

Figure 1-11. *Azure management methods*

Azure's visual tools provide full access to all functionality in a visually friendly manner. It may be less valuable to use visual tools when you're trying to deploy a large number of interdependent resources and have multiple configuration options.

In most cases, a code-based tool is the better choice when configuring Azure resources quickly and at scale. The correct commands and parameters may take some time to understand, but they can be saved into files and used repeatedly. Setup and configuration code can also be stored, versioned, and maintained in a source code-management tool such as Git. When developers write application code, they use this approach to manage hardware and cloud resources. It is called Infrastructure as Code (IaC).

In IaC, two approaches are available: imperative and declarative. The imperative code details each step required to achieve the desired result. Contrary to declarative code, imperative code specifies only the desired outcome, and it allows an interpreter to determine how to achieve it. It is crucial to distinguish declarative code tools from those based on logic, as declarative code tools provide a more robust way of deploying dozens or hundreds of resources simultaneously and reliably.

For managing your cloud environment, Microsoft offers a variety of tools and services, each geared toward a different scenario and user.

Management refers to the assignments and methods required to maintain IT applications and the resources supporting an organization's business. Azure has several services and tools that operate together to give complete management for cloud consumers. Figure 1-12 depicts the Azure management methods.

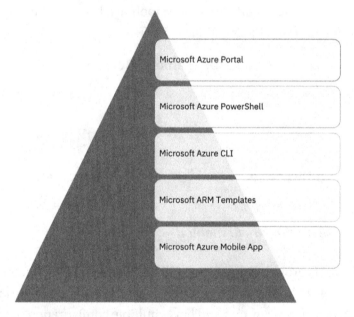

Figure 1-12. *Microsoft Azure management methods*

Microsoft Azure portal: Deploy, run, and monitor everything via a single management plane from web apps, databases, virtual machines, virtual networks, storage, and Visual Studio team projects to the aggregate cloud-native application from a unified console.

When you sign up for the Azure portal, you can take a tour of it. If you're not familiar with the portal, taking the tour is a good use of your time.

The Azure portal provides a web-based interface that accesses almost all Azure features. Azure's portal provides an intuitive GUI to view all of the services you are using, create new services, and configure them. This is how most people engage with Azure for the first time. As your Azure usage grows, you will likely choose a more repeatable, code-centric approach to managing your Azure resources. The initial view in Azure is shown in Figure 1-13.

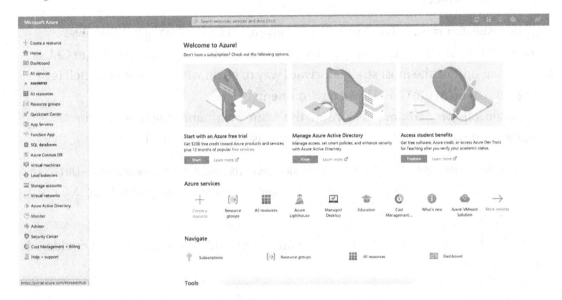

Figure 1-13. *Microsoft Azure portal*

Microsoft Azure PowerShell: Azure PowerShell is a kit of cmdlets for operating Azure resources immediately from the PowerShell command-line interface. Microsoft developed Azure PowerShell to make it easy to read, write, and execute code to provide powerful automation features for IT support functions. AVD administrators can use Azure PowerShell when they want to automate code.

Microsoft PowerShell 7.x and the following higher version are recommended.

Use the following command to check your PowerShell version:

```
$PSVersionTable.PSVersion
```

Use the following command to install the Azure PowerShell module (Az PowerShell module):

```
Install-Module -Name Az -Scope CurrentUser -Repository
PSGallery -Force
```

Use the following command to connect to an Azure account (Az PowerShell module):

```
Connect-AzAccount
```

Microsoft Azure CLI: The Azure CLI is convenient for deploying in Windows, macOS, and Linux environments. The Azure command-line interface, the Azure CLI, is an excellent option; the most straightforward way to begin with Azure PowerShell is by trying it out in an Azure Cloud Shell environment.

Use the following command to install the Azure command-line interface on Windows or download and deploy the latest release of the Azure CLI:

```
Invoke-WebRequest -Uri https://aka.ms/installazurecliwindows -OutFile
.\AzureCLI.msi; Start-Process msiexec.exe -Wait -ArgumentList
'/I AzureCLI.msi /quiet'; rm .\AzureCLI.msi
```

Use the following command to sign in with your cloud consumer account credentials in the browser:

```
az login
```

Microsoft Azure Cloud Shell: The Azure cloud shell is the completely online version, so there's no need of any deployment. Upon the first launch of the Cloud Shell, you choose the environment to be used. The Cloud Shell presents two choices: bash and PowerShell. Cloud consumers can change the choice after it is configured the first time.

To reach Azure Cloud Shell, click the Cloud Shell button in the Microsoft Azure portal. Figure 1-14 depicts the Azure Cloud Shell icon.

Figure 1-14. *Azure Cloud Shell*

Upon clicking the icon, the console loads. Once bash or the PowerShell environment is selected, you create an Azure storage account; however, you need an active subscription. Figure 1-15 depicts the Azure Cloud Shell at launch.

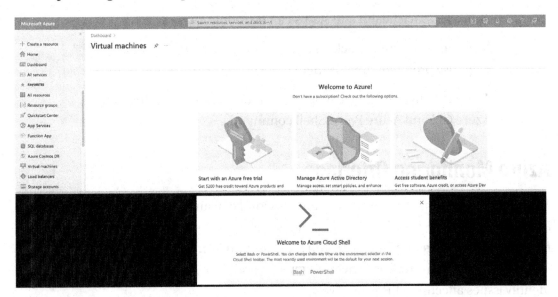

Figure 1-15. *Azure Cloud Shell with bash and PowerShell*

Type the following command to get knowledge about PowerShell in Azure Cloud Shell:

```
Get-Help.
```

Microsoft ARM templates: The Azure CLI and Azure PowerShell both allow Azure administrators/developers to set up and tear down one Azure resource or orchestrate an infrastructure comprised of hundreds of resources. However, there's a better way to do this.

Azure Resource Manager templates (ARM templates) allow Azure administrators/developers to describe resources in a declarative JSON format. As a result, the entire ARM template is verified before any code is executed, ensuring that the resources are correctly created and connected. The template then orchestrates parallel creation. Consequently, if Azure administrators/developers need 50 instances of the same resource, all of them will be created simultaneously. Developers, DevOps professionals, and IT professionals need to specify each resource's desired state and configuration in the ARM template, and the template takes care of the rest. Scripts can even be executed before or after a resource has been set up using templates.

Microsoft Azure Mobile App: While users are away from their computers, they can still access Azure resources via the Azure mobile app. Consumers can use the app for the following tasks:

- Azure resource health and status can be monitored.

- A web app or virtual machine can be restarted to catch alerts, diagnose problems, and fix them quickly.

- Azure resources can be managed for cloud consumers using the Azure CLI and Azure PowerShell commands.

Azure Monitoring Offerings

Microsoft Azure Monitor: Azure Monitor lets cloud consumers maximize the functional and non-functional KPIs of applications and services. It gives an end-to-end solution for gathering, interpreting, and acting on the data feed from the Azure tenant cloud and integrating it with on-premises environments. In addition, it offers golden signals to identify issues affecting KPIs proactively.

Azure Monitor can perform tasks such as metrics gathering, storing logs, and providing insights.

- **Metrics:** It automatically gathers metrics (defined key performance indicators) into Azure Monitor Metrics.

- **Logs:** It maintains diagnostic configurations, collecting platform logs, and key performance indicators in Azure Monitor Logs.

- **Insight:** Azure Insight is available for the cloud consumer's subscribed service and presents a well-defined monitoring experience for the consuming service.

- **Service health:** Microsoft runs an Azure status web page where cloud consumers can observe information in each region where Azure runs. While it is a healthy aspect of overall Azure health, the immense range of the web page doesn't make it the common powerful way to get an overview of the health of cloud consumer-specific services. Instead, Azure Service Health can provide cloud consumers with a picture of consumed resources.

To reach Azure Monitor services, click the Monitor button in the Microsoft Azure portal. Figure 1-16 depicts Azure Monitor.

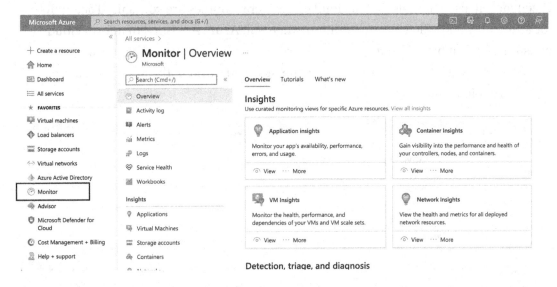

Figure 1-16. *Azure Monitor*

Figure 1-17 of the Azure Monitor dashboard provides an overview.

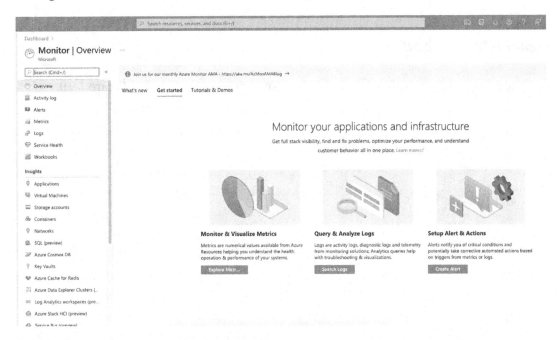

Figure 1-17. *Azure Monitor dashboard*

Microsoft Azure Advisor: Microsoft Azure Advisor offers recommendations and impacts of services regarding cost, security, reliability, performance, and operational excellence. It also guarantees that cloud consumer resources are configured accurately for availability and efficiency. In addition, Microsoft Azure Advisor can inform cloud consumers about predicaments in Azure services configuration to avoid trouble.

To reach Azure Advisor services, click the Advisor button in the Microsoft Azure portal as depicted in Figure 1-18.

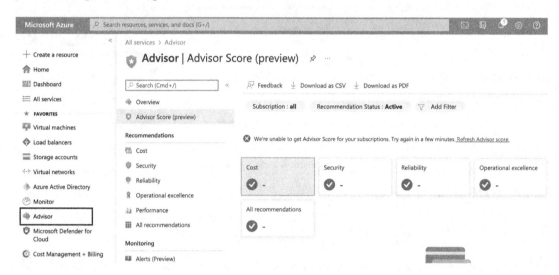

Figure 1-18. *Azure Advisor*

The Azure advisor dashboard provides an overview, as depicted in Figure 1-19.

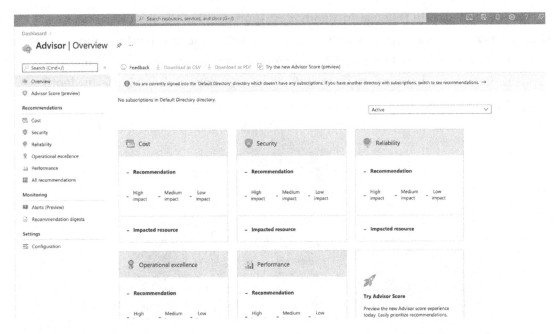

Figure 1-19. *Azure Advisor overview*

Azure Security and Compliance Offerings

Security is one of several critical aspects of any design. Assuring cloud consumers that their business applications and data are secure is essential. A data compromise can destroy an organization's reputation and create financial wickedness.

When end users, end user devices, and organization data are contained inside the organization's firewall, it's assumed to be trusted. This implicit trust can be an easy target for a malicious hacker.

Critical defense in-depth and identify key security technologies and methods to promote a defense-in-depth strategy into reality.

Identities, devices, infrastructure security, network protection, application security, and data encryption are essential and integral to any security design. Securing cloud consumers' networks from attacks and unauthorized access is vital.

Microsoft uses a layered path to security, both in datacenters and across Azure services. A key component to know is defense-in-depth. The zero trust model drives security researchers, engineers, and architects to design using an applied security approach and layered maneuvering to guard their resources provisioned across the cloud and on-premises with shared responsibility.

Defense-in-depth: Defense-in-depth is an approach that applies a series of tools to slow the advancement of an attack to acquire unapproved access to information. Each layer gets protected so that a subsequent layer is already in place to prevent further exposure if even one layer is compromised. Figure 1-20 depicts the defense-in-depth process.

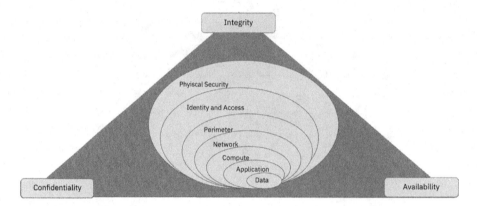

Figure 1-20. Defense-in-depth

Microsoft Azure offers a wide variety of security functionality via three security-integrated services:

- Protects against security threats via Microsoft Azure Security Center

- Detects and responds to security threats via Microsoft Azure Sentinel

- Stores and manages secrets via Microsoft Azure Key Vault

Azure Security Center: Azure Security Center (renamed to Microsoft Defender for Cloud) is a consolidated infrastructure security control system that extends the security posture. It provides exceptional threat protection across hybrid workloads running in the multi-cloud, including the cloud consumer's private cloud.

Keeping cloud consumers' IT resources protected is a collective work between the cloud service provider, Microsoft Azure, and the cloud consumers. Cloud consumers have to make sure data and app workloads are secure when running in the Microsoft Cloud. At the same time, when you move to IaaS, there is more customer responsibility than there was in PaaS and SaaS. Azure Security Center provides cloud consumers with a rich set of tools to strengthen their networks and secure their benefits.

Azure Security Center covers three common critical security difficulties:

- **Swiftly changing workloads:** Azure Security Center can address the strengths and challenges of the cloud.

- **Frequently complex attacks:** Cloud consumers must secure workloads in public cloud workloads.

- **Security professionals are few in number:** The number of security alerts and alerting rules is far higher than the number of security professionals with the required knowledge and practice to ensure that cloud consumers' environments are protected.

To reach Azure Security Center services, click the security center button in the Microsoft Azure portal. The Azure Security Center dashboard provides an overview, as depicted in Figure 1-21.

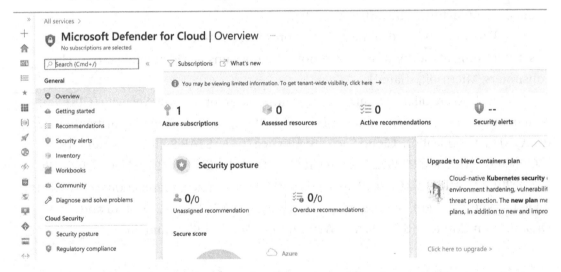

Figure 1-21. *Microsoft defender for Cloud*

Azure Key Vault: Azure Key Vault is a cloud-native service for securely saving and reaching secrets (keys). A key is anything cloud consumers want to control access to, such as API keys, passwords, certificates, or cryptographic keys.

The Key Vault service supports two types: vaults and managed hardware security module (HSM) pools. Azure Key Vault strengthens the Transport Layer Security protocol to guard data when moving among Azure Key Vault and clients.

Azure Sentinel: Azure Sentinel is Microsoft's cloud-native SIEM that presents exceptional security analytics for the entire cloud enterprise at a cloud scale. Microsoft's SIEM solution is designed as a cloud-native security-monitoring platform that uses the power of the cloud for analytics and detections. Azure Sentinel provides straightforward amalgamation with flags and statistics from security solutions despite Microsoft Azure or any other cloud inclusive of a private cloud. Azure Sentinel combines machine learning algorithms, global security investigation, and the extent and intensity of the essential security data available to Microsoft as a significant enterprise vendor. Azure Sentinel helps cloud consumers discover known and unknown attack vectors, recognizing threats across all steps.

Azure Compliance: Azure compliance has 90+ certifications, including covering 50 distinct global regions and countries, the US, the European Union, Germany, Japan, the United Kingdom, India, and China. And you get more than 35 compliance offerings particular to the requirements of critical industries, including government, education, finance, manufacturing, health, and media.

Regulatory compliance in Azure Policy presents built-in action representations to observe a listing of the controls and compliance domains based on obligations (cloud consumers, Microsoft, shared).

Microsoft Azure offers global coverage with Center for Internet Security (CIS) benchmarks, Cloud Security Alliance (CSA) STAR Attestation, Cloud Security Alliance (CSA) STAR Certification, Cloud Security Alliance (CSA) STAR Self-Assessment, ISO/IEC 20000-1:2018, ISO 22301:2019, ISO/IEC 27001:2013, ISO/IEC 27017:2015, ISO/IEC 27018:2019, ISO/IEC 27701:2019, ISO 9001:2015, System and Organization Controls (SOC) 1 Type 2, System and Organization Controls (SOC) 2 Type 2, System and Organization Controls (SOC) 3, and Web Content Accessibility Guidelines.

Getting Started with Azure VMware Solution

In this section, you'll learn what Azure VMware Solution is. Over the years, organizations that run virtualized environments on-premises have faced many challenges, including incurring significant capital expenditures, spending a lot of resources, and spending a lot of time managing and maintaining the servers. Additionally, in this model, licenses are typically purchased with elaborate and lengthy enterprise license agreements (ELAs), which are inflexible and unable to scale rapidly to meet ever-changing business requirements.

Is it possible to leverage cloud consumers' current investments while implementing virtualization in the cloud era?

In a partnership with Microsoft, VMware offers a streamlined approach for migrating VMware environments. VMware workloads can be deployed in a hybrid cloud architecture with Microsoft Azure Cloud, enabling cloud consumers to achieve significant benefits while using the familiar tools, resources, and capabilities of VMware deployments on-premises. VMware and Microsoft enable IT departments to create dynamic, virtualized pools of resources from static servers and networks. These resources can be provisioned on-demand based on evolving business and technical needs.

More and more organizations are moving to the cloud, and Microsoft and VMware's Azure VMware Solution, a jointly-engineered offering, speeds up the transition and reduces long-term costs. Microsoft develops, operates, and supports Azure VMware Solutions, backed by VMware and cloud-verified by the company. Figure 1-22 provide an overview of Azure VMware Solution.

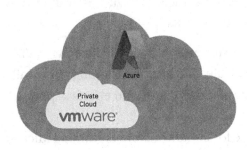

Figure 1-22. *Azure VMware Solution*

Key AVS Capabilities

- Cloud customers can immediately access Azure's high availability, disaster recovery, and backup services, minimizing risk and ensuring business continuity for their critical workloads.

- Whenever cloud consumers want to consolidate, retire, or expand their existing datacenters, they can access additional capacity on demand. When cloud consumers move to Azure, they will be able to use the same VMware tools they are already familiar with from on-premises environments, such as VMware vSphere, vSAN, and vCenter. vSphere-based applications can be redeployed to Azure without requiring refactoring.

- Cloud consumers can manage their existing environments with VMware tools they're familiar with, while modernizing their applications with native Azure management, security, and services. Taking on modernization one step at a time is easy with Azure VMware Solution. They can utilize native VMware tools and management experiences to build cloud competencies and modernize over time.

- AVS leverages VMware VCF for a VMware-compliant architecture.

- With the Azure hybrid benefit, cloud consumers can bring their own Windows Server and SQL Server licenses with Software Assurance to Azure. As part of the Azure VMware Solution, customers receive free extended security updates for Windows Server 2008 and SQL Server 2008 R2 for up to three years after the end-of-extended-support date. With Reserved Instances for Azure VMware Solution, cloud consumers can reduce costs.

AVS increases cloud consumers' productivity by moving VMware workloads to Azure and utilizing the elasticity, scale, and fast provisioning only available via the cloud. Cloud consumer productivitiy means saving time and efforts in phyiscal provisoning compute, storage and networks.

Azure is the best choice for cloud consumers running Microsoft Windows and SQL Server workloads, based on licensing and support options from Microsoft.

Cloud consumers can get on-demand access to additional capacity when they consolidate, retire, or expand existing datacenters.

They can move to Azure seamlessly using VMware's HCX technology and continue to manage their environment using the same VMware tools they already know, such as vSphere Client, NSX-T, Power CLI, or any popular DevOps toolchain.

They can ensure operational continuity when redeploying vSphere-based applications to Azure and avoid the complexity of application refactoring.

Using Microsoft's Azure operating platform and back-end infrastructure, it is possible to run VMware vSphere, VMware vSAN, and VMware NSX-T natively and at scale. Cloud consumers' workloads can run on a single-tenant, fully managed, bare-metal Azure infrastructure, eliminating the hassles of procuring, deploying, and managing a hardware infrastructure. Azure ExpressRoute is a high-speed, low-latency connectivity option for cloud consumers.

VMware Solutions for Azure are based on VMware Cloud Foundation, a comprehensive provider of compute, storage, networking, and management software deployed on Azure with integrated Azure services. By leveraging the global Microsoft Azure infrastructure, VMware customers can utilize their existing skills and tools. Using the Azure VMware Solution, VMware workloads can be seamlessly migrated or extended from on-premises to Azure without requiring costly rearchitecture or retooling of operations. Cloud consumers can build, run, manage, and secure applications across VMware environments and Microsoft Azure with familiar and established VMware tools, skills, and processes.

In Azure VMware Solution, a bare-metal Azure infrastructure is used to build vSphere clusters running on private clouds. Clusters can be expanded to 16 hosts over time, starting with a minimum of three hosts. vCenter Server and NSX Manager, the management tools for Azure VMware Solutions, are configured to be available 99.9% of the time.

A VMware-validated Azure VMware Solution includes ongoing testing and validation of enhancements and upgrades. It allows cloud consumers to focus on developing and running workloads in their private clouds while Microsoft manages and maintains their private cloud infrastructure and software.

Cloud-to-cloud networking allows Azure services or vNets to be integrated with private clouds via SLAs. Azure VMware Solution connects a cloud consumer's on-premises environment to the Azure VMware Solution private cloud. Figure 1-23 provides an integrated view of AVS.

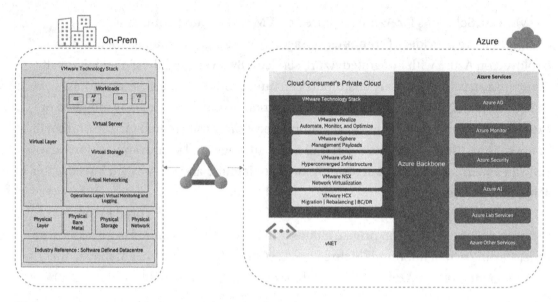

Figure 1-23. *Azure VMware integrated view*

Figure 1-23 shows the relationship between private clouds and virtual networks in Azure, Azure services, and on-premises environments.

VMware vSphere: Uses the server virtualization platform designed for modern hybrid clouds to run existing applications along with modern containerized applications in Microsoft Azure.

VMware vSAN: Improves business agility while reducing costs with VMware vSAN, the enterprise-class storage virtualization software.

Azure VMware Solution uses hyper-converged Azure infrastructure hosts. High-end hosts are equipped with the processor of Intel 18-core and dual 2.3GHz processors plus 576GB of memory. Additionally, high-end hosts have two vSAN disk groups with 15.36TB of SSD for VMware vSAN's basic capacity tier and 3.2TB (NVMe) of VMware vSAN's cache tier.

VMware NSX-T: Connects and secures apps across datacenters, clouds, and containers, all from one interface. Cloud consumers manage most cluster configurations or operations via vSphere and NSX-T Manager. Each host of a cluster has access to their local storage through vSAN. The solution includes four 25 Gbps NICs per ESXi host, two of which are designated for ESXi system traffic and two for workload traffic.

VMware HCX: Continuity and workload rebalancing are built into the tool for extending the on-premises environments of cloud consumers into the cloud.

An Azure VMware Solution private cloud can be connected to a cloud consumer's on-premises environment using ExpressRoute Global Reach. Cloud consumers connect circuits directly at the Microsoft Enterprise Edge (MSEE) level. Connecting via a virtual network (VNet) with an ExpressRoute circuit to on-premises requires an Azure subscription. Consequently, VNet gateways (ExpressRoute Gateways) cannot transmit traffic, which means cloud consumers can attach two circuits to the same gateway, but it won't transmit traffic between them.

The Azure VMware Solution environments each have their own ExpressRoute region (their own virtual MSEE devices), so cloud consumers can connect Global Reach to "local" peering locations. Azure VMware Solution customers can connect multiple instances to the same peering location in a single region.

An Azure VMware Solution provides an on-premises and Azure-based private cloud environment. Physical connections are provided through Azure ExpressRoute, VPN connections, or Azure Virtual WAN. There are, however, specific network address ranges and firewall ports needed to enable these services.

Building a private network results from deploying a private cloud for management, provisioning, and vMotion. Cloud users use the private networks to access vCenter, NSX-T Manager, and virtual machine vMotion or deployment.

Azure Monitor logs automatically generate once cloud consumers deploy the Azure VMware Solution into their subscriptions. In their private cloud, the Azure VMware administrator can

- Collect logs on each of their VMs.

- Install MMA agents on the Windows and Linux VMs.

- Make sure Azure diagnostics are enabled.

- Create queries and run them.

- Create queries as you would in a VM.

Azure VMware Solution monitoring patterns are the same as those for Azure VMs within the IaaS platform.

Key AVS Benefits

The cloud consumer can do the following:

- Take advantage of VMware workloads running on the global Azure infrastructure to gain scale, continuity, and fast provisioning.

- Maintain operational consistency using familiar technology including vSphere, HCX, NSX-T, and vSAN using VMware investments, skills, and tools.

- Azure is the best cloud for those who use Microsoft workloads, and it offers unmatched pricing benefits for Windows Server and SQL Server.

- Integrate Azure native management, security, and services with VMware applications to modernize them at their own pace.

- Use Azure VMware Solution as their disaster recovery site and have it become the primary site in the event of a disaster.

- Quickly scale out datacenter capacity on demand for seasonal, temporary, or regional needs with flexible payment plans.

- Redeploy vSphere-based workloads to Azure in a nondisruptive, automatic, and scalable manner, reducing their on-premises infrastructure footprint.

- Ensure disaster protection for on-premises virtual desktops by leveraging high-performance infrastructure and fast networking for virtual desktop infrastructure (VDI).

Key AVS Terminologies

In this section, you'll learn the top 10 terminologies used in the Microsoft Azure VMware Solution. Figure 1-24 gives a holistic view of the key terms.

Figure 1-24. *Azure VMware Solution termniologies*

Virtual Machines

Virtual machines (VMs) are used instead of physical machines to run programs and deploy apps. It is possible to run several virtual "guest" machines on a physical "host" machine. Even if they are running on the same host, virtual machines run their own operating systems and behave independently. A virtual macOS machine can, for example, run on a physical PC.

Hypervisor

Hypervisors, also called virtual machine monitors (VMM), are software tools that enable the creation and management of virtual machines. Virtually sharing resources like memory and processing among multiple guest virtual machines is possible with a hypervisor.

Containers

A container is a lightweight and standalone program that encapsulates the runtime environment, including the application and dependencies (libraries, binaries, and any additional configuration files), enhancing portability, scalability, security, and agility. Containers are highly efficient, enabling high resource utilization and high density. Even though containers can run almost any application, they are commonly associated with microservices, in which several containers run separate components or services. Container orchestration platforms such as Kubernetes are typically used to coordinate and manage the containers that make up an application.

Kubernetes

A container orchestration platform, Kubernetes facilitates the operation of a flexible web server framework in the cloud. Using Kubernetes, datacenters can be integrated into Azure public cloud providers or web hosting can be scaled. With Kubernetes, websites and mobile apps with complex custom code can be deployed on commodity hardware, lowering the cost of provisioning web servers with public cloud hosts and optimizing software development processes.

Virtual Networks

Using virtual networking, devices across different offices and datacenters can communicate with each other via computers, virtual machines, and virtual servers. Physical networks connect computers through cabling and other hardware, but virtual networks use software management to connect computers and servers over the Internet. In addition, virtualizing traditional network tools, like switches and network adapters, makes routing more efficient and configuration changes more manageable.

Hyperconverged Storage

The term *hyperconverged storage* refers to a type of hyperconverged infrastructure (HCI) in which storage, computing, and networking are integrated into a single virtualized system. Software-defined storage replaces dedicated hardware through flexible pools. A virtualization layer is installed on each node to share the resources within it across all nodes in a cluster, creating a large storage pool. SDN and load balancing determine which hardware is used to serve requests.

Using hyperconverged storage, administrators can manage resources more efficiently and reduce the total cost of storage ownership, often at a lower price than cloud service providers' native storage.

Bare-Metal Hypervisor

Hypervisors separate a computer's software from its hardware, allowing virtual machines to be created and managed. A hypervisor transfers requests between physical and virtual resources, making virtualization possible. Hypervisors installed directly on a physical machine, between the hardware and the operating system, are called bare-metal hypervisors. The firmware of bare-metal hypervisors is embedded at the same level as the motherboard basic input/output system (BIOS). Some operating systems require this to enable the operating system on a computer to access and use virtualization software.

Software-Defined Storage

With software-defined storage (SDS), provisioning and management of storage are independent of the underlying hardware. Separate storage pools can be managed as one logical device since they are managed as a single physical pool. Storage is aggregated between all disks in the compute hosts, and then the disks are pooled, formatted with object file systems, and allocated to VMs and file services.

Software-Defined Networking

Software-defined networking (SDN) enables networks to communicate with their underlying hardware infrastructure using software-based controllers or application programming interfaces (APIs). Unlike traditional networks, which rely on dedicated hardware devices for network control (i.e., routers and switches), this model relies on software to manage traffic. Software-defined networking is capable of creating and maintaining virtual networks, firewalls, and load balancing.

Virtual Desktop Infrastructure

A virtual desktop infrastructure (VDI) is a technology that provides and manages virtual desktops using virtual machines. Desktop environments are hosted on a centralized server and deployed to end users on demand.

Inner Engineering of AVS Components

Azure VMware Solution is based on vSphere, and Microsoft Azure now offers VMware's enterprise-class software-defined datacenter (SDDC) software. Using the AVS solution, any application can run on vSphere-based private, public, or hybrid cloud environments. VMware offers it as an elastically scalable, on-demand, on-premises service delivered, sold, and supported through Microsoft Azure.

The VMware Azure VMware solution integrates compute, storage, and network virtualization technologies (vSphere, VMware vSAN, and VMware NSX). It is combined with VMware vCenter Server management and optimization; it provides a complete cloud solution built on a next-generation, elastic, bare-metal Azure infrastructure.

Azure VMware Solution is a managed environment, so Microsoft performs all upgrades and maintenance procedures.

A private cloud based on Microsoft Azure can be used by enterprises and modern applications using the Azure VMware Solution. Azure VMware Solution is based on the VMware Cloud Foundation and thus offers a comprehensive set of software-defined services for compute, storage, network, container, and cloud management. This offering is built on a proven stack of software-defined technologies, including VMware vSphere with Tanzu, VMware vSAN, and VMware NSX-T Datacenter. An agile, reliable, and efficient cloud infrastructure ensures consistent cloud operations across private and public clouds. Figure 1-25 shows the AVS building blocks.

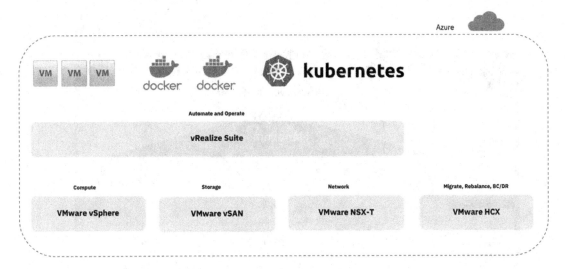

Figure 1-25. *Azure VMware Solution building blocks*

Let's get started. VMware vSphere is a virtualization platform that combines resources like CPU, storage, and networking to aggregate bare-metal hypervisors into computing infrastructures. Cloud consumers have access to tools for administering the datacenters that are part of that environment via vSphere, which manages these infrastructures as a unified operating environment.

The VMware vSphere product family includes VMware ESXi and vCenter Server, and it is designed to build and manage virtual infrastructures. The vCenter Server system provides key administrative and operational functions, such as provisioning, cloning, and VM management features essential for a virtual infrastructure.

Virtualization software is composed of ESXi and vCenter Server. Virtual machines, containers, and appliances can be built and run on ESXi. vCenter Server allows cloud consumers to manage and pool the resources of multiple hosts connected in a network. Figure 1-26 shows the AVS vSphere overview.

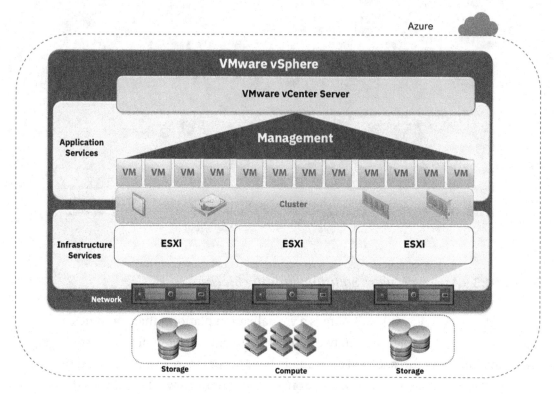

Figure 1-26. *Azure VMware Solution VMware vSphere overview*

There are four major components that make up a VMware vSphere implementation:

Compute: Resources made up of physical hosts and clusters with processors, memory, and I/O interfaces

Storage: Resources made of high-performance local disks based on best RAID configurations, SAN, network-based storage systems, and VMware vSAN (applicable to Azure VMware Solution)

Network: Resources made of physical and logical network connectivity, including virtualized security solutions based on VMware NSX-T

Management: Resources that provide basic and advanced VMware systems management, focusing on VMware vCenter Server Appliance, VMware vRealize Operations Manager, and VMware vRealize Log Insight. These systems offer services or interfaces for managing hosts, clusters, virtual machines, compliance and patch management, virtual networking, monitoring and alerting, virtual storage, backups, logging, and replication.

The compute building block is a key block in the VMware vSphere virtual infrastructure, consisting of ESXi hosts (CPU and RAM), virtual machines, resources pools, HA, and DRS clusters.

ESXi host: The ESXi host is a physical server running the VMware vSphere ESXi operating system (the hypervisor) in the compute building block. The ESXi host is a fundamental component that hosts virtual machines and other associated components such as virtual switches and datacenters.

Virtual machine: The VM is one of the compute block's basic components. A VM is made of a set of files, namely a configuration file (.vmx), virtual disk files (.vmdk), a swap file (.swap), and log files.

Cluster: A cluster is a group of ESXi hosts with a shared network and storage. There are four main features in a cluster: vMotion, a distributed resource scheduler (DRS), high availability (HA), and fault tolerance (FT).

vMotion: vMotion allows administrators to move a running virtual machine from one physical host to another without powering it down.

Distributed resource scheduler: The distributed resource scheduler (DRS) from VMware aggregates CPU and RAM resources from all hosts in a cluster and intelligently allocates resources to virtual machines based on predefined rules that reflect business needs and changing priorities. With VMware Distributed Power Management (DPM), you can automate power management and minimize power consumption across servers in a VMware DRS cluster. While DRS is standard on all VMware deployments, DPM is not widely recommended.

DRS clusters extensively leverage vMotion functionality to migrate the virtual machines from one ESXi host to another to balance the load across the hosts within the cluster.

High availability: vSphere high availability is a feature in vCenter, at the cluster level, that provides higher availability levels for virtual machines than each ESXi host can provide individually. The vSphere HA feature is designed to provide an automatic restart of VM(s) on an ESXi host that goes down to a different ESXi host in the same cluster. HA starts to recover VMs in as little as 60 seconds.

One common misconception about HA is that it uses vMotion to provide seamless availability to virtual machines. HA does not use vMotion; it's used only by DRS because it requires both the source and target hosts to be up and running. When an ESXi host fails, the virtual machines running on that host also fail (except when they are protected with fault tolerance, which has severe restrictions). HA is only there to ensure that those virtual machines are restarted automatically on the remaining cluster hosts.

Fault tolerance: Fault tolerance (FT) creates a second virtual machine to work in tandem with the virtual machine on which fault tolerance is enabled. There are two virtual machines located on different hosts in the cluster that run in sync with each other. When the first virtual machine fails, the second virtual machine replaces it with the least amount of service interruption as possible. Legacy FT provides access to the same VMDK storage for VM instances.

Legacy FT does not protect issues related to VMDK problems (corruption, access, etc.). vSphere 6 introduced options for storage redundancy and multiprocessor support, with limitations. It does not widely recommend the FT feature.

Kubernetes deployments in multi-cloud environments can be made more accessible with the VMware Tanzu Standard, which centralizes operation and governance across clusters and teams in on-premises, public clouds, and edge deployments. Customers can run their containerized workloads in the cloud with Tanzu Standard on Azure VMware Solution, with consistent operation and management to support their infrastructure modernization and app development.

VMware Horizon on Azure VMware Solution also provides seamless integration of virtual desktops and applications across a hybrid cloud.

Azure VMware Solution continuously monitors both the VMware components and the underlay, and Azure VMware Solution repairs the damaged elements as soon as a failure is detected. If Azure VMware Solution detects a degradation or loss on an Azure VMware Solution node, the host remediation process is initiated.

Host remediation involves replacing faulty nodes with new, healthy nodes in the cluster. As soon as possible, VMware vSphere maintenance mode is applied to the faulty host. When VMware vMotion is enabled, the VMs are moved from the faulty host to other available servers in the cluster, potentially resulting in zero downtime for live migrations of workloads. If the faulty host cannot be placed in maintenance mode, it is removed from the cluster.

In addition to monitoring the host's conditions, Azure VMware Solution also monitors

- Processor grade

- Memory grade

- Storage grade

- Connection and power grade

- Hardware fan grade

- Hardware system board status

- Hardware voltage

- Hardware temperature status

- Hardware power status

- Errors occurring on the disks of a vSAN host

- Network connection and connectivity failure

Private clouds with vSphere clusters are available via Azure VMware Solution. In those clusters, Azure hosts are dedicated bare-metal machines.

The same NSX-T Manager and vCenter server can manage multiple clusters within a private cloud, and Azure subscriptions can manage private clouds. Private clouds can be managed in any number within a subscription, and private clouds are initially limited to one per subscription.

For every private cloud created, a vSphere cluster is created by default. The Azure portal and API enable cloud consumers to add, delete, and scale clusters. Cloud consumers can choose the type of node that will fit their organization's needs based on core, memory, and storage requirements, and Microsoft offers node configurations based on these requirements.

Next, let's discuss virtual storage area networks (vSANs). A vSAN is a software-based distributed storage platform that combines compute and storage resources of VMware ESXi hosts. Azure bare metal hardware choices are more limited when designing and scaling a vSAN cluster.

A vSAN combines ESXi hosts' compute and storage resources in a software-based platform. With vSAN, users can manage their storage resources easily.

The vSAN storage system is native to the vSphere hypervisor, so there is no need to deploy virtual appliances or the vSphere Installation Bundle (VIB) on each host in the cluster.

Validated Design for Software-Defined Datacenter (SDDC) design decisions forms the basis of the VMware vSAN core design. Based on the design, a flexible and highly scalable HCI storage solution is created to be incorporated into the product, such as the SDDC. The design of a component should be interchangeable with another similar element if it is not suitable for any reason for the business or technical requirement.

The Hyperconverged Infrastructure (HCI) market leader VMware vSAN continues to be the vSAN software. The vSAN solution is proven to be an excellent fit for all workloads. Currently, vSAN runs traditional applications such as Microsoft SQL Server, SAP HANA, Cassandra, and next-generation applications such as Splunk, Cassandra, and MongoDB. It also runs container-based services orchestrated through Kubernetes. Many factors contribute to vSAN's success, such as its performance, flexibility, ease of use, robustness, and pace of innovation.

Disaggregated tools and specialized skill sets are often associated with traditional infrastructure deployment, operations, and maintenance paradigms. Using familiar tools for deployment, operation, and management of private cloud infrastructure, vSphere and vSAN simplify these tasks. VMWare vSAN is the cornerstone of the VMWare Cloud Foundation, which accelerates a customer's Azure cloud journey.

VMware's software-defined storage solution, built from the ground up for vSphere virtual machines, is called vSAN.

vSphere Client and vCenter are used to provision, configure, and manage locally attached disks in a vSphere cluster. Storage and compute for VMs run on the same x86 server platform running the hypervisor, as vSAN is embedded within it.

An HCI deployment based on vSAN can have anything from a 2-node setup to a 64-node cluster based on cloud consumers' requirements. As a disaster recovery solution, vSAN supports a stretched cluster topology. Customers of vSAN can mount a vSAN datastore remotely to another vSAN cluster, separating storage and compute, and customers can scale both compute and storage independently. Figure 1-27 shows a VMware vSAN overview.

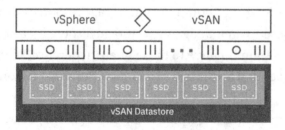

Figure 1-27. *VMware vSAN*

The vSAN solution integrates with the entire VMware stack, including vMotion, HA, DRS, and more. Setting and modifying on-the-fly VM-level policies that control storage provisioning and SLA management is possible. It is the ideal storage platform for VMs because of its enterprise-class features, scale, and performance.

Flash drives (an all-flash configuration) or a combination of flash drives and magnetic disks (hybrid configuration) contribute cache and capacity to the vSAN distributed datastore.

Disk groups range from one to five per host. Each disk group contains one cache device and a capacity device. Figure 1-28 shows the VMware vSAN disk classification.

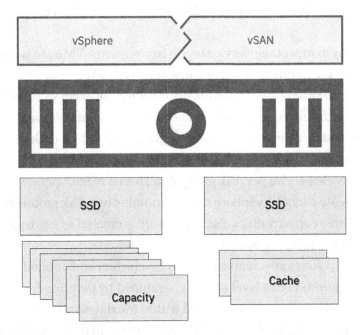

Figure 1-28. *VMware vSAN disk classification*

The flash devices in the Cache tier are primarily used for writes, but they can also serve as reading cache for buffered writes in all-flash configurations. In an all-flash vSAN configuration, flash devices fall into two categories:

- Capacity is lower, but cache devices have higher endurance and are more cost-effective.

- Cost-effective and low-endurance devices for the Capacity layer

The Cache layer performs writes, which are then destaged to the Capacity layer. This increases the usable life of lower endurance flash devices in the Capacity layer while maintaining performance.

As part of a hybrid configuration, one flash device and one or more magnetic drives are configured as a disk group. The capacity of the disk group can be as high as seven drives. There may be one or more disk groups based on the number of flash devices and magnetic drives contained in a vSphere host.

Magnetic drives provide the datastore's capacity, while flash devices act as a reading cache and write buffer. As a read cache, vSAN uses 70% of the flash capacity, and as a write cache, 30%.

For applications to meet their service level requirements, VMware is constantly working to improve the performance and consistency of vSAN.

Azure VMware Solution uses native, locally installed, all-flash vSAN storage. vSAN uses all local storage from every host in a cluster to create a datastore, and data-at-rest encryption is enabled by default. vSAN datastores are enabled for deduplication and compression by default.

With 1.6TB of NVMe cache per disk group and 15.4TB of SSD capacity per host, all disk groups use NVMe cache. A vSphere cluster contains two disk groups containing a cache disk and three capacity disks. Each datastore is created as a private-cloud deployment and is immediately available.

vSAN datastore policies are created on vSphere clusters and applied to vSAN datastores. The required service level can be guaranteed by determining how the VM storage objects are allocated and provisioned within the datastore. A minimum of 25% spare capacity must be maintained on the vSAN datastore to maintain the service-level agreement.

Azure storage services can be used to store workloads running in Azure's private cloud for cloud consumers. Azure VMware Solution offers cloud consumers access to various storage services, as depicted in Figure 1-29.

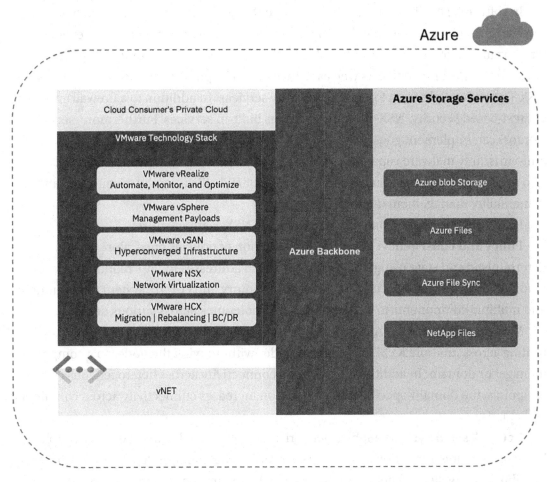

Figure 1-29. *Azure VMware Solution with Azure Cloud native storage services*

Next, let's discuss NSX-T. The NSX-T architecture has built-in separation of the data, control, and management planes. This separation delivers multiple benefits, including scalability, performance, resiliency, and heterogeneity.

VMware NSX-T fulfills the future application frameworks. In addition to vSphere, NSX-T environments may include other hypervisors, containers, and bare metal for prospective cloud consumers' needs.

NSX-T is designed to manage heterogeneous endpoints and technology stacks in application frameworks and architectures. vSphere may be used in conjunction with other hypervisors, containers, bare-metal operating systems, and public clouds. IT and development teams can choose the technologies that are best suited for their applications using NSX-T. Development organizations can also manage, operate, and consume NSX-T.

In software, NSX-T gives users full access to the network services (such as switching, routing, firewalling, and load balancing) provided by a network hypervisor (network virtualization). Programmatic assembly of these services produces unique, isolated virtual networks in seconds. As well as network and endpoint-based security services, NSX-T provides a platform for various security services. In addition to a firewall and context-based security, NSX-T includes various built-in services. Furthermore, security vendors can implement guest introspection, network introspection, and agentless anti-virus/anti-malware capabilities using these frameworks, which are integrated into service-chained next-generation firewalls, IDS/IPS, file integrity monitoring, and vulnerability management deployments.

Four fundamental attributes characterize the NSX-T architecture:

Policy and consistency: Supports the definition of policies once, along with a deterministic end state using a RESTful API, which addresses today's requirements for automated environments. The NSX-T has an inventory and control system that is unique and multiple components to determine desired outcomes across various domains.

Network connectivity: Allows for consistent logical switching and distributed routing across multiple KVM and vSphere nodes without tying the nodes to a compute manager or domain. In addition to providing connectivity across heterogeneous endpoints, the domain-specific implementation increases connectivity across containers and clouds.

Network security: This enables network connectivity with a unified security policy. It allows the implementation of services such as load balancing, edge (gateway) firewalls, distributed firewalls, and network address translation among multiple compute domains. The integrity of the overall framework established by security operations requires consistent security between VMs and container workloads.

Insight: Monitors collect metrics and track flow across domains through a standard set of tools. VMs and containers have drastically different tools for completing similar tasks, so visibility between them is essential for operationalizing mixed workloads.

These attributes enable heterogeneity, app alignment, and extensibility to support diverse requirements.

Here is a brief introduction to NSX-T Datacenter and its components. Similar to how server virtualization creates, takes snapshots, deletes, and restores Software-based network such as Portgroups, segements and etc. The equivalent of a network hypervisor with network virtualization provides Layer 2 through Layer 7 network services (such as switching, routing, access control, firewalling, and quality of service) in software. The result is the ability to assemble these services programmatically into unique, isolated virtual networks within seconds. Management, control, and data are implemented as separate but integrated planes in NSX-T. Agents, modules, and processes implement the three planes. Figure 1-30 shows Azure VMware Solution VMware NSX-T.

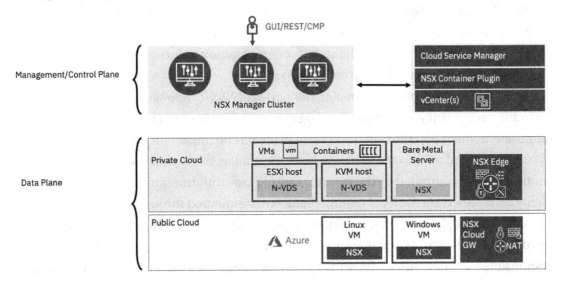

Figure 1-30. *Azure VMware Solution VMware NSX-T*

Management plane: The management plane manages all system management, control, and data plane nodes, thus providing a single point of API entry into the system. It also persists user configurations, handles user queries, and performs operational tasks.

The user configuration is manipulated and persisted by NSX-T using the management plane. Data plane elements receive that configuration from the control plane, whereas the control plane is responsible for distributing it. Depending on where data exists, specific data can belong to multiple planes. Additionally, the management plane queries the control plane and sometimes the data plane directly for information about status and statistics.

As configured by the user via, only the management plane represents the true state of the configured (logical) system. The NSX-T GUI or RESTful API can be used for making changes.

The NSX-T Datacenter offers the capability to create clusters of managers to ensure the high availability of the APIs and user interfaces. Redundant load distribution and redundancy can be provided by external balancers or an NSX virtual IP provided by NSX. Azure NSX administrators also need to manage fewer virtual appliances due to merging the management plane and the central control plane into this new management cluster.

Control plane: It controls messages for network virtualization. Consumers of cloud services isolate the control plane's communications from the data plane's transport networks by creating secure physical networks (VLANs).

Based on the configuration in the management plane, the control plane calculates the runtime state. The control plane propagates topology information reported by the data plane elements by pushing the stateless configuration to forwarding engines.

NSX-T splits the control plane into two parts:

CCP: The central control plane. Cluster nodes of NSX-T Manager are used for CCP, providing redundancy and scalability. Logically, the CCP is separate from all data plane operations, so a failure in the control plane has no impact on existing data plane operations. Based on the configuration from the management plane, some ephemeral runtime state is computed by the central control plane. Information about data plane elements reported via the local control plane is disseminated through this plane.

LCP: The local control plane using transport nodes. The LCP runs adjacent to the data plane it controls and is connected to the CCP. This part of the data plane is responsible for programming forwarding entries, monitoring local link status, computing most ephemeral runtime states based on updates from the data plane and CCP, and pushing forwarding engines. Data plane elements that host the LCP share their fate.

Data plane: It maintains packet-level statistics, reports topology information to the control plane, and performs stateless forwarding or transformation of packets based on control plane tables.

The data plane carries the following traffic:

- Workload data

- NSX-T's virtual switch, distributed routing, and distributed firewall are N-VDS. In a physical network, data flows over designated transport networks.

Next, let's discuss vRealize supported components in Azure VMware Solution. Azure VMware Solution tests and supports both on-premises and cloud versions of vRealize software. Here are the versions of vRealize that VMware and Microsoft tested when writing this book for deployments in on-premises datacenters:

- VMware vRealize Operations Manager 8.3

- VMware vRealize Automation 8.3

- VMware vRealize Network Insight (vRNI) is 6.1.

Moreover, vRealize Operations Cloud, vRealize Automation Cloud, and vRealize Network Insight Cloud are supported. On-premises and cloud versions of the vRealize Log Insight software were not supported in Azure VMware Solution when writing this book.

Figure 1-31 shows a VMware vRealize Suite overview.

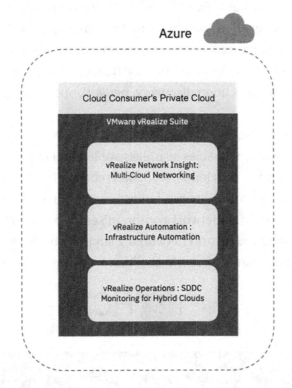

Figure 1-31. *Azure VMware Solution VMware vRealize Suite*

vROPS offers intelligent remediation and predictive analytics, and AI/ML capabilities enable self-driving IT operations management across private, hybrid, and multi-cloud environments.

A VMware infrastructure administrator can monitor system resources with vRealize Operations Manager, an operations management platform. Application-level resources (physical or virtual) can also be infrastructure-level resources. Each Azure VMware Solution private cloud includes a dedicated deployment of vCenter, NSX-T, vSAN, and HCX. VMware administrators typically monitor and manage VMware private cloud components through vRealize Operations.

Connecting VMware workloads to Azure VMware Solution (AVS) is supported by vRealize Automation. AVS helps Microsoft integrate VMware environments.

A VRA offering enables self-service clouds, multi-cloud automation, management, and security through DevOps. VRealize Automation helps enhance IT agility, productivity, and efficiency to prepare for the future of cloud consumers' business.

In a vRealize Network Insight Cloud, cloud consumers can add their vCenter and VMware Cloud NSX Manager deployed in Azure VMware Solution (AVS). In a vRealize Network Insight Cloud, native Azure components are not supported.

Using VRNI, a cloud consumer's network can be securely and confidently managed with intelligent application discovery, network optimization, analytics, and troubleshooting.

Next, let's discuss VMware HCX components in Azure VMware Solution.

The VMware HCX platform enables seamless application migration across cloud consumer datacenters and Azure clouds, workload rebalancing, and business continuity.

vSphere HCX on Azure Cloud allows seamless integration of VMware Solutions deployments in vSphere vCenter networks on-premises. By extending vSphere vCenter networks into the Azure Cloud, hybrid networking supports bidirectional virtual machine (VM) mobility. Figure 1-32 shows the Azure VMware Solution HCX.

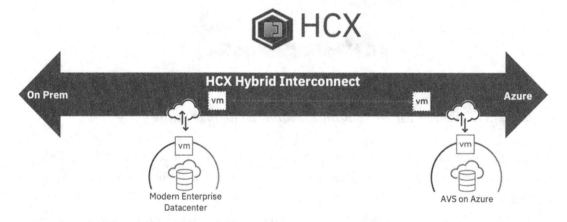

Figure 1-32. *Azure VMware Solution HCX*

The following are various use cases that get addressed by VMware HCX:

- **Application migration:** Virtual machines running on vSphere can be scheduled and migrated between datacenters without requiring a reboot by cloud consumers.

- **Change platforms or upgrade vSphere versions:** In HCX, workloads can be migrated from vSphere and non-vSphere (KVM and HyperV) environments across datacenters and clouds to current vSphere releases without upgrading.

- **Workload rebalancing:** Rebalancing workloads allows customers to move applications and workloads across regions and cloud providers, thereby offering scaling, keeping costs down, and remaining vendor neutral.

- **Business continuity and protection:** By replicating workloads across HCX sites, administrators can protect workloads. On-demand migrations are possible, or they can be scheduled for business or maintenance needs.

HCX from VMware includes a virtual management component and, depending on the license, up to five different types of VMware HCX Interconnect appliances. In VMware HCX, the source site should configure and activate services, and the destination site should deploy the virtual appliances as peers.

The following are five different types of appliances:

- HCX-IX Interconnect appliance

- HCX WAN Optimization appliance

- HCX Network Extension Virtual appliance

- HCX Sentinel Gateway appliance

- HCX Sentinel Data Receiver appliance

Let's explorer each of them.

HCX Cloud and Connector Installer: An HCX source environment and an HCX destination environment are considered separately in the HCX site-to-site architecture. Each environment requires a different HCX installer: HCX Connector or HCX Cloud. HCX Connector is always used as the source. In cloud-to-cloud deployments, HCX Cloud is typically used as the destination. However, it can also be used as a source. Cloud providers deploy HCX Cloud, and tenants deploy HCX Connector on-premises if they are using HCX-enabled public clouds.

HCX operations pair source and destination sites.

The source and destination environments deploy HCX to the management zone next to the vCenter Server, providing a single plane (HCX Manager) for managing VMware HCX. This HCX Manager provides the framework for managing HCX service virtual machines across both the source and destination sites. Each VMware HCX task is authorized using the existing vSphere SSO identity sources. Mobility, extension, and protection actions can be initiated from the VMware HCX UI or the vCenter Server Navigator screen's context menu.

A tenant can deploy both source and destination HCX Managers in the NSX Datacenter Enterprise Plus (HCX for Private-to-Private deployments).

HCX-IX Interconnect appliance: As a replication and vMotion service appliance, the HCX-IX appliance provides strong encryption, traffic engineering, and mobile virtual machines over the Internet and private lines to the destination site.

The Mobility Agent service is installed as a host object on the vCenter Server with the HCX-IX appliance. The Mobility Agent is the mechanism HCX uses to migrate virtual machines to a new location using vMotion, Cold, and replication-assisted vMotion (RAV).

HCX WAN Optimization appliance: By applying WAN optimization techniques such as data deduplication and line conditioning, VMware HCX WAN Optimization improves the performance characteristics of private lines or internet paths. The onboarding process to the destination site is accelerated through internet connections without waiting for direct connect/MPLS circuits. Performance is closer to a LAN environment.

HCX Network Extension Virtual appliance: With HCX Network Extension, cloud consumers can extend Layer 2 fast (4–6Gbps) from environments using vSphere distributed switches and VMware NSX. With the HCX Network Extension, cloud consumers can keep the same IP and MAC addresses when migrating virtual machines. Mobility optimized networking in HCX Network Extension eliminates "tromboning" between migrated virtual machines on different extended segments and virtual machines on native NSX-T networks at the destination.

HCX Sentinel Gateway appliance: Cloud consumers can migrate guest (non-vSphere) virtual machines from on-premise datacenters to the cloud with VMware HCX OS Assisted Migration (OSAM). A few components make up OSAM: HCX Sentinel software that runs on each virtual machine to be migrated, Sentinel Gateway (SGW) appliances that connect and forward guest workloads in the source environment, and Sentinel Data Receiver (SDR) appliances in the destination environment.

HCX Sentinel Data Receiver appliance: The HCX Sentinel Data Receiver (SDR) appliance receives, manages, and monitors data replication operations at the destination environment when used with the HCX Sentinel Gateway appliance.

The HCX Enterprise Edition for Azure VMware Solution is generally available.

Finally, let's discuss Azure security and compliance in Azure VMware Solution.

The Azure VMware Solution uses vSphere role-based access control for access and security. vSphere SSO LDAP capabilities can be integrated with Azure Active Directory (Azure AD).

- CloudAdmin is the role assigned to a local user in vCenter built into Azure VMware Solution. In comparison to other VMware cloud solutions, the CloudAdmin role has vCenter privileges that are different.

- Active Directory administrators can grant users of Azure VMware Solution permission by linking an identity source to their local CloudAdmin user.

- The administrator cannot access the administrator user account of an Azure VMware Solution deployment. vCenter administrators can assign Active Directory users and groups to their CloudAdmin roles.

- Microsoft supports and manages specific management components that are unavailable to private-cloud users. Clusters, hosts, datastores, and distributed virtual switches make up these components.

- Data-at-rest encryption is enabled by default for vSAN storage datastores through the Azure VMware Solution. Key Management Service (KMS) is used for encryption and supports vCenter key management. The keys are encrypted and wrapped by a master key in Azure Key Vault. If a host is removed from a cluster, data on SSDs is immediately invalidated.

Summary

In this chapter, you explored the fundamentals of cloud computing and Microsoft Azure, getting started with Azure VMware Solution, essential Microsoft AVS terminologies, and the well-framed framework for AVS building blocks.

In the next chapter, you will read about performing assessments and requirements gathering with Microsoft AVS.

CHAPTER 2

Solution Overview of AVS

As VMware's preferred public cloud provider, AVS supports vSphere workloads in the Azure Cloud. In VMware and Microsoft's hybrid cloud solution, customers can move to the cloud and modernize their applications quickly and easily, enabling faster time-to-market and innovation.

AVS solutions enable cloud consumers to accelerate adoption of the cloud without the burden of having to reformat existing assets for the cloud. The Azure VMware Solution makes it possible to run cloud consumers' VMware technology stacks on Azure as if it were on-premises, so no app refactoring or different skillsets are needed.

AVS delivers scalable processing and high throughput networking with low latency. Cloud consumers can migrate datacenters to the cloud to easily deploy rapid data center evacuation, disaster recovery, and application modernization.

This chapter provides the component-level solution overview of AVS. It covers the following:

- Overview of AVS

- Key elements of AVS

- Compute overview of Azure VMware Solutions

- Storage overview of Azure VMware Solutions

- Network overview of Azure VMware Solutions

- AVS workload and application mobility

- AVS management and operations

- AVS security

© Puthiyavan Udayakumar 2022
P. Udayakumar, *Design and Deploy Azure VMware Solutions*, https://doi.org/10.1007/978-1-4842-8312-7_2

Overview of Azure VMware Solutions

The Microsoft Azure VMware solution combines VMware's proven enterprise-grade software defined datacenter with elasticity, flexibility, and the global presence of the Azure Cloud. Combining these technologies allows users to standardize on-premises and on-cloud infrastructures. Cloud consumers do not need to make modifications or refactor workloads to migrate.

By centralizing on-premises and cloud administration, AVS ensures consistency and operational efficiency. Tools and processes are the same, so there's nothing new to learn. AVS runs on the latest hardware that improves performance, resulting in cost savings compared to a traditional on-premises infrastructure such as vSphere with non-converged compute networking and storage. The hyperconverged infrastructure of AVS can be used to lower prices by adding storage and networking. In addition to a significant amount of platform lifecycle automation in Azure, cloud-based vSphere increases consolidation ratios, operations, and security. Figure 2-1 depicts an overview of Azure VMware Solution.

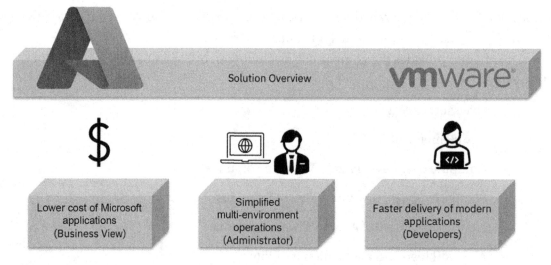

Figure 2-1. *Overview of Azure VMware Solution*

If an organization utilizes Windows Server or SQL Server, Microsoft has specific cost savings for AVS to incentivize businesses to adopt the technology. These include free security updates for Windows Server 2008 r2 and SQL Server 2008 r2 for four years beyond the end-of-the-extended-support date for these products. Extended security updates typically cost around 75-125% of the base software license cost per year, making running legacy Microsoft platforms on the cloud prohibitively expensive.

VMware on-premises does not receive the same service. It does not provide free security updates. If IT organizations want to stay as secure as possible, they must update security. According to Microsoft, the extended security updates for SQL Server 2012 r2 and Windows Server 2012 r2 will be provided free of charge by Azure and AVS. The Azure hybrid benefit program also allows customers to bring their existing Windows Server and SQL Server licenses with software insurance to Azure and AVS after their extended support dates in 2022 and 2023. Microsoft licensing costs are reduced by 40% due to this. For Windows and SQL Server licenses purchased after October 2019, no other VMware hyperscale service lets you bring your own licensing options.

As part of AVS, Microsoft also allows the deployment of downloadable Office 365 and VDI desktops. Other non-Microsoft VMware hyperscale services cannot run downloadable Office 365 applications that integrate Microsoft tools. AVS subscriptions are managed by the Azure portal, which uses Azure credits to purchase AVS. The portal also simplifies initial and day-to-day operations for administrators. The Azure portal provides integrated audit logging alerting, metrics management, and a unified Azure services bill included as an Azure Resource Manager template.

With Azure Monitor for application developers, developers can also modernize existing vSphere applications with Azure's IoT services and develop and deploy applications via Azure APIs. Developers have access to all Azure services, including AVS, through a single pane of glass because of VMware's SDDC and vCenter integration with Azure. Utilizing Azure services from within the AVS SDDC environment is also more accessible and secure by integrating VMware and Azure identity management.

You might be asking yourself, well, that's all great information, but what is Azure VMware Solution?

As vSphere runs on bare metal, VMware's AVS combines compute, networking, and storage on dedicated bare metal hosts within the Microsoft Azure Cloud. Consumers of cloud computing enjoy the same level of performance and resilience that they have on-premises. Validated by VMware and jointly developed with Microsoft, the Azure service provides the initial environment, periodic updates, fixes, maintenance of the hypervisor, maintenance of the server, and management of any network failures. It is fully integrated with Azure's native services and available as a standalone cloud service. Cloud consumers are not required to have anything from VMware on-premises; however, if they have any VMware technologies, they can maximize the value of that offering and easily migrate workloads from on-premises to the cloud or connect via HCX in a hybrid cloud configuration. Figure 2-2 depicts the Azure VMware Solution logical view.

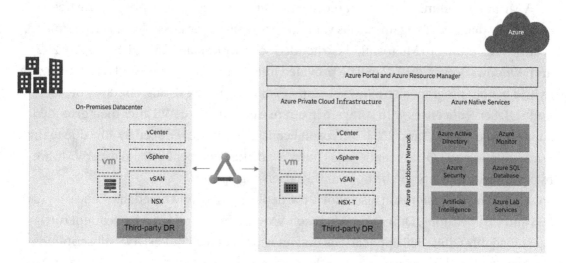

Figure 2-2. *Azure VMware Solution logical view*

With vSAN storage, AVS hosts can scale performance and reliability as they add more hosts. NSX-T offers software-defined networking in the AVS private cloud for easy interoperability with on-premises networks. The AVS private cloud hosts vCenter, which is used to manage VMware components.

Cloud datacenters with VMware AVS are located in more countries than any other cloud service offered by VMware. At the time of writing, 20 of the more than 60 regions of Azure offer Microsoft's AVS service.

Azure is continually adding new AVS regions. AVS's broad geographic coverage is essential for cloud consumers to ensure compliance with data sovereignty regulations. Microsoft and VMware have committed to delivering cloud services that follow industry best practices for security and compliance. In addition to adhering to rigorous security standards, each company also extends its coverage to specific industries.

In Azure Cloud, VMware Solutions offers bare metal and hypervisor access and administrative access to vCenter, NSX-T, and many more add-on services. The VMware environment deployed in Azure Cloud possesses the same control, security, and functionality as its on-premises counterpart. As an entirely native VMware environment, AVS does not require any modifications to existing tools or processes. It is only accessed through the cloud.

Microsoft and VMware have created solutions based on VMware Cloud foundation solutions to address the concern that security is one of the biggest reasons for hesitation in cloud adoption. AVS VCF runs in a single, dedicated environment, eliminating "noisy neighbors" and data corruption.

The VMware hardware attestation for Microsoft Azure enables workloads to run on trusted servers with role-based access and Intel TXT, which provides encryption at the chip level. The Azure Virtual Compute Facility includes leading-edge security solutions. Clients who access hypervisors and bare metal can use the technical, business, and personnel controls to meet compliance and auditing requirements.

In nutshell, Azure VMware solutions gives cloud consumers the ability to run VMware workloads natively on the Azure platform. They can

- Take advantage of the global Azure infrastructure to get continuity, speed, and scale for VMware workloads

- Utilize their existing VMware investments, skills, and tools, including VMware VCF, vSphere, vSAN, vCenter, and other providers' tools

- Take advantage of the data locality in the Azure cloud to seamlessly migrate apps to Azure-native management, security, and services

- Enjoy unmatched Windows and SQL Server pricing

AVS has five primary use cases that customers can use for their digital transformations. Figure 2-3 depicts the Azure VMware Solution use cases.

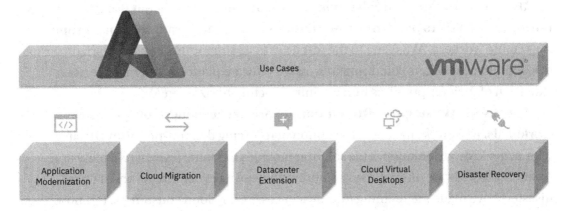

Figure 2-3. *Azure VMware Solution use cases*

Use case 1: Modernizing applications is simplified if migrated to AVS. Workloads can be incrementally refactored to cloud-native standards using SaaS, PaaS, the Azure Kubernetes service, or directly on AVS with its support. You can enable True Hybrid capabilities, such as streamlining DevOps across VMware and Azure. You can optimize and standardize VMware administration for Azure services and solutions applicable to all cloud customers' workloads. You can access public cloud services without expanding cloud consumers' datacenters or reengineering cloud consumers' applications. Azure VMware Solution helps cloud consumers identify and access control policies and log and monitor them.

Use case 2: Cloud customers who need to move to the cloud from CapEx to OpEx or aging hardware. In the past, IT expenses were primarily CapEx, including outright purchases of hardware and software and maintenance equipment. Business owners who buy these items outright have total ownership of their systems, but this comes at a cost. The problem with CapEx purchases in IT is that they often become outdated before they have time to pay for themselves, so the initial investment isn't always recouped before the further expense is incurred.

Over the last decade, businesses have steadily reduced their IT CapEx in favor of operating expenses such as cloud services.

Use case 3: The data center extension needs extra capacity or retains Windows Server and SQL Server software beyond the end-of-support dates. Customers would need to pay prohibitive prices to Microsoft to receive security updates to stay on premises.

Use case 4: Desktop virtualization in the cloud was a significant use case for AVS during the COVID 19 pandemic when customers needed to rapidly expand support for remote workers. AVS came to the rescue with its support for VMware horizon virtual desktops that customers could run on a native VMware platform and manage as an extension of their on-premises horizon infrastructure horizon on AVS.

Use case 5: AVS supports DR solutions to protect customers' on-premises workloads. AVS gives customers the option of replacing their off-premises DR sites with Azure VMware Solution. This solution provides the same level of reliability and testability as VMware on-premises solutions. Increasing cyber threats and natural disasters have made maintaining uptime a necessity for cloud consumers. It is now imperative that Microsoft and VMware have a resiliency strategy. Customers can reduce downtime with three resiliency tools: VMware HCX, JetStream Disaster Recovery, and Zerto (disaster recovery).

Key Elements of Azure VMware Solutions

Let's discuss a deployment overview for AVS and what is deployed in a private cloud. The steps for deploying Azure VMWare Solutions to deliver VMWare-based private clouds within Microsoft Azure will be described in this section. Microsoft Azure's private cloud hardware and software deployments are fully integrated and automated.

The Azure portal, Azure CLI, or Azure PowerShell can deploy and manage the private cloud. In Figure 2-4, the private cloud is seen within its Azure resource group and connected to another VNet in the same region that runs native Azure services. The private cloud is outlined within its Azure resource group and connected to another VNet with Azure services in the same region. Figure 2-4 depicts the Azure VMware Solution private cloud integrated view.

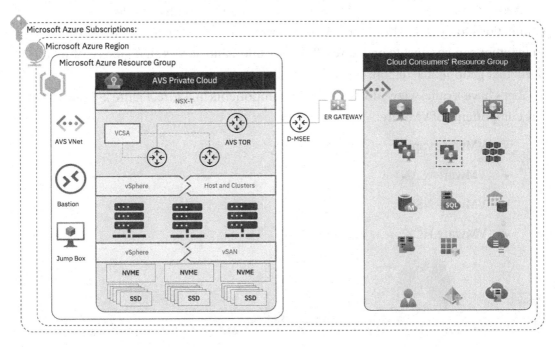

Figure 2-4. *Azure VMware Solution private cloud integrated view*

The Azure VMware Solution combines VMware compute, networking, and storage running on bare metal hosts within Microsoft Azure.

Here's a quick view of Azure core components.

Azure subscriptions: Subscriptions are a billing boundary in Azure. To deploy any Azure resource, a user needs a valid subscription. Subscriptions associated with

Microsoft Enterprise Agreements or Cloud Solution Provider Azure plans support Azure VMware Solution.

Azure regions: Azure regions are collections of datacenters linked by a dedicated, low-latency network that hosts Azure services. Azure services are not available in all regions.

Azure resource groups: The purpose of a resource group is to simplify the management of multiple Azure resources by grouping them into one container object. All resources within the group can be affected by policies and lifecycle actions.

Azure VNets and virtual network gateway: Private networks within Azure are built using Azure virtual networks. Azure VNets allow resources to securely communicate with each other, the Internet, and on-premises resources. Virtual network gateways allow routes to be exchanged between VNets.

Azure ExpressRoute: Microsoft Azure ExpressRoute circuits enable private connections to its global backbone. Through an ExpressRoute connectivity provider, a customer can connect to an ExpressRoute location and access all regions within a particular geopolitical region.

Let's have a quick view of VMware core components in Azure. Figure 2-5 illustrates key components of VMware:

- VMware vSphere

- VMware vSAN

- VMware NSX-T

- VMware HCX

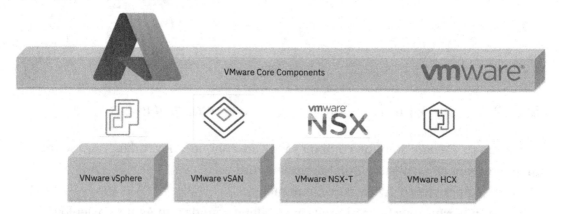

Figure 2-5. *Azure VMware Solution – VMware core components*

AVS core capabilities are provided by VMware vSphere, VMware vCenter, VMware vSAN, VMware NSX-T, and VMware HCX. The core capabilities of VMware products that have been certified with AVS can be extended with VMware services. Virtual machines can be migrated to AVS using VMware HCX.

vRealize portfolio products can manage, monitor, and automate AVS, VMware SD-WAN and NSX Advanced Load Balancer. Tanzu Kubernetes Grid, Tanzu Mission Control, and VMware Tanzu Standard provide a platform for application modernization, presenting consistent Kubernetes runtime and management capabilities.

The virtual desktop solution supported by AVS is VMware Horizon. The primary disaster recovery solution for the cloud is VMware Site Recovery Manager. Horizon Cloud on Azure is another option, a separate solution that offers Horizon as a service SaaS on Azure.

In AVS, the CloudAdmin role is assigned to a local user called CloudAdmin. This role provides access to manage the environment. It does not have access to Microsoft-specific management components, such as ESXi hosts, clusters, and datastores. Active Directory users and groups can be assigned the CloudAdmin role using the CloudAdmin user.

HCX Advanced is deployed by default for no additional charge. HCX Enterprise can be upgraded through a support ticket with Microsoft. HCX offers many benefits over HCX Advanced, such as scheduled bulk migrations between on-premises and AVS.

When the AVS private cloud is provisioned, an ExpressRoute circuit is created, connecting it to the Microsoft dedicated Enterprise Edge routers, allowing access to Azure services. An ExpressRoute gateway enables AVS to connect to existing Azure VNets. AVS private clouds should be connected to on-premises datacenters via ExpressRoute Global Reach. Site-to-site VPN connections can be used without an ExpressRoute connection between the datacenter on-premises and Azure.

Four elements need to be prepared and planned well enough before kick-starting the deployment:

- Subscription

- Resource group

- Subscription contributor

- Network

Figure 2-6 depicts the Azure VMware Solution private cloud deployment prerequisites.

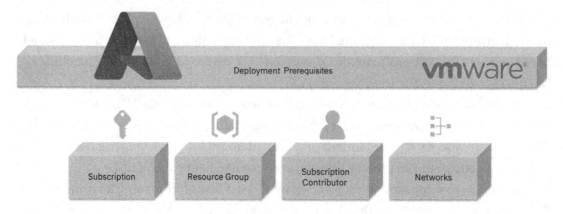

Figure 2-6. *Azure VMware Solution private cloud deployment prerequisites*

It is necessary to identify several things before deploying the private cloud object in Microsoft AVS Solution. Cloud consumers must place a subscription into which they want AVS to be deployed; they can use an existing subscription if that subscription is associated with an enterprise agreement (EA) or cloud solution provider plan (CSP), or create a new one.

Next, they must identify a resource group. Generally, AVS administrators can create a new resource group for AVS and related resources. Alternatively, AVS administrators can use an existing resource group. It is also necessary for AVS administrators to identify the administrator who will enable and deploy the private cloud. They should assign this individual the role of Contributor.

AVS architects need to think about network requirements. AVS administrators require a slash 22 network for AVS deployment, divided into smaller subnets for vCenter Next, VMotion, and HCX. This block should not overlap with any existing cloud consumers' network segment on-premises. Azure, and a VNet defined connect AVS into if cloud consumers generally want to connect to Azure native services.

AVS administrators must create a virtual network that hosts the jump box to access the private cloud from Azure. For workload VMs defined in NSX-T post-deployment, AVS administrators also need to identify one or more network segments.

HCX might need some on-premises segments to be created after deployment if cloud consumers want to use HCX for migrations and network extension.

In addition, AVS administrators should determine whether cloud consumers are connecting via a VPN or an Express route and adjust the configuration accordingly. Most enterprise customers will use the Express route, but a VPN is also supported.

Administrators must also configure firewall rules to access on-premises resources from AVS or to access AVS from on-premises.

Compute Overview of Azure VMware Solutions

Azure is a platform of choice for companies because of its computing services. Applications and services can be hosted on Azure. Azure compute provides the infrastructure needed to run cloud consumer applications. You can take advantage of compute capacity in the cloud and scale as needed. Cloud consumer applications can be containerized, Windows and Linux VMs can be deployed, and VMs can be migrated to Azure with flexibility. Cloud consumers can deploy where and how they want with comprehensive support for hybrid environments. In addition, Azure compute includes a full-featured identity solution, so cloud consumers can benefit from managed end-point protection and Active Directory support to secure access to on-premises and cloud applications. Pay-as-you-go and Azure Hybrid Benefits enable you to deploy apps and save.

Some of the computing services provided by Azure are listed in Table 2-1.

Table 2-1. *Computing Services Provided by Azure*

Name of Services	Service Function
Azure Virtual Machine	Windows or Linux VM hosted in Azure
Azure Virtual Machine Scale Sets	With autoscaling, cloud consumers can create thousands of VMs in minutes while maintaining high availability.
Azure Spot Instances	Provision unused compute capacity for cloud consumers workloads to get deep discounts
Azure Functions	An event-driven and serverless compute service
VM Hosted on Azure VMware Solution	VMs running in dedicated host provisioned and isolated from other tenants running in Azure VMware Solution
App Services	Providing managed hosting services for web applications, mobile apps, REST APIs, or automated business processes
Azure Spring Cloud	Host Spring Boot apps with a managed service
Azure Kubernetes Services	Containerized applications running on Kubernetes
Batch	The execution of large-scale parallel and high-performance computing applications (HPC) via a managed service
Container Instances	This is the most straightforward way to run a container in Azure without creating any virtual machines and without having to adopt a higher-level service.
Azure Dedicated Host	Using physical servers only for cloud consumers to deploy virtual machines or containers for cloud consumers

Physical servers that the Azure Dedicated Host provides host Azure virtual machines. Azure's physical cloud servers are dedicated to each organization and workload, and capacity isn't shared with other tenants. Compliance requirements are met as a result of this host-level isolation. In provisioning the host, cloud consumers gain visibility into and control over the placement of their VMs and can define the host's maintenance policies.

The AVS administrator should deploy at least three virtual machines on various hosts to ensure high availability. Cloud consumers can choose from several Azure Dedicated Host options to customize their fault isolation boundaries with cloud infrastructure.

Within an Azure region, availability zones are unique physical locations, and datacenters within each zone are outfitted with independent power, cooling, and networking. All hosts in a host group will be placed within a single availability zone once the group is created. Cloud consumers need to create multiple host groups (one per zone) and spread their hosts accordingly to achieve high availability across zones.

All VMs created on that host must be created in the same availability zone if a cloud consumer assigns a host group to a zone. It is possible to create hosts in specific fault domains. Hosts in different fault domains will be placed on other physical racks in the data center as they are with VMs in a scale set or availability set. Cloud consumers must specify the fault domain count when creating host groups. When creating hosts within a host group, a cloud consumer assigns a fault domain to each host. A fault domain is not assigned to VMs.

Fault domains are not the same as colocation, and two hosts sharing the same fault domain do not necessarily mean they are near each other. A fault domain is scoped to a host group. The cloud consumer should avoid assuming anti-affinity between two host groups (unless they are in different availability zones). A VM running on a host with a different fault domain will have its managed disk services deployed on multiple storage stamps to increase fault isolation.

The cloud consumer can combine both capabilities to achieve even more fault isolation. Cloud consumers specify the availability zones and fault domains for each group of hosts, assign a fault domain to each host in the group, and assign availability zones to each VM.

A hosted Azure Dedicated Host supports Azure standard HDDs, standard SSDs, and premium SSDs at the time of writing this book.

AVS compute perspective: Resources made up of physical hosts and clusters with processors, memory, and I/O interfaces.

Figure 2-7 depicts the Azure VMware Solution's core compute.

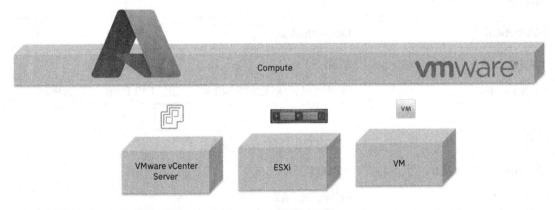

Figure 2-7. *Azure VMware Solution – core compute*

A private cloud is built up of nodes that serve as compute nodes. A node is made up of the following:

- A host, where a VMware ESXi hypervisor is installed on bare metal

- Private clouds can be provisioned or reserved on the host.

- Azure provides the service in the region.

From provisioned nodes, cloud consumers create their own private cloud. The minimum number of nodes needed for a private cloud is three of the same SKU. Adding additional nodes expands the private cloud. Administrators can add nodes to an existing cluster through the Azure portal or create a new cluster.

Nodes with provisioned capacity provide pay-per-use capacity. By provisioning nodes, you can scale VMware clusters for cloud consumers quickly. To scale back cloud consumers' VMware clusters, you can add nodes or remove a provisioned node. Every month, provisioned nodes are billed to the subscription where they are provisioned.

- By paying with a credit card, cloud consumers subscribe to Azure immediately.

- They will be billed for Azure the following month.

In addition to bare-metal server hosts for the vSphere clusters, vCenter Server, NSX-T, and vSAN, AVS private clouds offer various Azure underlay resources that are required for connectivity/operation. There is a default limit of one AVS private cloud per subscription, but this can be scaled through a support ticket.

As of this writing, AVS supports only one type of host, detailed in Table 2-2.

Table 2-2. *AV36 Host Configuration*

Components	Configuration
Instance size	AV36
Processor type	Dual Intel Xeon Gold 6140 @2.3 GHZ I 18 Cores, HT enabled
Core(s)	36
RAM	576GB (50.15GB reserved)
ESXi minimum version	6.7 U3 P05
ESXi edition	Enterprise Plus

(continued)

Table 2-2. (*continued*)

Components	Configuration
vCenter minimum version	6.7 U3
Clusters per private cloud	12
Minimum hosts per cluster	3
Maximum hosts per cluster	16
Maximum hosts per private cloud	96
vCenter per private cloud	1
vSAN capacity limit	75% of total usable space
Cache	2 *1.6 TB NVMe
Capacity	8 *1.92 TB SSD
All flash storage	15.36 TB
NVMe cache	3.2 TB
vSAN minimum version	6.7 P05
vSAN minimum edition	Enterprise
Network interface card (uplink)	2 x Dual port 25 GbE

AVS private clouds are made up of a single cluster of 3-16 hosts. AVS private clouds can be configured with up to 12 clusters and 96 hosts. vCenter, NSX Manager, and HCX components are placed on the first cluster of AVS management VMs. AVS Host and it is maximum capacities are listed in Table 2-3.

Table 2-3. *Host Max Configuration for CPU, RAM, and Storage*

Host	CPU	RAM	Storage
3	108	1.5 TB	46 TB
8	288	4 TB	122 TB
16	576	8 TB	245 TB
32	1,152	16 TB	491 TB
64	2,304	32 TB	983 TB
96	3,456	49 TB	1.4 TB

Storage Overview of Azure VMware Solutions

Microsoft Azure Storage is a cloud storage platform designed for modern data storage scenarios. Azure offers a massively scalable object store for data objects, a file system for the cloud, a messaging store for reliable messaging, and a NoSQL store for NoSQL data. Benefits include durability and high availability, security, scalability, management, and accessibility.

- **Durability:** In a hardware failure, redundancy will ensure the safety of cloud consumers' data. Cloud consumers can also replicate data across datacenters or geographical regions to protect against local catastrophes or natural disasters. If a disaster hits, the replicated data will remain reliable.

- **Secure:** Azure Storage accounts are encrypted when data is written to them. Azure Storage lets cloud consumers control who can access their data at fine-grained levels.

- **Scalable:** Azure Storage is designed to be massively scalable to meet today's performance and data storage needs.

- **Managed:** Cloud consumers can rely on Azure for hardware maintenance, updates, and critical issues.

- **Accessible:** Over HTTP or HTTPS, Azure Storage data can be accessed from anywhere globally. .NET, Java, Node.js, Python, PHP, Ruby, Go, and others provide Azure Storage client libraries, as well as a mature REST API. Azure Storage supports scripting in Azure PowerShell or Azure CLI. And the Azure portal and Azure Storage Explorer provide easy visual solutions to work with data in the cloud.

VMware vSAN is used by default as cluster-wide storage in Azure VMware Solutions private clouds by AVS. Host storage is used in a vSAN datastore, and information at rest is encrypted by default. Azure Storage resources can be utilized to extend the storage capabilities of cloud consumers' private clouds.

Azure Storage resource such as Blob Storage, File Sync, Azure Files, Azure Netapp Files, and Azure Disk Poo can be integrated with AVS as well.

AVS Storage perspective: Resources made up of high-performance local disks based on the best RAID configuration.

Figure 2-8 depicts the Azure VMware Solution's core storage.

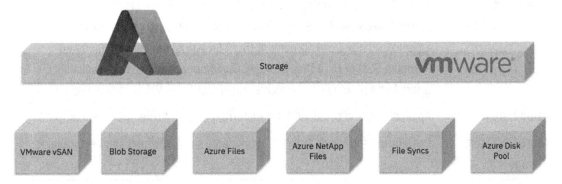

Figure 2-8. *Azure VMware Solution – core storage*

Among the storage services Azure provides, a few are listed in Table 2-4.

Table 2-4. *Azure Storage Functions*

Name of Services	Service Function
Blob Storage	A massively scalable object store for binary and text data. Blob Storage's archive tier has the lowest possible cost. Offline data might need to be copied to a Cool, Hot, or Premium tier to enable access. A Cool tier provides low-cost, instant access to offline data.
Azure Files	Using Azure Files, users can manage native SMB file shares without running virtual machines. Any Azure virtual machine or on-premises computer can mount an Azure Files share as a network drive.
Azure NetApp Files	Metered Azure NetApp Files is a high-performance service that offers enterprise-class performance. Across all workload types, Azure NetApp Files is highly available by default. Service and performance levels can be selected, and this service can set up snapshots.
File Sync	File Sync in Azure Files allows cloud consumers to centralize their file shares. File Sync from Azure offers the same flexibility, performance, and compatibility as an on-premises file server.

(*continued*)

Table 2-4. (*continued*)

Name of Services	Service Function
Azure Disk Pool	Azure disk storage offers high-performance, persistent block storage to power Azure VMs. Azure Disk Pool provides the industry's only single-instance service-level agreement (SLA) for virtual machines running on Premium SSD or Ultra Disk Storage. Customers can have high availability using Azure disks with availability zones and Azure VM fault domains.
Azure Databox	Applications and solutions for transferring data to Azure and edge computing
Azure Data Lake Storage	For high-performance analytics workloads, a scalable and secure data lake

VMware's software-defined storage solution, vSAN, was designed from the ground up for virtual machines running on vSphere. vCenter and the vSphere Web Client can provision and manage local disks abstracted and aggregated in a vSphere cluster. Figure 2-9 depicts the Azure VMware Solution's vSAN storage.

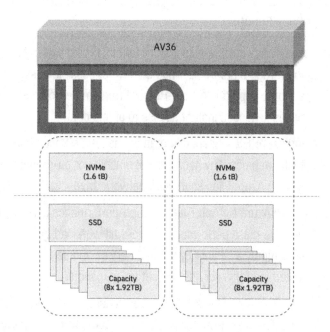

Figure 2-9. *Azure VMware Solution – vSAN storage*

Virtual storage area networks (vSANs) are hypervisor-converged, meaning storage, compute, and management are delivered from the same x86 server platform running the hypervisor. The VMware stack is fully integrated. Provisioning of VM storage and management of storage SLAs can be controlled by VM-level policies that can be set and modified on demand. Cluster-wide vSAN datastores use local storage in each host, and data-at-rest encryption is enabled by default.

vSAN datastores are built using local storage on each cluster host. With a raw, SSD-based capacity of 15.4TB per host, all disk groups include an NVMe cache tier of 1.6TB. A cluster's raw capacity tier equals the per-host capacity multiplied by the number of hosts. For example, in the vSAN capacity tier, four hosts provide 61.6TB of raw capacity.

In a cluster-wide vSAN, local storage is used in cluster hosts. During a private cloud deployment, all datastores are created and are immediately available. With the vSAN privileges below, the CloudAdmin user and all CloudAdmin role users can manage datastores:

- Datastore.AllocateSpace

- Datastore.Browse

- Datastore.Config

- Datastore.DeleteFile

- Datastore.file management

- Datastore.UpdateVirtualMachineMetadata

VMware vSAN is used as storage in Azure VMware Solution. VMware vSAN is a distributed, object-based file system software layer that runs natively in the ESXi hypervisor. vSAN aggregates a host cluster's local or direct-attached capacity devices into a unified storage pool shared by all hosts in the cluster.

Virtual machines are stored according to storage policies in vSAN. These policies determine how virtual machine storage objects within a datastore are provisioned and allocated to guarantee a certain level of service.

On a host cluster, vSAN is enabled by creating a single vSAN datastore using disks from all participating hosts, and it is assigned a default storage policy.

Default storage policies for the private cloud cluster include RAID-1 (mirroring), FTT-1 (failure to tolerate), and thick provisioning. With this configuration, the cluster continues to grow unless the storage policy is changed. FTT-1 accommodates a single host failure in a three-host cluster.

The FTT-1 protocol accommodates the failure of a single host in a cluster of three hosts. Microsoft monitors failures regularly and replaces hardware when necessary from an architecture perspective.

Administrators who are uncertain if the cluster will expand to four or more should deploy using the default policy. Microsoft recommends expanding a cluster after initial deployment if you are certain that the cluster will grow. In the VM settings, change the disk's storage policy to either RAID-5 FTT-1 or RAID-6 FTT-2 when the VMs are deployed to the cluster.

vSAN storage policies determine the performance and availability of the provisioned storage. RAID-1 FTT1-1 is the fastest but uses the most storage and RAID 5 FTT-1 is fast and more space efficient while RAID-6 FTT-2 is the most available and space efficient but can be slower in large sequential reads from disk.

Azure VMware Solution provisioning types are classified into two categories:

Thick: Space that has been assigned, fully provisioned, or reserved in advance. The system is protected because the space on the vSAN datastore is already reserved, even if it is full. An AVS administrator can create a 10GB virtual disk with thick provisioning. A virtual disk's total storage capacity is preallocated on its physical storage, which consumes all of the datastore's space. A VM can't share the datastore space with another VM.

Thin: Consumes the space it needs initially and then grows to match the data space demand used by its datastore. AVS administrators can create VMs instead of thick provisioning (outside of the default). The cloud consumer's VM template should use thin provisioning for a deduplication setup. This can be used when capacity growth projections are uncertain.

Data-at-rest encryption : Data-at-rest encryption is enabled by default in vSAN datastores using keys stored in Azure Key Vault. For key management, the encryption solution utilizes Azure KMS. The data on SSDs is invalidated immediately when a host is removed from a cluster.

Cloud administrators can use Azure Storage services within their private clouds. Storage accounts, table storage, and blob storage are among the storage services. Azure Storage services aren't connected via the Internet to the workloads. Cloud consumers can use SLA-based Azure storage services on their private clouds with this connectivity.

VMs deployed in AVS can access native Azure Storage services such as storage accounts and blob storage.

The connection of workloads to Azure Storage services doesn't traverse the Internet. Figure 2-10 depicts the Azure VMware Solution's network integrated view.

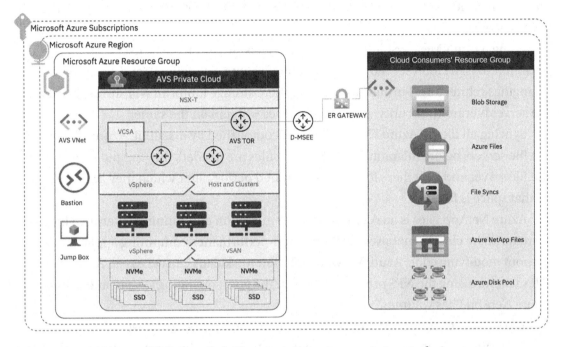

Figure 2-10. *Azure VMware Solution – native storage intgrated view*

The Azure backbone provides high-speed, low-latency private and secure connectivity and enables cloud consumers to use SLA-based Azure Storage services in their private cloud workloads.

Microsoft has a cloud-based object storage solution called Azure Blob Storage. Massive amounts of unstructured data are best stored in blob storage. Unstructured data, such as text or binary data, does not conform to a particular model or definition.

VMs and data can be stored in Azure Blob Storage, enabling enterprise-grade DR at a reduced cost of operation.

Azure Blob Storage is more than just a journal or "cold data tier" and can be used as a repository for all VMs, data, configuration metadata, and recovery policies.

Azure Files provides cloud-hosted file shares accessible with the Server Message Block (SMB) or Network File System (NFS) protocols. Using an AVS private cloud, Azure Files file shares can be mounted concurrently. NFS shares can be mapped to VMs within AVS.

Windows, Linux, and macOS clients can access SMB Azure file shares. NFS files can be accessed using Linux or macOS clients. Moreover, SMB Azure file shares can be cached on Windows Servers using Azure File Sync for fast data access near where the data is needed.

Using Azure VMware Solutions and Azure Files simultaneously, users can realize a vSphere-based cloud solution without replatforming, changing IP addresses, or changing architecture. Furthermore, the vSphere storage footprint will shrink, but the file server hierarchy, security, and available files will remain the same.

Syncing all files to Azure File Storage is accomplished by installing Azure FileSync on the file servers before migrating to AVS. When files are needed, they are pulled down to the file server and kept there for a predetermined period, after which they are removed so that space is freed.

Azure NetApp Files is an Azure service for migration and running enterprise file systems in the cloud: databases, SAP, and high-performance computing applications without modifying code. Azure VMware Solution workloads can access an Azure NetApp Files volume using the NFS protocol. VMs run the guest operating system and access Azure NetApp Files volumes.

You can attach Azure VMware Solution disk pools to AVS ESXi hosts. AVS administrators can utilize disk storage for Azure VMware Solutions for optimal performance and cost; at the time of writing, this is in preview.

Applications and workloads backed by Azure Disks can access persistent block storage through Azure disk pools. Whenever the capacity consumption reaches 75%, Microsoft sends an alert. Moreover, AVS administrators have access to capacity consumption metrics that are integrated with Azure Monitor.

Network Overview of Azure VMware Solutions

With Azure virtual networks, Azure resources such as virtual machines, web apps, and databases can communicate with each other and with users on the Internet and with cloud clients on-premises. Azure networks are resources that are used to link Azure resources.

Consumers of cloud services can create multiple isolated virtual networks by using virtual networks. Cloud consumers can use public or private IP address ranges to define a private IP address space. Cloud consumers can allocate each subnet part of the defined address space.

For name resolution, cloud consumers can use the name resolution service built into Azure. Users of the cloud can also configure their virtual networks to use either an internal or external DNS server.

Azure VMs are automatically connected to the Internet. Incoming connections to the cloud can be enabled via public IP addresses or public load balancers. Cloud consumers can connect via the Azure CLI, Remote Desktop Protocol, or Secure Shell for VM management.

For communication between Azure resources in a secure manner, Azure consumers have two options:

- Azure virtual networks connect VMs and other Azure resources, including Azure Kubernetes Service, App Service Environment for Power Apps, and Azure virtual machine scale sets.

- Connecting to other Azure resource types, including Azure SQL databases and storage accounts, is also possible via service endpoints. Users can use this approach to link multiple Azure resources to virtual networks to improve security and optimize routing between resources.

Cloud consumers can connect resources in their on-premises environments with resources in Azure by using Azure virtual networks. Cloud consumers can create both local and cloud-based networks. To achieve such connectivity, cloud consumers can use three methods:

- **Point-to-site VPN:** A typical virtual private network connection is from a PC outside the cloud consumer's organization back into the cloud consumer's corporate network. Connecting the client computer to the Azure virtual network is achieved by initiating an encrypted VPN connection.

- **Site-to-site VPN:** A site-to-site VPN links your on-premises VPN device or gateway to the Azure VPN gateway as part of a virtual network. A device in Azure can appear as if it is on a local network. Connectivity over the Internet is encrypted.

- **ExpressRoute:** Azure ExpressRoute is the perfect solution for environments where cloud consumers require higher bandwidth and increased security. Azure ExpressRoute provides dedicated private connectivity without going over the Internet.

In Azure, traffic is routed between subnets on any virtual network connected to the Internet and virtual networks to on-premises networks. Similarly, customers can override those settings and control routing:

- **Route table:** Defining routes in a route table allows cloud consumers to control how traffic should be directed. Cloud consumers can create their own route tables that control how packets are routed between subnets.

- **Border Gateway Protocol (BGP):** With the BGP, on-premises BGP routes can be propagated to Azure virtual networks using Azure VPN gateways or ExpressRoute.

Azure virtual networks provide cloud customers with the following options for filtering traffic between subnets:

- **Network security groups:** Azure network security groups contain multiple security rules for inbound and outbound connections. The cloud consumer can define rules based on source and destination IP addresses, ports, and protocols to allow or block traffic.

- **Network virtual appliances:** Compared to a hardened network appliance, a network virtual appliance is a specialized VM. A network virtual appliance performs a specific network function, such as managing a firewall or optimizing wide area networks (WANs).

Virtual network peering allows cloud consumers to connect virtual networks. Peering allows resources within virtual networks to communicate with one another. With Azure, cloud consumers can create a global interconnected network with these virtual networks located in different regions.

Users can define routing using UDR, and UDR is a major upgrade to Azure's virtual networks. Administrators can control routing tables between subnets within a VNet and between VNets, allowing them to better control network traffic.

Networks are provided as a service, but they are not free. Public IP addresses, global/regional peering, and inbound/outbound data transfers between availability zones cost money. Although nominal, the cost is not free. However, transferring data between resources within the same virtual network is free. Managing, planning, and calculating subscription costs are essential for operating an Azure subscription.

When cloud consumers deploy to Azure, they must consider some significant configuration activities. The basic capabilities deployed in an Azure datacenter are provided by network connectivity, firewalls, DMZs, and other networking devices and configurations.

A lot depends on the solution's requirements being created or migrated to Azure. In a typical design, the following components are present: inbound and outbound port/firewall rules, network security groups, enabling security via Azure Security Center, and other load balancing rules.

A key function of Azure networking is to link resources and provide access to applications. Azure has options for connecting the outside world to its services and features hosted in the global datacenters of Microsoft. Table 2-5 lists key Azure networking services.

Table 2-5. *Azure's Key Networking Services*

Name of Service	Service Function
Azure Protection Services	Protects cloud-based applications using Azure's network services: load balancing, private links, DDoS protection, firewalls, group security policies, web application firewalls, and virtual network endpoints
Azure Connectivity Services	The following Azure networking services can be used with on-premises resources: virtual networks (VNets), virtual WANs, ExpressRoute, VPN gateways, virtual network NAT gateways, Azure DNS, peering services, and Azure Bastion.
Azure Delivery Services	Using any of these or a combination of these Azure networking services, cloud consumers can deliver applications in the cloud: Content Delivery Network (CDN), Azure Front Door Service, Traffic Manager, Application Gateway, Internet Analyzer, and Load Balancer.
Azure Networking Services	Utilize any of these networking services in Azure to monitor cloud consumers' network resources: Network Watcher, ExpressRoute Monitor, Azure Monitor, and VNet Terminal Access Point (TAP).

Network: Resources made up of physical and logical network connectivity, including virtualized security solutions based on VMware NSX-T.

Before we get started, see Table 2-6 for key Azure networking terminologies.

Table 2-6. *Key Networking Terminologies*

Terminologies	Descriptions
Subscription	Microsoft subscriptions entitle users to use one or more cloud platforms or services.
Virtual network (VNet)	Fundamental building block for a cloud consumer's private network in Azure. Connects VMs to an incoming VPN connection.
ExpressRoute	Private connections between Azure datacenters and infrastructure on cloud consumers' premises or in a colocation environment
Microsoft Enterprise Edge (MSEE)	High availability with two routers in an Active/Active configuration. Routers that connect directly to a datacenter allow connectivity providers to connect their circuits.
Virtual network gateways – VPN or ER	VPN connection between an Azure virtual network and an on-premises network Connects Azure virtual networks to on-premises networks via ExpressRoute
Azure Firewall	Deploys a high-security, high-availability firewall with unlimited scalability
Azure Virtual WAN	Develops a unified WAN, connecting local and remote sites
Azure Network Watcher	Monitors and diagnoses conditions on a network scenario basis

A VMware Azure Solution provides an on-premises or Azure-based private cloud environment. Connectivity is provided through Azure ExpressRoute, VPN connections, or Azure Virtual WAN. Nevertheless, these services require specific network address ranges and firewall ports to function. Figure 2-11 depicts the Azure VMware Solution's core network connectivity.

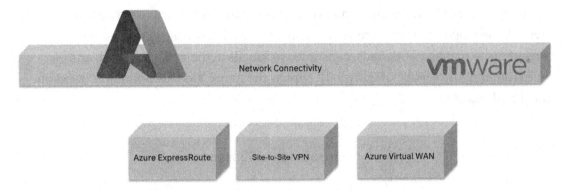

Figure 2-11. *Azure VMware Solution – core network connectivity*

AVS private clouds come preconfigured with NSX-T networking and connectivity. The on-premises deployment of NSX-T is not required. Active-Active is the mode used by the t0 gateway, and the t1 gateway uses Active-Standby. Cloud gateways let cloud consumers connect network segments with logical virtual switches and provide east-west and north-south connectivity.

The NSX-T objects can then be configured within the Azure portal once the AVS cloud is deployed. Azure VMware administrators have a simplified view of NSX-T operations that they might use daily.

The Azure portal currently allows the configuration of four components:

- **Component 1: Segments**. Azure administrators can create network segments that display in the NSX-T manager and vCenter.

- **Component 2: DHCP**. If the Azure VMware administrator intends to use DHCP to provide addresses to AVS workloads, they can create a DHCP server or DHCP relay.

- **Component 3:** A VMware administrator can set up port mirroring in Azure to help troubleshoot network problems.

- **Component 4:** A DNS VMware administrator can create and manage DNS forwarders to send DNS requests to designated DNS servers for resolution.

In addition, Azure VMware administrators retain access to the NSX-T management console to use advanced settings and other NSX-T features such as configuring routing firewalls and micro-segmentation.

Azure VMware Solution consumers can connect the Azure virtual network to their private cloud infrastructure. Azure VMware Solution private clouds allow cloud consumers to manage workloads, consume workloads in their private cloud, and access other Azure services. Figure 2-12 depicts the Azure VMware Solution's backbone integrated view.

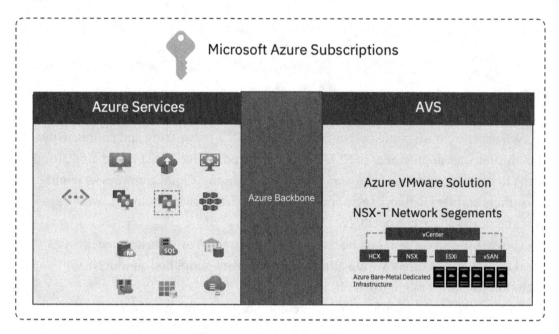

Figure 2-12. *Azure VMware Solution – backbone integrated view*

Figure 2-12 illustrates how essential network interconnections are established during a private cloud deployment. Azure VMware Solution provides connectivity between a virtual network in Azure and a private cloud using ExpressRoute on the back end. It is primarily used to enable the following:

- From VMs in cloud consumers' Azure subscriptions, inbound access to vCenter Server and NSX-T manager is available.

- Private clouds can access Azure's services outbound.

- They can also pass workloads inbound to Azure.

Azure VMware Solution can be integrated with on-premises datacenters and Azure virtual networks. Let's take look at the options. The bare metal hosts used for AVS are different from the server fleet that hosts other Azure services. Each host is in its own zone within Microsoft's datacenters.

The following are the functions enabled by this interconnectivity:

- VMs in cloud consumers' Azure subscriptions have inbound access to vCenter Server and NSX-T manager.

- VMs can access Azure services on a private cloud.

- Workloads running in the private cloud can be accessed from the outside.

Figure 2-13 depicts the Azure VMware Solution's ExpressRoute.

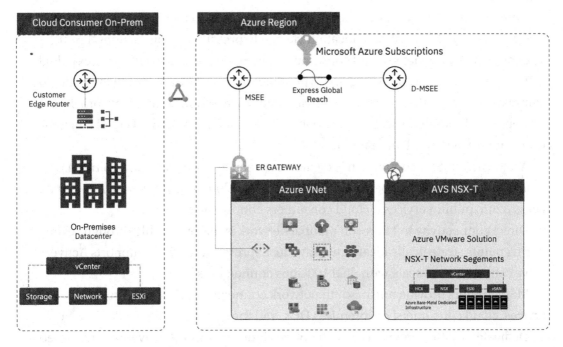

Figure 2-13. *Azure VMware Solution – ExpressRoute*

Through Microsoft ExpressRoute, cloud consumers can connect cloud on-premises networks to the Microsoft cloud through a private connection. Cloud consumers of Microsoft cloud services such as Azure and 365 can connect to ExpressRoute.

An IP VPN (any-to-any) network, an Ethernet point-to-point network, or a cross-connect through a colocation facility can provide connectivity. There is no public Internet connectivity for ExpressRoute. Because of this, ExpressRoute connections offer reliability, higher speeds, and consistent latency than typical shared Internet connections.

With respect to Layer 3 connectivity, Microsoft connects cloud consumers' on-premises networks, cloud consumers' instances in Azure, and Microsoft public addresses using BGP, a dynamic routing protocol. Multiple BGP sessions are established between Microsoft and cloud consumers' networks for different traffic profiles.

Cloud consumers' AVS private clouds are connected to the dedicated Microsoft Enterprise Edge (MSEE) when they deploy the existing ExpressRoute circuit between on-premises and Microsoft Azure. Cloud consumers can then connect that to an ExpressRoute gateway in their existing Azure VNet to allow resources within that Azure viewer to communicate with AVS.

Connectivity providers and cloud consumers connect to two Microsoft Enterprise Edge routers at an ExpressRoute location via two ExpressRoute connections. From the connectivity provider's/cloud consumer's network edge, Microsoft requires a dual BGP connection, one to each MSEE. It is possible that cloud consumers will not deploy redundant devices/Ethernet circuits on their end. More often, connectivity providers will deploy redundant devices to ensure that Microsoft has handed off cloud consumers' connections in a redundant manner.

A dedicated MSEE connection is created between an Azure VMware Solution private cloud and the Azure global backbone when a private cloud is provisioned. AVS can then access Azure public services if cloud consumers choose the Internet.

Direct connectivity to Microsoft's global network is made possible through several peering points strategically located worldwide. ExpressRoute Direct supports Active/Active connectivity at scale with dual 100Gbps connections.

MSEE routers provide north/south network connectivity among Azure native services, cloud consumers' on-premises DCs, and the Internet.

Dedicated MSEEs provide connectivity for cloud consumers' private clouds based on AVS running in an Azure environment to connect to Azure native services and on-premises via MSEE.

ExpressRoute Azure services provide private, secure, high-speed, low-latency connections among the on-premises network and Microsoft Azure.

Azure resources can communicate with AVS resources through an ExpressRoute gateway configured in an existing VNet, a virtual network gateway that exchanges IP routes among the network and routes network traffic.

To connect to the jump box through the Azure bastion, you usually creates a VNet with a jump box virtual machine and an ExpressRoute gateway connected to an AVS ExpressRoute. Most enterprises already have an ExpressRoute circuit between their on-premises data center and the Azure region. Those ExpressRoute circuits can be peering with the private ExpressRroute circuit supporting AVS to allow connectivity between the on-premises resources connected VNet and AVS.

Global Reach peer ExpressRoute circuits together to avoid hopping over a VNet.

Private networks are created for management, provisioning, and vMotion in an AVS private cloud. NSX-T Manager, vCenter, and vMotion or deployment of virtual machines can be accessed through these private networks. Private clouds can be connected to on-premises environments with ExpressRoute Global Reach. An ExpressRoute circuit to the Azure subscription on-premises is required to connect to the virtual network.

Connectivity From On-Premises to AVS via ExpressRoute

The customer network can communicate with the Azure VNet as depicted in Figure 2-13, and the Azure VNet can connect to AVS, but the customer network cannot connect directly to AVS yet. Figure 2-14 depicts the Azure VMware Solution's ExpressRoute without Global Reach.

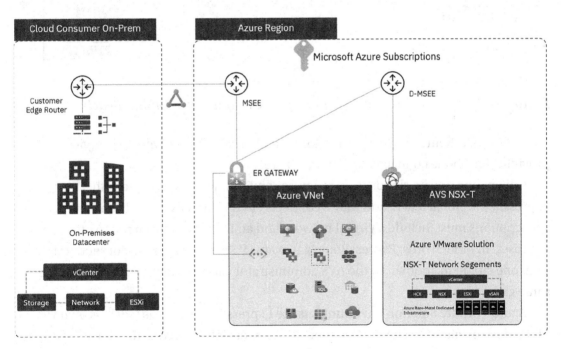

Figure 2-14. *Azure VMware Solution – ExpressRoute without Global Reach*

To connect directly to AVS, the cloud consumer must configure ExpressRoute Global Reach to peer the ExpressRoute circuit supporting the customer connection to the ExpressRoute circuit supporting AVS. Figure 2-15 depicts the Azure VMware Solution's ExpressRoute with Global Reach.

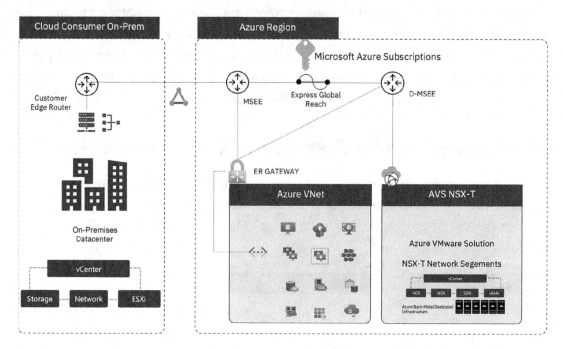

Figure 2-15. *Azure VMware Solution – ExpressRoute with Global Reach*

The ExpressRoute between AVS D-MSEE and MSEE is part of the AVS service providing backbone connectivity to/from Azure.

Connecting private clouds to on-premises environments is possible with ExpressRoute global reach, and MSEE connects circuits directly. Cloud consumers' subscriptions must include a virtual network and an ExpressRoute circuit to on-premises. In other words, ExpressRoute gateways (VNet gateways) cannot send traffic from one circuit to another, so the AVS administrator cannot attach two circuits to the same gateway.

Azure VMware Solution environments are ExpressRoute regions (each its own virtual MSEE device), allowing cloud consumers to connect global reach to the "local" peering location. With this feature, multiple Azure VMware Solution instances can be connected to the same peering location in the same region.

In the absence of an ExpressRoute, cloud consumers can use the site-to-site VPN to connect to on-premises. Traffic flows through an Azure VPN tunnel through the Internet and an ExpressRoute gateway to the dedicated Microsoft Edge that VMware and Microsoft recommended for deployments of non-production or POC.

Over VPN, HCX was initially not supported; however, HCX 4.2 now supports it. Figure 2-16 depicts the Azure VMware Solution's VPN connectivity.

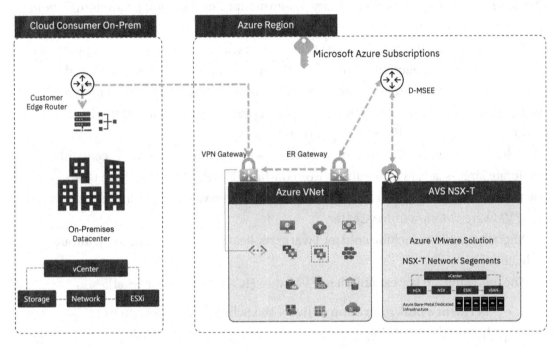

Figure 2-16. *Azure VMware Solution – VPN connectivity*

At the time of writing, AVS supports the configuration maximums listed in Table 2-7.

Table 2-7. *AVS Supported Configuration for Networking*

Components	Configuration
Azure VMware Solution ExpressRoute maximum linked private clouds	4
Azure VMware Solution ExpressRoute port speed	10 Gbps
Public IPs exposed via vWAN	100

Azure virtual WAN public IP addresses provide internet access to virtual machines deployed on a private cloud. By default, internet access is disabled for new private clouds.

AVS Workload and Application Mobility

VMware HCX is an application mobility platform that simplifies application migration, rebalancing workloads, and optimizing disaster recovery across datacenters and clouds.

Cloud migration is dependent on several factors: staff readiness, current processes, IT support, and management. Through AVS, cloud consumers gain access to and manage VMware environments using familiar VMware tools without retraining or even replatforming the hypervisors. As a result, cloud consumers maintain direct administrative access to VMware vSphere interfaces.

Using the VMware HCX Enterprise functionality, organizations can successfully accelerate large-scale, live migrations from on-premises to Azure with little to no downtime. VMs are migrated from on-premises to Azure without any interruption when using VMware vMotion from vCenter.

Migration options include cold and warm replication or live migration without replication,

The following are key capabilities of VMware HCX (what license level):

- **Perform a bulk migration of live VMs:** Schedule the movement of hundreds of VMs in parallel.

- **Use simple migration planning tools:** To quickly identify the application and workload relationships and logically group VMs for efficient migration.

- **Cloud and data center mobility:** VMs can be moved between local datacenters and Azure AVS private clouds or across cloud regions or providers to maximize resource utilization.

- **Migrate with no downtime:** There is no need to rearchitect IP addresses.

- **Migration of non-vSphere workloads:** Migrate KVM and Hyper-V workloads to the current vSphere versions compatible with the entire VMware Cloud, VMware Cloud Foundation, VMware Cloud Provider Program, and IaaS offerings.

- **Work across the WAN and LAN:** Provide a unique infrastructure model based on the workload requirements, mixing public, private, and hybrid clouds.

- **Extend network and IP space seamlessly for cloud consumers:** Reduce complexity and ensure compliance with IP addressing policies, security policies, and administrative boundaries.

To accelerate data center modernization and cloud transformation, VMware HCX enables high-performance, large-scale mobile app deployment across VMware vSphere and non-vSphere environments.

VMware HCX enables interoperability across KVM, Hyper-V, and vSphere 6.0+ to current vSphere versions. Live and bulk migrations can be performed without redesigning the application or rearchitecting the network.

Cloud consumers can modernize existing on-premises datacenters using the complete software-defined data center (SDDC)/VMware Cloud Foundation stack, managed services, or IaaS.

Migrating to a new platform can be driven by the need to move a set of available applications. Cloud adoption is the most common use case for a first wave migration using VMware HCX today, whether it is through a private cloud on-premises using VMware Cloud Foundation or adopting a VMware-based public cloud service such as VMware Cloud on AWS or Azure VMware Service or a combination of these services in support of a multi-cloud strategy.

It is rarely straightforward to move many virtual machines. By replatforming !!is relocating a better word? applications to current vSphere versions as part of the migration process or transforming workloads from KVM and Hyper-V environments, HCX is designed to support these brownfield migrations.

AVS private clouds and on-premises application footprints cannot be rebalanced actively without the ability to connect multiple clouds and become software-centric, service-driven businesses. A secure, high-throughput, WAN-optimized, always-on, secure, hybrid interconnect is at the core of HCX, continuously moving workloads across cloud regions, cloud providers, and on-premises datacenters.

Business continuity and disaster recovery (BC/DR) are optimized through a HCX hybrid interconnect, which offers on-demand migration. The cloud enables consumers to back up virtual workloads and migrate large-scale workloads to avoid disasters on-demand, on a schedule, and through scheduling.

HCX-enabled vSphere environments can be moved to and from using multiple HCX migration technologies. Legacy and modernized sites are compatible with HCX, and it provides the following virtual machine mobility:

- Up to four virtual machines can be transferred simultaneously using HCX bulk migration using the vSphere Replication protocol. Rebooting the virtual machines into the target site can be transformed to the latest VM hardware/tools. Virtual machines can have their vNIC IP addresses updated as part of the migration process by using bulk migration.

- HCX vMotion allows you to move virtual machines individually using VMware vMotion. With HCX Network Extension, applications sensitive to downtime can be migrated with zero downtime.

- The VMware NFC protocol is used for HCX cold migration. Powered-off virtual machines are automatically transferred using this migration type.

- With HCX vMotion with vSphere replication, virtual machines prepared in parallel will fail over with zero downtime (currently in preview with VMware Cloud on AWS).

- HCX OS-assisted migration is a migration solution (currently in beta) that enables migrations from non-vSphere (KVM) environments to vSphere using an agent in Windows/Linux VMs.

By replicating data to an HCX-enabled provider or private cloud, VMware HCX helps protect on-premises applications. VMware HCX can restore the networking layer in a disaster. Since traffic routes are kept before the disaster, there is minimal downtime and high-speed disaster recovery. There is no reconfiguration of IPs, eliminating complexity and enabling partial or complete site recovery.

Through various migration methods, VMware HCX cloud consumers can migrate VMware workloads from on-premises datacenters running vSphere 6.0 or later to Azure VMware Solution and other connected sites. Figure 2-17 depicts the Azure VMware Solution's HCX interconnect.

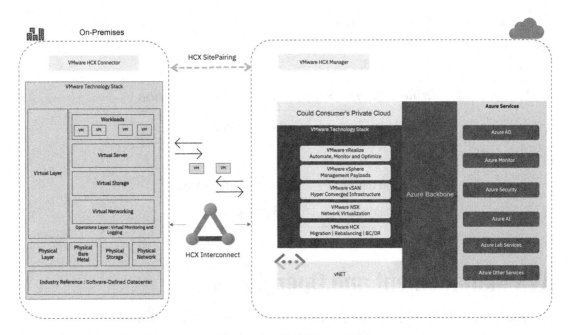

Figure 2-17. *Azure VMware Solution – HCX interconnect*

Once the cloud consumer's AVS private cloud is deployed, the HCX cloud manager
can be deployed and configured automatically through the Azure portal's Add-ons tab.

After that, the cloud consumers need to download, activate, and configure the HCX
connector in their VMware environments on-premises. They can ensure a secure bidirectional connection between the environments and incorporate several features,
including a built-in VPN with Suite B encryption, traffic engineering, LAN optimization,
and deduplication and compression.

By extending on-premises networks into the cloud, workload migrations can be
facilitated without the need to reconfigure IPs, and WAN optimization between on-
premises and AVS can also be achieved, as well as deduplication and compression,
which can reduce bandwidth and migration time.

For workload mobility and cloud migration, VMware HCX 4.2.2 advanced is deployed. It must be added through the Add-ons panel after private cloud provisioning to use this feature. See Table 2-8.

Table 2-8. *AVS Supported HCX Configuration*

Components	Configuration
HCX	4.2.2
HCX edition minimum	Enterprise/Advanced
HCX site pairings	25 (any edition)

AVS Management and Operations

Azure administrators interact with the cloud environment, deploy dozens of resources, configure individual services with scripts, and view detailed reports on usage, health, and costs. There are two broad categories of management tools at a high level: visual tools and code-based tools. Figure 2-18 depicts the Azure VMware Solution's management block.

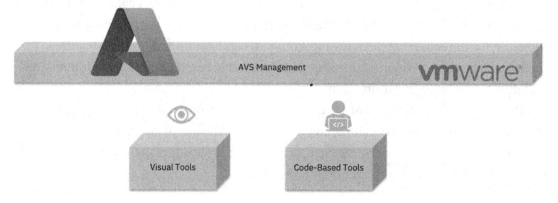

Figure 2-18. *Azure VMware Solution – management block*

Azure's visual tools make it easy for cloud consumers to visually access all its functionality. Visual tools, however, may not be as helpful when setting up a large deployment of interdependent resources with configuration options.

A code-based tool is usually the better choice for setting up and configuring Azure resources quickly. The correct commands and parameters can be saved into files and used again and again once they have been entered, even though understanding them might take a bit of time. A source code-management tool such as Git allows setup and configuration code to be stored, versioned, and maintained along with application code. This method of managing hardware and cloud resources, which developers use when writing application code, is called Infrastructure as Code.

Infrastructure as Code can be viewed as either imperative code or declarative code. Code that specifies each necessary step to achieve a specific outcome is imperative code. On the other hand, declarative code only defines the desired effect, leaving it up to the interpreter to decide how to do it. A declarative approach is more reliable for deploying dozens or hundreds of resources simultaneously and reliably, so tools based on declarative code are essential.

Azure portal users, Azure PowerShell users, Azure CLI users, and Azure Cloud Shell users must select and use a tooling option.

Microsoft Azure management tools enable administrators, developers, and managers to interact with the cloud environment to perform tasks such as deploying dozens or hundreds of resources at once, configuring individual services programmatically, and viewing detailed reports on usage, health, and costs.

Depending on the situation, Microsoft Azure provides a range of management tooling options. Azure administrators can monitor, manage, and protect VMs using native Azure services in a hybrid environment (Azure, Azure VMware Solution, and on-premises).

It is Azure's responsibility to manage the lifecycle of the private cloud software stack, while Azure administrators monitor and manage it. Azure is also responsible for providing and configuring the Azure infrastructure. When a failure occurs, or more or fewer resources are needed for cluster scaling, it is responsible for adding or removing hosts and networks. Azure VMware Solution handles the patching and updating of private cloud software.

It also monitors, manages, and protects VMs in Azure VMware Solution and on-premises VMs with Microsoft Azure native services. Microsoft Azure native services can be integrated with Azure VMware Solution. Azure VMware Solution supports the Azure native services depicted in Figure 2-19.

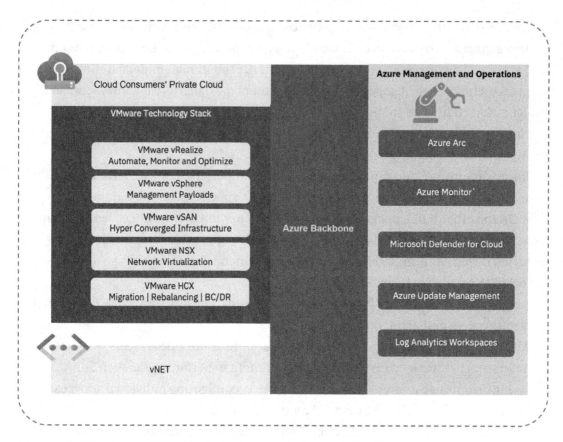

Figure 2-19. *Azure VMware Solution – monitoring block*

Azure Arc: Microsoft Azure Arc enables the management of any infrastructure, including Azure VMware Solutions, on-premises, or other cloud services. Azure Arc-enabled servers allow cloud customers to manage Windows and Linux servers and virtual machines hosted outside of Azure, on cloud consumers' corporate network, or in another cloud provider.

Azure Monitor: AVS and on-premises telemetry are collected and analyzed by Azure Monitor. There is no deployment required. Azure VMware Solution or on-premises VMs can be monitored via Azure monitor. Log Analytics workspaces in Azure Monitor enable cloud consumers to collect logs and performance counters using Log Analytics agents and extensions.

The Azure Monitor allows administrators to collect and analyze data from other sources for analysis, visualization, and alerting. The cloud consumer can also create alert rules to detect issues within the AVS environment, including high resource use, missing patches, low disk space, and heartbeats of AVS VMs. By sending an alert to IT Service

Management (ITSM) tools, cloud users can automatically respond to detected events. Ops administrators can also receive notifications via email during the detection process.

As part of the Azure VMware Solution, both the VMware components and the underlay are continuously monitored. When Azure VMware Solution detects a failure, it takes action to repair the failed components. Azure VMware Solution initiates host remediation by detecting node degradation or failure.

Host remediation involves replacing the faulty node with a healthy one in a cluster. Whenever possible, the defective host is placed in VMware vSphere maintenance mode. Through VMware vMotion, the VMs can be moved from the faulty host to other available hosts in the cluster, potentially resulting in zero downtime for the live migration of workloads. The host is removed from the cluster if it cannot be placed in maintenance mode.

Monitoring conditions on the host are performed by Azure VMware Solution:

- Processor and memory status

- Connection and power state

- Hardware fan status

- Network connectivity loss

- Hardware system board status

- Errors on the disk(s) of a vSAN host

- Hardware voltage and temperature status

- Hardware power status

- Storage status and Connection failure

Additional Azure Monitor tasks include

- Seamless monitoring

- Better infrastructure visibility

- Instant notifications

- Automatic resolution

- Cost efficiency

Microsoft Defender for Cloud: Microsoft Defender for Cloud increases data center security and protects hybrid workloads in the cloud and on-premises against advanced threats. It assesses the vulnerability of Azure VMware Solution VMs, generates alerts when necessary, and forwards them to Azure Monitor for resolution. By way of an example, it estimates the number of missing operating system patches, security misconfigurations, and endpoint protection issues. Customers of Microsoft Defender for Cloud can also define security policies.

Advanced threat protection is provided by Microsoft Defender for Cloud, including

- File integrity monitoring

- Fileless security alerts

- Operating system patch assessment

- Security misconfigurations assessment

- Endpoint protection assessment

Azure Update Management: The Azure Update Management function in Azure Automation allows cloud users to manage operating system updates on Windows and Linux machines. Azure Monitor receives patching deviation alerts and alerts the user to remediate the problem. Cloud consumers' Log Analytics workspaces must be connected to Azure Update Management to assess the status of updates on their VMs.

Log Analytics Workspaces: Workspaces for Log Analytics store log data. Data repositories and configurations vary by workspace. Azure VMware Solution VMs can be monitored by using the Log Analytics agent. The Log Analytics Workspace agent collects data about changes to installed software, Microsoft services, Windows registry and files, and Linux daemons on monitored machines. Azure Monitor Logs receives data from the agent and processes it when available. As Azure Monitor Logs receives data, it applies logic to it, records it, and makes it available for analysis. To support deploying Log Analytics agents on VMs, use the Azure Arc-enabled servers VM extension. Using the VM extension support for Azure Arc enabled servers, you can quickly deploy the Log Analytics agent. Figure 2-20 depicts the Azure VMware Solution management and operations integrated view.

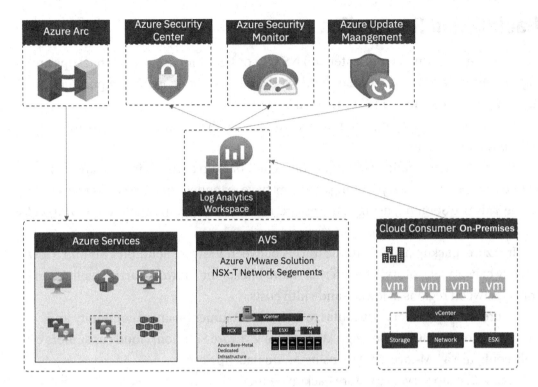

Figure 2-20. *Azure VMware Solution – management and operations integrated view*

Log Analytics agents can be connected to Azure, Azure VMware Solution, and on-premises virtual machines to collect log data. Azure Monitor Logs sends log data to the Log Analytics workspace, where it is stored. For new and existing VMs, cloud consumers can deploy the Log Analytics agent by using Arc-enabled servers.

Log Analytics workspaces collect logs, and cloud consumers can use Log Analytics workspaces with Defender for Cloud to assess the vulnerability status of Azure VMware Solution VMs and raise an alert if a critical vulnerability is found. The system estimates, for example, the number of operating system patches to install, security misconfigurations, and endpoint protections to install.

Microsoft Sentinel can be integrated into the Log Analytics workspace for alert detection, threat visibility, hunting, and threat response.

The Defender for Cloud connector is used to connect Defender for Cloud and Microsoft Sentinel. Microsoft Sentinel receives the vulnerability and creates an incident, which is then mapped with other threats from Defender for Cloud. Cloud consumers can also use the scheduled rules query to detect unwanted activities and report them as incidents.

Backup and Restoration

Backups are performed for vCenter and NSX-T configurations daily, and backups are kept for three days. In the Azure portal, cloud consumers can open a support request via Azure Portal if they need a restore from a backup.

Continuous monitoring is performed on Azure VMware Solution's VMware and underlay components.

Backup and restoration solutions from Azure backup partners in VMware-based environments are industry-leading. Partners have extended their solutions to include Azure VMware Solution, using Azure as a repository for backups and a storage target for long-term archiving and retention.

In Azure, backup network traffic travels between VMware Solution VMs and a low-latency backup repository. The internal Azure backplane network carries replication traffic between regions at lower bandwidth costs.

Azure Backup Server contributes to a cloud consumer business continuity and disaster recovery (BCDR) strategy. With Azure VMware Solution, cloud consumers can only configure a VM-level backup using Azure Backup Server.

Azure Backup Server can store backup data to

- **Disk:** Azure Backup Server stores short-term backup data in disk pools.

- **Azure:** Data stored in Azure Backup Server disk pools can be backed up to Microsoft Azure using Azure Backup for short-term and long-term storage off-premises.

Use Azure Backup Server to restore data to the source or an alternate location. Cloud consumers can restore data to an alternate location if the original data is unavailable because of planned or unexpected issues.

Microsoft and VMware recommend performing the following for backup and recovery domain:

- Ensure regular automated backups

- Encrypt backup data

- Validate all backups, including customer-managed keys

- Mitigate the risk of lost keys

Shared Responsibility

Microsoft Azure VMware Solution is a VMware-validated solution that undergoes ongoing testing and verification related to vSphere upgrades and enhancements. Microsoft manages cloud consumers' private cloud infrastructures and software. Having Microsoft handle this responsibility allows cloud consumers to focus on developing and running workloads within their private cloud and using Azure native resources. With the Azure VMware Solution private cloud and VMware software upgrades, cloud consumers can ensure their private cloud deployments have the latest security, stability, and features.

The VMware Cloud Infrastructure Services providers all have a shared responsibility model, which defines distinct roles and responsibilities between the VMware Cloud Infrastructure Services provider and the organization that consumes the service.

Cloud consumers and Microsoft are involved in the Azure VMware Solution under the shared responsibility model.

In the Microsoft cloud, ongoing maintenance, security, and management are abstracted, leaving cloud consumers in charge of the most important things, such as guest OS provisioning, applications, and virtual machines. Customers can also consider bringing their lifecycle processes and configuration management techniques to Azure. The Azure VMware Solution infrastructure is more under the control of Microsoft in this model, eliminating specific operational responsibilities.

Azure VMware Solution assumes responsibility for the underlying infrastructure when it deploys in Azure. Unless a support ticket is opened, IT departments cannot gain root access to ESXi hosts or join vCenter to a domain without seeking support. It means that central IT personnel have control over all on-premises VMware environments, changing standard operating procedures and process flow for IT departments.

By managing a traditional VMware environment, operations engineers can focus on innovation within the applications and workloads that define their business charters. Besides Azure VMware Solution, it allows for a more comprehensive digital transformation. Figure 2-21 depicts Azure VMware Solution's security and shared responsibility view.

Components	Deployment	LifeCycle	Configuration
		Microsoft Responsibility	Cloud Consumer Responsibility
Phyiscal Infrastructure	X	X	X
Regions	X	X	X
Availabiltiy Zone	X	X	X
Edge Locations	X	X	X
Hardware	X	X	X
Compute	X	X	X
Network	X	X	X
Storage	X	X	X
vSphere Lifecycle	X	X	X
vSAN Lifecycle	X	X	X
NSX-T Lifecycle	X	X	X
VM-Guest OS and Applications	X	X	X
VM-Appliances	X	X	X
VM-Security	X	X	X
VM-Backup	X	X	X
Firewall and Network Configuration	X	X	X

Figure 2-21. *Azure VMware Solution – security shared responsibility view*

The cloud consumers' responsibilities are to deploy and configure their SDDCs, virtual machines, and data. Customers are responsible for configuring network firewalls, ExpressRoute, and VPNs, managing virtual machines (including guest security and encryption), and applying appropriate controls for users using Azure role-based access controls (or Azure Active Directory), along with vCenter roles and permissions.

The Azure VMware Solution service is protected by Microsoft software and systems. Computing, storage, and networking software comprise the SDDC, along with the service consoles used to provision Azure VMware Solution.

The full service's physical facilities, security, infrastructure, and hardware are under Microsoft's control.

Microsoft is responsible for managing Azure infrastructure, including physical infrastructure, Azure Regions, Azure Availability Zones, and end-to-end management of compute, network, storage, rack, power bare metal hosts, and network equipment.

Microsoft is responsible for the Azure VMware Solution SDDC lifecycle including ESXi patching and upgrading, vCenter Server patching and upgrading, NSX patching and upgrading, and vSAN patching and upgrading. SDDC Networking (NSX) including Tier-0 Router, connectivity from Tier-0 to Azure Network. SDDC Backup/Restore including Backup and Restore vCenter Server, Backup and Restore NSX Manager. SDDC Health includes replacing failed hosts.

Azure VMware Solution is secured and protected by Microsoft. It consists of the compute, storage, and networking software that makes up the SDDC and the service consoles that enable Azure VMware Solutions to be provisioned.

Microsoft guarantees that Azure VMware Solution will be available at least 99.9% of the time.

Microsoft guarantees that NSX Manager and vCenter Server (management tools for VMware) will be available at least 99.9% of the time.

For Azure VMware Solution in the Azure cloud to provide the above specified uptime, cloud consumers must maintain the following minimum configurations:

- There is one failure to tolerate for clusters with 3 to 5 hosts and two failures to tolerate for clusters with 6 to 16 hosts.

- Cluster storage retains a slack capacity of 25%.

- Microsoft has not been prevented from meeting its availability commitment due to consumer actions under the Elevated Privilege mode.

- Virtual machines can be started on the cluster since there is enough capacity.

- The calculation of total available uptime excludes scheduled maintenance.

Unified licensing and consumption:

- Keeping licenses and resources in one place eliminates unnecessary complexity.

Azure Hybrid use benefits:

- The core pack can be licensed on-premises.

- Fully utilize existing Windows Server and SQL Server licenses when possible. Azure Reserved Instances and AHUB help you save up to 80%.

- Azure offers three years of extended security updates for Windows Server 2008 and 2008 R2. It only upgrades when necessary.

- PaYG pricing is available and invoiced as other Azure services based on monthly usage.

- Reservations can be discounted programmatically.

Microsoft handles many low-level operational tasks, leaving the customer to manage their workloads.

Cloud consumers are responsible for deploying software-defined data centers (SDDCs), including sizing host count, management network range, and HCX network range.

They are also responsible for configuring the SDDC Network and Security (NSX) including Tier-1 routers, firewall, IPsec VPN, NAT, public IP addresses, network segments, distributed firewalls, and network extensions (via HCX or NSX).

They are also responsible for configuring the SDDC network and Security (VSAN), including defining and maintaining VSAN VM policies and adding hosts to keep adequate "slack space." Deploying VMs includes installing operating systems, patching operating systems, installing antivirus software, installing backup software, and installing configuration management software.

They are also responsible for migrating VMs including HCX configuration, HCX updates, Live vMotion, cold migration, and content library sync.

They are also responsible for managing VMs including installing software, implementing backup solutions, and implementing antivirus solutions.

AVS Security

Any environment must have security. Workloads deployed in Azure by cloud consumers' organizations should be secure. Without this, an attacker may be able to use cloud consumers' Azure resources to mine cryptocurrency at their expense or gain access to sensitive customer information, which would result in massive fines or sanctions for the company. In addition, it could result in reputation damage. Security concerns are increasing, whether using a hybrid cloud or a multi-cloud approach, due to the challenges presented by remote workers and the frequency and sophistication of nation-state attacks. For hybrid cloud planning, security and compliance are viewed as critical and as the first considerations.

With Azure Virtual Services, cloud migrations can access Azure's built-in security capabilities across all layers and resources of the cloud. It's easy to turn on throughout every development lifecycle stage, from native controls to scalable security operations.

The security offered by Azure is holistic. The cloud consumer's organization needs to be protected, not just Azure. Integrating built-in controls and services allows cloud consumers to protect workloads efficiently. AVS workloads are protected against rapidly evolving threats via the Azure Monitoring and Security Center, which makes cloud consumers feel confident during their cloud journey.

Azure VMware Solution security allows cloud consumers to run their VMware-based workloads in a secure and trustable environment.

VMware-based solutions from Microsoft Azure security partners cover many aspects of the security ecosystem, such as threat protection and security scanning. Cloud consumers have adopted many solutions integrated with VMware NSX-T for their on-premises deployments. Figure 2-22 depicts Azure VMware Solution's security and compliance integrated view.

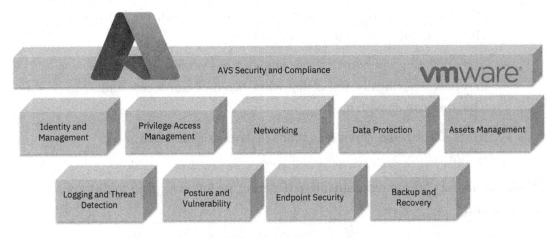

Figure 2-22. *Azure VMware Solution – security and compliance*

As organizations migrate to AVS with Azure, they need to know a new attack vector. Security threats also exist for an AVS workload if it is not protected and secured per industry standards and recommendations.

One of the most daunting tasks for landlords is tenant security. Since Microsoft Azure is a public tenant, Microsoft and its AVS cloud customers share a certain amount of responsibility.

Corporate data used to be protected primarily by network perimeters, firewalls, and physical access controls. With the proliferation of bringing your own device (BYOD), mobile apps, and cloud-based applications, network perimeters have become increasingly porous.

Most cloud-related security breaches begin with a compromised user identity. When attackers gain access to a network through a compromised credential, they can escalate privileges or gather intelligence for further attacks. Secure identity is essential in any discussion about cloud security.

Security is increasingly being determined by identity. As a result, securing AVS solutions and data requires proper authentication and privilege assignment.

Authentication and authorization are two fundamental concepts that need to be understood when discussing identity and access control. They determine everything else that occurs and occur sequentially in every identity and access process:

- The authentication process establishes the identity of a person or service seeking to access a resource. An identity and access control principle is created by challenging a party for legitimate credentials. These credentials prove the person's identity.

- Authenticating a person or service determines what level of access they have. Specifically, it specifies what data they can access and what they can do with it.

- Azure AD provides services to manage authentication and authorization.

Microsoft and VMware recommend performing the following for identity and management:

- Standardize Azure AD as the central identity and authentication system.

- Manage application identities securely and automatically.

- Use Azure AD single sign-on (SSO) for application access.

- Eliminate unintended credential exposure.

Cloud consumers can restrict standing administrator access to privileged roles discover and review who has access using Privileged Identity Management (PIM) in Azure AD.

To reduce the chances of misappropriation, can organizations limit who has access to secure information or resources:

- An attacker gaining access to the system

- Accidentally affecting a sensitive resource by an authorized user

Users still need to perform privileged operations in Azure AD, Azure, Microsoft 365, or SaaS apps. Cloud consumers can grant users just-in-time privileged access to Azure and Azure AD resources and monitor what they do with their privileged access.

Microsoft and VMware recommend performing the following for privilege access management:

- Protect and limit highly privileged users.

- Review and reconcile user access regularly.

- Use privileged access workstations.

- Follow the least privilege principle.

- Choose approval process for Microsoft support.

A virtual network is a logically isolated private network that can be created using the Azure cloud platform. Cloud computing services such as IaaS and PaaS use isolated networks, which must be isolated or controlled by customers. The perimeter (the outer boundary between the untrusted public internet and Azure virtual network resources consumed by cloud consumers) is where these private networks are protected from attacks.

Azure Firewall is an intelligent network firewall that protects cloud workloads residing on Azure with a cloud-native approach.

Microsoft and VMware recommend performing the following for networking:

- Implement security for internal traffic.

- Connect private networks.

- Establish private network access to Azure services.

- Protect applications and services from external network attacks.

- Simplify network security rules.

- Secure domain name services (DNSs).

- Only allow trusted networks.

- Use Azure firewall premium.

- Deploy and configure network security groups on a VNet.

- Review and implement recommendations within the Azure security baseline for Azure VMware Solution.

The importance of data security is growing. Cloud consumers are obliged to handle their data carefully, including under strict regulations. The data of cloud consumers shouldn't end up in the wrong hands.

Microsoft and VMware recommend performing the following for data protection:

- Protect sensitive data.

- Encrypt sensitive information in transit.

- Encrypt sensitive data at rest.

All assets in a cloud infrastructure can be seen and managed using cloud asset management. This is an automated and secure way to manage cloud infrastructure. Businesses can track their cloud assets while maintaining smooth cloud infrastructure.

Microsoft and VMware recommend performing the following for assets management:

- Ensure the security team has visibility into risks to the assets.

- Ensure the security team has access to asset inventory and metadata.

- Use only approved Azure services.

- Use only approved applications in compute resources.

Logging and threat detection discusses how to detect threats on Azure and enable, collect, and store audit logs. As part of this process, Azure will enable detection, investigation, and remediation processes with controls that ensure high-quality alerts can be generated with native threat detection; it will also collect logs with Azure Monitor, centralize security analysis with Azure Sentinel, synchronize time, and keep logs for a specified period.

Microsoft and VMware recommend performing the following for logging and threat detection:

- Enable threat detection for Azure resources.

- Enable threat detection for Azure identity and access management.

- Enable logging for Azure network activities.

- Enable logging for Azure resources.

- Centralize security log management and analysis.

- Configure log storage retention.

- Use approved time-synchronization sources.

Controls for evaluating and improving the Azure security posture are included in position and vulnerability management. Azure security configuration tracking, reporting, and correction include vulnerability scanning, penetration testing, and remediation.

Microsoft and VMware recommend performing the following for posture and vulnerability:

- Establish secure configurations for Azure services.

- Sustain secure configurations for Azure services.

- Establish secure configurations for computing resources.

- Sustain secure configurations for computing resources.

- Securely store the custom operating system and container images.

- Perform software vulnerability assessments.

- Rapidly and automatically remediate software vulnerabilities.

- Conduct regular attack simulation.

An Azure SDK Import module is provided for configuring and enabling anti-malware protection as part of Azure service deployment. Endpoint protection for Azure provides anti-malware protection for Azure services in the cloud running on the Azure OS. During the deployment of Azure role VMs, anti-malware is installed and updated.

An AVS VM is protected from potentially harmful software with Microsoft Endpoint Protection for Azure, including viruses and spyware.

Microsoft and VMware recommend performing the following for endpoint security:

- Use endpoint detection and response (EDR).

- Use centrally managed modern anti-malware software.

- Ensure anti-malware software and signatures are updated.

Summary

In this chapter, you got an overview of AVS, explored key elements of AVS and got a compute overview of Azure VMware Solutions, a storage overview of Azure VMware Solutions, and a network overview of Azure VMware Solutions. You also learned about AVS workload and application mobility, management, operations, and security.

In the next chapter, you will read about the design methodologies of Azure VMware Solution; AVS network topology and connectivity; AVS identity and access management; AVS security, governance, and compliance; AVS management and monitoring; AVS business continuity and disaster recovery; and AVS platform automation.

CHAPTER 3

Design Essentials of AVS

VMware's Microsoft Azure VMware Solution is a first-party Microsoft Azure product that provides one-tenant, vSphere-based private clouds on Azure. There are four VMware technologies: vSphere, NSX-T, vSAN, and HCX. VMware environments can continue to run on-premises with Azure VMware Solution running in Azure datacenters. An environment can be set up in a few hours once the VM resources have been migrated. Azure VMware Solution provides management, networking, and storage services.

Migrating organizations can choose between options provided by Azure VMware Solution. Moving VMware resources to a dedicated Azure cloud environment reduces complexity, minimizes negative effects on business continuity, and accelerates the migration process. Businesses can adopt cloud technology at their own pace with Azure VMware Solution, and as their business evolves, cloud services can be added incrementally.

By the end of this chapter, you should understand the following:

- Azure's well-architected framework

- The AVS Solution building block

- AVS network topology and connectivity

- AVS identity and access management

- AVS security, governance, and compliance

- AVS management and monitoring

- AVS business continuity and disaster recovery

- AVS platform automation

© Puthiyavan Udayakumar 2022
P. Udayakumar, *Design and Deploy Azure VMware Solutions*, https://doi.org/10.1007/978-1-4842-8312-7_3

Azure's Well-Architected Framework

Cloud computing has revolutionized the way businesses solve their business challenges and how workloads and security are designed. A solution architect is not solely responsible for delivering business value through the application's functional requirements. The design must ensure that the solution is scalable, resilient, efficient, and secure.

The well-defined framework for AVS Solution provides services, availability, security, flexibility, recoverability, and performance required for AVS cloud consumers. The following are key design principles can be followed in your AVS design.

The architecture must be able to create IT adoption, implementation, and design frameworks that support delivering business processes. The decision frameworks that the architecture develops should be followed when planning, designing, implementing, and improving a technology system. A system architecture balances and aligns business requirements with the technical capabilities needed to implement those requirements. The system and its components are designed to balance risk, cost, and capability.

Developing high-quality solutions on Azure is made more accessible by Azure's well-architected framework. When it comes to designing architecture, there is no one-size-fits-all solution. However, some universal concepts are applicable regardless of the cloud provider, the architecture, or the technology.

Concepts such as these are not all-inclusive. Focusing on these features will help AVS solutions architects build a solid, reliable, and flexible foundation.

Superficial design characteristics enable AVS architects/engineers to provide AVS solution with reliability, availability, flexibility, recoverability, and performance required for the solution. Figure 3-1 depicts the key design principles followed at each level of AVS Solution.

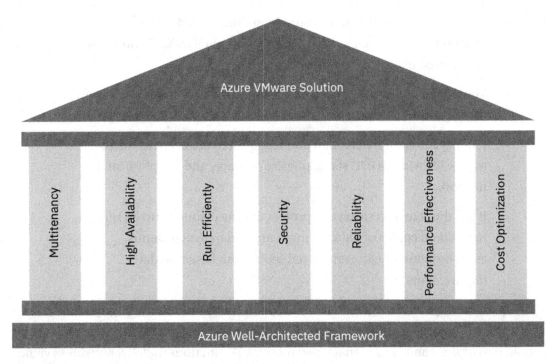

Figure 3-1. *Key design principles for simplicity*

Multitenancy: The design allows isolation of resources and networks to deliver applications with quality. It includes

- Complete isolation of computing, storage, and network resources to be managed by dedicated clusters and resource pools. Logical isolation is obtained at the virtual machine or container level, using a distributed cluster or shared resource pool.

- Application and data segregation is wanted for the multi-tenant atmosphere to ensure that one tenant cannot enter other tenants' data. The deployment of modern protection to isolate data is needed to achieve the segregation.

High availability: The design should avoid any single point of failure across the design.

- An IT function is highly available when it can withstand an individual's crash or multiple elements. Deployment of automated recovery and lessening disruption at every panel of the IT function architecture is key.

- In the design, the AVS administrator/architect needs to introduce redundancy by having varied resources for equal tasks. Redundancy is deployed in standby mode or active mode.

- The design philosophy is that when one fails, the rest can consume a more considerable part of the IT workload.

- It offers automated detection and response to the event as much as possible via a SDDC stack, physical storage, and the physical network.

- It has durable data storage to protect data availability and integrity. Redundant copies of data are implemented by synchronous, asynchronous, or Quorum-based replication based on data requirements.

Run efficiently: The design should focus on running and monitoring systems to deliver client business value and continually improve processes and procedures. It should have the capability to manage and monitor IT functions to deliver business value and continually improve supporting processes and procedures

The operation and processes needed to keep workloads in production are run efficiently. Deployments must be reliable, predictable, and automated to reduce human error. Routine processes must not slow down the deployment of new features and bug fixes. Cloud users must quickly roll back or roll forward if an update has problems. This means the following:

- AVS administrators need to have a yielded opinion of SRE workload, their role in it, and participated business goals to set the preferences that will empower business accomplishment. Distinct preferences will increase the benefits of SRE efforts.

- AVS administrators need to determine internal and external end users' needs involving key decision-makers, including business, DevOps, DevSecOps, and AVS teams, to decide where to concentrate purposes. Estimating end users' needs will guarantee that AVS has an absolute belief of the support that is wanted to design business upshots.

- AVS administrators need to estimate implications to the business and manage this information in risk records.

- AVS administrators need to evaluate risks and tradeoffs amid clashing interests or alternative passageways.

- AVS administrators need to promote innovation to expedite knowledge and engage the AVS team.

- AVS administrators need to adopt passageways that develop feature enhancement into production, enabling rehost, refactoring, agile feedback on quality, and bug fixes.

Security: The design must focus on protecting client information and systems. Security is the ability to protect the information, systems, and assets while delivering business value through risk assessments and mitigation strategies.

Design thinking about security is required throughout the entire lifecycle, from design and implementation to deployment and operations. The Azure platform protects against various threats such as network intrusion and DDoS attacks. But it would be best if cloud consumers still built security into the AVS infrastructure, data, and applications. This involves the following:

- Confidentiality, integrity, and availability of apps, data, and infrastructure

- Preserving identities using roles, for illustration, IAM roles, implementing fine-grained authorization

- Preventing traffic using ports/IP ranges, such as security groups and dividing internal and external traffic using a CIDR range

- A nocturnal trend using network flow log analysis to detect behavior, such as VPC flow log analysis using Cloud Workload Protection

- Endpoint safeguarding using anti-malware/antivirus agents, such as Endpoint Point safeguard and Cloud Workload Protection Agent

- Centralized log analysis to detect exceptions or DDoS attacks by adopting traffic trends or unnatural sources of traffic

- IDS/IPS approach by having all traffic forwarding within the gateway to such a method and then blocking/allowing traffic

- Protection in transit and an at-rest method such as using SSL deploy and encrypting disk at the storage

- An orderly process to handle any security incident and have the possible information to discover such incidents and a suitable response

Reliability: The design should focus on preventing and quickly recovering from failures to meet business and client demand. A system can recover from IT function disturbances, dynamically procuring computing support to meet the need, and moderating interruptions such as misconfigurations or temporary network issues.

A resilient system can recover from failures and continue to function. When a loss occurs, resiliency aims to restore the application to its previous state. Accessibility refers to whether cloud consumers can access their workload at any time. It includes

- Design for availability since it is estimated as a percentage of uptime and describes the proportion of time an IT function is working as expected

- Queue-based load leveling, which is a well-known design pattern that uses a queue as a buffer among a task and a setting that it uses to monitor increasing workloads

- Availability zones to defend against data center failures and provide heightened high availability to end users

- Circuit breaker patterns that take a variable volume of time to harden when connecting to a remote IT function

- An efficient mechanism for discovering breakdowns and recovering speedily and efficiently, which is essential to maintaining resiliency

- Leader Election, a well-known design pattern to organize the actions completed by a group of colluding assignment instances in a dispersed application by choosing one instance as the leader that assumes liability for managing the additional instances

Performance effectiveness: The design should focus on using computing resources efficiently. The capability to use computing resources efficiently meets system requirements and maintains that efficiency as demand changes and technologies evolve.

The performance efficiency for cloud consumers is their ability to scale their workload to meet their users' demands efficiently. Scaling appropriately and deploying

PaaS offerings with scaling capabilities are the two main ways to improve performance and efficiency. This involves

- Provisioning sufficient computing resources based on capacity requirements

- Deploying solutions in a hybrid cloud in multiple availability zones

- Adopting serverless structures to exclude the necessity to manage and maintain IT resources

- Directly carrying out stated testing with automatable resources with a wide variety of computing resources

- Integrating functional and non-functional tests into the agile development process to know when bottlenecks become an issue in production

- Integrating a content delivery network, distributing cached files across servers worldwide, and developing international end users

- Deploying server-side caching to remove the number of calls hitting the database and dramatically increasing search queries

- Using prefetching procedures to foretell what developments users are about to accept and begin the loading before they start the event

Cost optimization: The design focuses on avoiding unnecessary costs. It's about the capacity to run IT functions to deliver business value at the most moderate price point. It involves

- Knowing and measuring where the money is being spent

- Deciding the most relevant and right amount of resource standards

- Examining spend over a period of time

- Scaling to engage business demands without overspending

- Advantages from economies of scale

- Examining attribute expenditure

- Examining associate managed services to lessen the cost of ownership

Solution Building Block for Azure VMware Solutions

Solution Building Block for Azure VMware Solutions provides a references framework for the Azure VMware Solution. It's building block consist of three foundational elements: Sizing Consideration for Azure VMware Solution, Azure Landing Zone for Azure VMware Solution, and Azure VMware Solution Networking. Figure 3-2 depicts the solution building block for AVS.

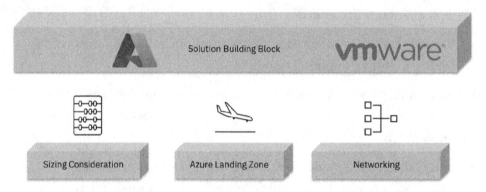

Figure 3-2. *Solution Building Block of AVS*

Let's do deep dive into each building block.

Sizing Consideration for Azure VMware Solution

A VMware offering running on Azure infrastructure is called Azure VMware Solution. By using Azure VMware Solution, on-premises VMware environments can be extended to the cloud. A VMware environment on-premises can also be migrated to Azure VMware Solution. Azure VMware Solution can be connected to an on-premises environment via various options.

Cloud consumers need to understand how the capacity of the overall cloud solution will assist them in making both technical and business decisions. These sections focus on critical design considerations in capacity planning. The following potential areas demand focus on the sizing.

- **Assess an existing VMware environment:** On-premises VMware environments typically grow organically over time. On-premises VMware environments are great for customers who want to know how great they are, such as RVTools, DICE tools, etc. You must assess the situation objectively to eliminate all guesswork in the decision-making process.

- **Determine the relationship between application components:** Customers may only need to use Azure VMware for some workloads. When customers plan for a subset of workloads, they can ensure that all the dependencies are considered.

- **A VMware on-premises environment may have different configuration requirements than the Azure VMware Solution environment:** A VMware on-premises environment might have a different set of software requirements. To help cloud consumers make the right decisions ahead of time, they consider whether the Azure VMware Solution can meet that requirement.

- **Understanding monthly and annual costs:** Customers want to know how much they will pay annually. A capacity planning exercise can help provide them with potential costs.

Figure 3-3 depicts an overview of the planning and sizing approach for Azure VMware Solution.

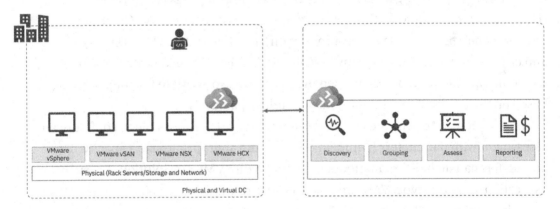

Figure 3-3. *Planning and sizing approach*

The following are the critical phases of Azure VMware Solution sizing:

- **Discovery:** This phase collects an inventory from an on-premises VMware installation.

- **Grouping:** Cloud consumers use this phase for grouping logically related VMs (like an app and a database).

- **Assessment:** During this phase, groups of virtual machines are assessed for suitability and potential remediation.

- **Reporting:** In this phase, the assessment score is consolidated with the estimates of costs.

Discovery: Azure Migrate can be used in two ways by cloud consumers. The first mode of Azure Migrate generates OVA (Open Virtualization Appliance) templates. An Azure Migrate VM can be bootstrapped with this template on an on-premises VMware site. The Azure Migrate instance sends inventory data from on-premises to Azure once it is configured. Uploading on-premises inventory data can be done using a CSV file formatted in a predefined manner. In the CSV file, four mandatory fields are expected: name of the VM/server, number of cores, memory, and eligible operating system. In addition to disk count and disk IOPS, other optional fields (such as throughput, etc.) could improve sizing accuracy. A CSV file can be generated using VMware tools such as RVTools.

Grouping: The VMware inventory details can be grouped once they have been gathered. After VMs are discovered, cloud consumers can organize and manage them quickly by grouping them. Among the possible groupings are workloads (HR, eCommerce, and so forth, license groupings, RedHat, SQL, SAP Oracle, etc.), environments (production vs. non-production), locations (US, EU, and so on), and criticality (mission-critical, small-scale, etc.). Using Azure Migrate, VMware environments can be analyzed for dependency. It is also possible to group VMs together based on the information obtained via dependency analysis.

Assessment: VMs that are grouped can be assessed. It is possible to configure an assessment with parameters helpful in determining appropriate size/capacity. The parameters can include details about the target Azure VMware Solution site, such as location and node type. VMware Solution VMs running on Azure must have the following settings (FTT, RAID, and CPU oversubscription). An assessment can be performed based on two aspects.

The first is a performance-based assessment of on-premises VMware VMs based on their performance profiles. Performance history can be selected as far back as one month for capturing a performance profile. An assessment can be fine-tuned even further by selecting a specific percentile within an evaluation (such as 50th, 90th,

99th, etc.). The capacity margin can be increased by multiplying the capacity with a comfort factor.

Secondly, the solution must be on-premises. This criterion uses the existing specs of the VM (CPU, memory, etc.) for its evaluation. The capacity can be increased if necessary.

Reporting: Reporting provides final results after an assessment is complete, including cost and readiness. There is a summary of the number of VMware virtual machines assessed, the average estimated cost per VM, and the total estimated costs for all VMs.

The reporting also contains a clear breakdown of Azure VMware Solution readiness across multiple readiness states (Ready, Not Ready, Ready with Conditions, etc.). There are specific reasons why some VMs may require remediation before migration.

Managing and orchestrating the migration plan becomes very easy in this way. Several Azure VMware Solution nodes are also provided in the reporting, and the Azure VMware Solution also reports anticipated CPU, memory, and storage utilization.

Azure Landing Zone for Azure VMware Solution

In this section, you'll explore Azure landing zones. Cloud computing is the basis and backbone of digital transformation in all its forms. Landing zones are the foundation for a successful shift to the cloud.

Any project that involves the cloud can be compared to laying a foundation. In designing and constructing any building, architects must consider everyday decisions. They have many things in common, like concrete, rebar, and conduits for bringing in utilities such as plumbing or electricity. There are some common elements and considerations among foundations, but other references can make them unique and wildly different. Unlike a house, a stadium has a larger and more complex foundation. Building a bridge's foundation may require stricter governance and performance standards. A solid foundation begins with an understanding of what it will support.

In Microsoft Cloud adoption strategies, landing zones serve as a fundamental component. Besides scalability, security, governance, networking, and identity, it builds an Azure environment that accounts for and underpins those functions. Azure landing zones allow enterprises to migrate applications, modernize, and innovate.

Cloud landing zones ensures that cloud consumers' target environments are well designed, deployed, secured, and governed to achieve consistency across their domains and that they fulfill every demanding dynamic business requirement in an agile manner and let the cloud consumers focus on staying compliant and controlling costs to invest where it matters.

Microsoft Azure landing zones result from a multi-subscription Azure environment that addresses scale, security governance, networking, and identity. With Azure landing zones, enterprises can migrate applications, modernize their infrastructure, and innovate. In these zones, all platform resources necessary to support the customer's application portfolio are considered, without distinction between IaaS and PaaS.

One solution does not fit all technical environments. Cloud consumers have several options for implementing Azure landing zones to meet their deployment and operational needs as their cloud portfolios grow.

Scalable: Azure landing zones don't care which workloads or resources are deployed to each landing zone; they all provide repeatable environments with consistent configurations and controls.

Modular: All Azure landing zones offer a modular approach to creating cloud consumer environments based on a standard set of design areas. Azure SQL Database, Azure Kubernetes Service, and Azure Virtual Desktop are only a few examples of the capability of each design area to support the distinct requirements of individual technology platforms.

Figure 3-4 depicts the cloud architecture portfolios.

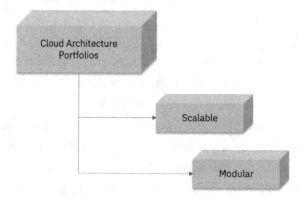

Figure 3-4. *Cloud architecture portfolios*

A modular architecture is designed for enterprise-scale deployments. By leveraging this technology, cloud consumers can start with a foundational landing zone control pane that supports their application portfolios, whether they are migrating or developing and deploying new applications to Azure. No matter what scale point cloud consumers are at, the architecture can scale alongside them.

The enterprise-scale architecture represents the design paths and target states of the Azure environments. Cloud consumer organizations must map their Azure journey by making various design decisions as the Azure platform evolves.

All enterprises do not adopt Azure the same way, and customer-specific Cloud Adoption Frameworks for Azure enterprise-scale landing zones exist. Depending on the cloud consumer organization's situation, the technical considerations and design recommendations for enterprise-scale architecture may require trade-offs. As long as cloud consumers follow the core recommendations, they will be on a path to effectively scale their organization's demands.

Landing zones are coupled to Microsoft's Cloud Adoption Framework, which helps organizations make the proper governance, strategy, and security decisions when migrating to Azure. Figure 3-5 depicts the environment design elements.

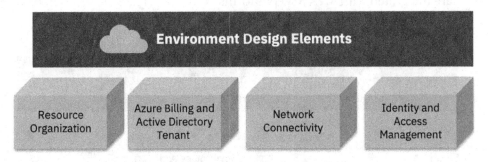

Figure 3-5. *Cloud environment design elements*

- **Resource organization:** The method by which cloud users organize their resources to allow for business growth, considering needs around management groups, subscriptions, business areas, and different teams.

  - **Cloud subscription:** The method by which cloud consumers adopt public clouds like Azure, considering they need to create three different landing zones.

- **Azure billing offers and Active Directory tenants:** Azure billing and Azure Active Directory (Azure AD) are the two highest alignment levels across all cloud Azure deployments within this critical area.

- **Multi-tenancy:** Ensures tagging policies are enforced across multiple cloud tenants and provides standardized tenants for different security profiles (dev/staging/prod).

- **Network connectivity:** Network implementation provides high availability, resiliency, and scalability. By combining networking patterns with external data centers, cloud consumers can create hybrid systems and multi-cloud adoption models. Before designing network connectivity, consider the following questions: What will the topology of the network be? Where will the resources be located?

- **Identity and access management:** The foundation of any fully compliant cloud architecture is IAM, the primary security boundary. Roles and access controls are defined to implement the principle of least privilege. All hosted production applications and cloud consoles are integrated with MFA SSO platforms.

Figure 3-6 depicts the compliance design elements.

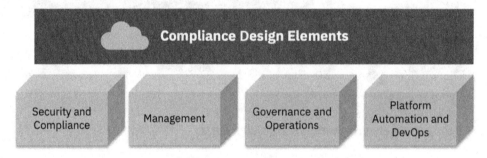

Figure 3-6. *Cloud compliance design elements*

- **Security and compliance:** Cloud users can enforce global and account-level security controls proactively and deductively by using landing zones. Landing zones can also be used to implement data residency and compliance policies across the enterprise.

- **Management:** A foundation is established here for managing operations across Azure, hybrid, or multi-cloud environments.

  - **Business continuity and disaster recovery:** The smooth functioning of applications depends on resilience, and BCDR is a critical element of strength. By using BCDR, cloud consumers can protect cloud consumers' data via backups and recover cloud consumers' applications in the event of an outage.

- **Governance and operation:** What are the cloud consumers' plans for managing, monitoring, and optimizing their environment? How will cloud consumers maintain visibility within the environment and ensure it operates as required?

- **Platform automation and DevOps:** Consumers of cloud services can increase productivity, scalability, and reliability by using automation. Cloud landing zones automate CI/CD pipelines based on Terraform, ARM, or cloud formation templates to deploy multi-account subscription structures in minutes.

The Azure VMware Solution can be deployed within a new or existing landing zone environment. By promoting a segregated Azure environment and shared services, landing zones help consumers avoid operational overhead and reduce costs.

In a landing zone environment, running the Azure VMware Solution addresses the following use cases:

- **Using an existing Azure tenancy infrastructure:** VMware solutions can be integrated into existing Azure tenants. Customers can bill and account for their goods by using their existing ownership chain.

- **Using existing shared landing zones:** Customers can reuse their existing shared landing zones, which run services such as network connectivity, monitoring, and so on, with Azure VMware Solution environments. In addition to reducing costs, reuse increases operational efficiency.

- **Separation of governance rules:** Different governance requirements may exist in dev/test and production environments. It is possible to provide the desired level of control for VMware Azure Solution environments by setting up separate landing zones.

Azure's enterprise-scale landing zones provide prescriptive deployment guidance for configuring Azure platform components (like identities, networks, and management) and application and workload components, such as Azure VMware Solution. It is easy to manage and scale Azure VMware Solution workloads due to a well-defined correlation between Azure platform components and Azure VMware Solution. Figure 3-7 depicts a landing zone overview and the Azure VMware Solution.

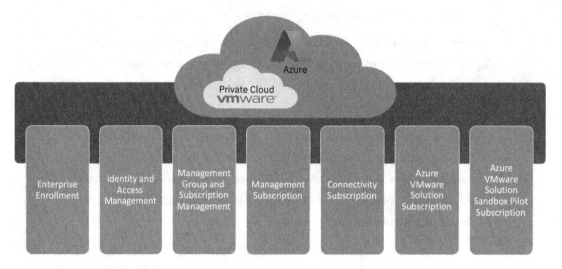

Figure 3-7. *Azure Landing Zone for AVS*

The Azure enterprise-scale landing zone components for Azure VMware Solution deployment are discussed below.

Enterprise enrollment: Microsoft Azure VMware Solutions subscriptions are enabled through enterprise enrollment's hierarchical structure. Through this organization, they can reflect hierarchies within the organization (geographical, divisional, functional, and so on). Accounts that hold Azure VMware Solution subscriptions can be set up with a cost budget and associated alerts, and customers can also specify who owns the subscriptions. Figure 3-8 depicts the Azure landing zone enterprise enrollment.

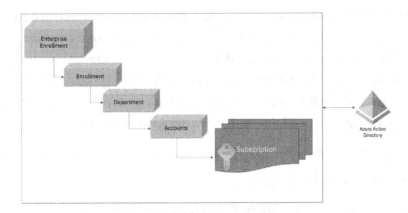

Figure 3-8. *Azure landing zone - enterprise enrollment*

As per Microsoft's landing zone design best practices, enterprise enrollment is one of the two highest levels of alignment across all cloud consumer Azure deployments, offering Azure billing to consumers and connecting that offer to their Azure AD tenant.

This design area should evaluate design options for cloud consumers. Azure Active Directory tenant association is best suited for a cloud consumer's overall environment.

Identity and access management: Multiple operations are available through the Azure VMware Solution Resource Provider (RP). Partners and customers want access to these operations controlled by roles. Cloud consumers can create such parts via identity and access management. Furthermore, these roles can be configured with additional functions such as just-in-time (JIT) access and access reviews. As part of identity and access management, Azure AD Domain Services (AAD DS) or Active Directory Domain Services (AD DS) can be configured for workloads requiring Windows authentication. Figure 3-9 depicts the Azure landing zone identity and access management.

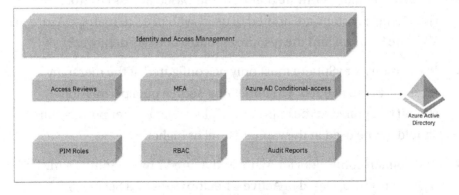

Figure 3-9. *Azure landing zone- identity and access management*

As per Microsoft's landing zone design best practices, identity and access management is the next highest level of alignment across all cloud consumers' Azure deployment. The design area sets a foundation for managing identity and access.

This design area should evaluate design options for cloud consumers' identities and access foundations. The following are minimum requirements for cloud consumers to consider when synchronizing identities with Azure Active Directory:

- User authentication

- Granting access to resources

- Determining any separation of duties requirements

Azure VMware Solution's identity requirements vary depending on its implementation in Azure.

As soon as cloud consumers deploy Azure VMware Solution, the new environment's vCenter contains a local user called CloudAdmin. The user CloudAdmin has several permissions in vCenter. Using the principle of least privilege, cloud consumers can also create custom roles in the cloud consumer Azure VMware Solution environment. Here are Microsoft's recommendations for AVS design:

- Deploy an Active Directory Domain Services (AD DS) domain controller as part of the enterprise-scale landing zone for identity and access management in the identity subscription.

- Set a limit on how many cloud consumers can assign the CloudAdmin role for each subscription. For Azure VMware Solution users, use custom roles and least privilege.

- Ensure that Azure VMware Solution role-based access control (RBAC) permissions are limited to users who need to manage Azure VMware Solution and the resource group where it's deployed.

- Permissions for vSphere must only be configured at the hierarchy level if they are needed. VM folder or resource pool permissions should be applied at the appropriate place. Datacenter permissions should not be used at the vSphere level or higher.

- The domain controllers for Azure and Azure VMware Solution AD DS traffic must be updated in Active Directory Sites and Services.

- vCenter and NSX-T can be managed using Active Directory groups and RBAC. Custom roles can be created and assigned to Active Directory groups by cloud consumers.

Management group and subscription management: Resources of VMware Solutions running in Azure can be deployed into an Azure subscription in a management group or a subscription management. The Azure enterprise-scale landing zone defines operational governance requirements and applies them to management groups. A management group allows Azure VMware Solution subscriptions to be subjected to Azure policy for any operational governance requirements. During Azure VMware Solution migration, an example of enforcing policy requirements is preventing the deployment of VPN connectivity. By distributing Azure VMware Solution workloads across multiple subscriptions, customers and partners can circumvent limits associated with Azure VMware Solution subscriptions. Figure 3-10 depicts the Azure landing zone management group and subscription management.

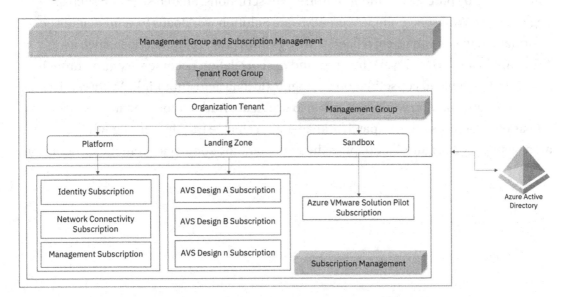

Figure 3-10. *Azure landing zone - management group and subscription management*

As per Microsoft's landing zone design best practices, management group and subscription management is the next component of alignment across all cloud consumers' Azure deployments. The design area sets a foundation for organizing resources in the cloud according to consistent design patterns.

This design area should set all compliance-related design decisions on resource organization decisions. Planning resource organization involves establishing consistent patterns in the following areas:

- Naming standards

- Tagging standards

- Subscription design

- Management group design

Focus on utilizing a subscription design that aligns with the Azure landing zone concept as a starting point. Assigning subscriptions or landing zones based on workloads or applications supports separation of duties and subscription democratization.

Management subscription: The platform management group includes the management subscription. Shared management and monitoring services can be consolidated by purchasing and monitoring subscriptions. Shared services, such as Log Analytics Workspace, allow Azure VMware Solution workloads to send diagnostic information, which can be correlated with logs from other Azure services, such as Azure Application Gateway. Debugging and log correlation become very easy through the centralization and consolidation of diagnostic data across multiple Azure services. Azure VMware Solution workloads can also use Azure Automation Update Management for various purposes, such as patch management, change tracking, configuration management, etc. Figure 3-11 depicts the Azure landing zone management subscription.

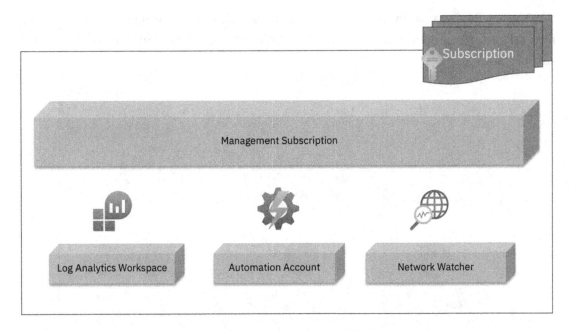

Figure 3-11. *Azure landing zone - management subscription*

As per Microsoft's landing zone design best practice, management subscription is the next alignment component across all cloud consumers' Azure deployments. The design area sets a foundation for operations management across cloud consumer Azure, hybrid, or multi-cloud environments.

Throughout the cloud consumers' cloud platforms, this design area focuses on operational management requirements and implements those requirements consistently across all workloads. This design area should primarily address operations tooling, and cloud consumers can manage the collective portfolio of workloads with a set of standard tools and processes. The operational baseline is referred to as this initial set of operations tools.

Management baselines are required to provide visibility, compliance, platform, and workload management and protect and recover capabilities in the cloud.

Connectivity subscription: Azure VMware Solution includes a connectivity subscription that centralizes network requirements across all Azure workloads. Azure VMware Solution can run workloads using shared services like Azure Virtual WAN, Application Gateway, etc. Reusing these services can help customers reduce costs (instead of creating new services exclusively for Azure VMware Solution). As part of a connectivity subscription, any network resources are available to limited roles, such as NetOps (Network Operations), for holistic network management. Debugging and troubleshooting networking issues become manageable and accountable when access to network resources is controlled. Figure 3-12 depicts the Azure landing zone connectivity subscription.

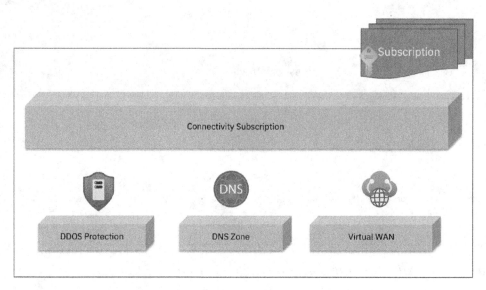

Figure 3-12. *Azure landing zone - connectivity subscription*

As per Microsoft's landing zone design, the best practice connectivity subscription is the next alignment component across all cloud consumers' Azure deployments. The design area sets a foundation for network connectivity across cloud consumers' Azure environments.

Azure VMware Solution subscription: Subscribers of Azure VMware Solutions are part of the landing zone management group, which makes it possible to reap the benefits of Azure policies applied at that management group. For example, Azure VMware Solutions can be restricted to specific Azure regions; budgets must be enabled before deployment. Multiple subscriptions for Azure VMware Solution allow cloud consumers to manage and scale workloads without being constrained by Azure subscription limits. Figure 3-13 depicts the Azure landing zone subscription.

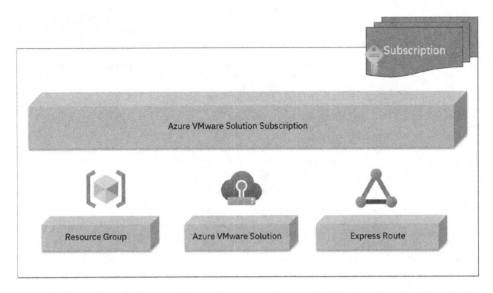

Figure 3-13. *Azure landing zone- Azure VMware Solution subscription*

Azure VMware Solution sandbox pilot subscription: Under the Sandbox management group, sandbox subscriptions are deployed as a playground for experimenting with Azure services. Likewise, a sandbox subscription prevents production workloads from being impacted. Sandbox subscriptions for VMware solutions on Azure have less restrictive policies, allowing cloud consumers to have greater control over the service. It's impossible to use the VMware Solution sandbox subscription for production deployment if cloud consumers create a separate subscription. Figure 3-14 depicts the Azure landing zone pilot subscription.

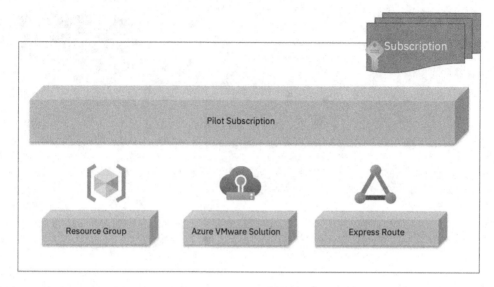

Figure 3-14. *Azure landing zone - pilot subscription*

This completes the core design essential elements required for the Azure AVS landing zone design. In next section, you'll explore AVS network topology and connectivity.

Azure VMware Solution Networking

The concept of terminology is crucial to understanding contexts and Azure's specialized networking components. The transmission of information will be more effective if you understand the terminology used in technical and Azure contexts. Listed below are the key terms used most frequently throughout this section:

- Azure virtual networks (VNets) are logically isolated sections of the Azure cloud from which you can launch Azure resources.

- Private networks in Azure are built using Azure virtual networks. VMs and Azure virtual networks enable Azure resources to connect to the Internet and internal data centers securely. As with a traditional network, a virtual network has consumers in a cloud data center but offers the benefits of Azure, such as scalability, availability, and isolation.

- Azure VNet routing describes how traffic is routed between subnetworks and subnetworks.

- Network virtual appliances (NVAs) are network devices that perform functions such as connectivity, application delivery, WAN optimization, and security. They include Microsoft Azure Firewall and Microsoft Azure Load Balancer.

- Microsoft Azure Virtual WAN is a network service that combines routing, security, and many networking functions under one operational interface.

- In hub-spoke networks, a hub virtual network connects many spoke virtual networks. Datacenters on-premises can also be connected through the hub. Workloads can be isolated using the spoke virtual networks that peer with the hub.

- Cloud networks can be scaled with the help of VXLAN (virtual extension LAN). Utilizing Layer 3 (L3) technology, VXLAN extends a local area network into a virtual network.

- A virtual LAN or broadcast domain can be extended by extending the Layer 2 domain across two sites. Many names for L2 extensions include data center interconnect (DCI), data center extension (DCE), stretched Layer 2 network, stretched VLAN, extended VLAN, stretched deploy, or Layer 2 VPN.

- In the open systems interconnection model (OSI), layer 4 (L4) represents the fourth layer. In L4, data is transmitted or transferred transparently between end systems, and error recovery end-to-end along with flow control is L4's responsibility.

- In the OSI model, layer 7 (L7) is the topmost and seventh layer known as the application layer. In Layer 7, the parties communicating are identified, and the quality of the service between them is evaluated. L7 handles privacy and user authentication, and L7 identifies any data format constraints. This layer handles application-specific data. It is responsible for API calls and responses. HTTP, HTTPS, and SMTP are the most common L7 protocols.

Azure VNet Concept and Microsoft Azure Best Practices

Azure VNets are private networks that you create in the cloud. Each Azure subscription has its own logically isolated and dedicated cloud. Virtual private networks (VPNs) can be configured and managed in Azure VNets. Alternative solutions can be created by linking Azure VNets to your on-premises IT infrastructure and creating hybrid or hybrid cross-premises solutions. Providing the CIDR blocks don't overlap, you can link a VNet with another VNet and an on-premises network if the CIDR blocks don't overlap. In addition, administrators can control VNet settings and segment subnets.

Azure connects resources securely to the Internet and on-premises networks. Azure Virtual Networking allows for communication between Azure resources, communication between Azure resources and on-premises resources, filtering network traffic, routing network traffic, and integration of Azure services.

By understanding the concepts and best practices, you can easily deploy virtual networks and connect cloud resources. The following section explains the key concepts.

Address space: IP addresses for VNets must be unique, either public or private (RFC 1918). Azure assigns each virtual network a private IP address from the address space you specify. There can be multiple virtual networks in the same subscription, and each virtual network may have its subnet.

Take into account when designing and deploying this list of non-routable addresses: 10.0.0.0 - 10.255.255.255 (10/8 prefix)

- 172.16.0.0 - 172.31.255.255 (172.16/12 prefix)

- 192.168.0.0 - 192.168.255.255 (192.168/16 prefix)

One of the most crucial configurations for a virtual network is the address space. The entire network would be divided into subnets using the entire IP range. The following address spaces cannot be added to your virtual network:

- 224.0.0.0/4 is used for Azure multicast.

- 255.255.255.255/32 is used for Azure broadcast.

- 127.0.0.0/8 is used for Azure loopback.

- 169.254.0.0/16 is used for Azure link-local.

- 168.63.129.16/32 is used for Azure internal DNS.

Also, having overlapping address spaces will prevent you from connecting virtual networks.

Subnets: A subnet allows you to segment a virtual network into one or more subnetworks, each receiving a portion of the virtual network's address space. Once a subnet has been created, Azure resources can be deployed within that subnet. As in a traditional network, you can segment your VNet address space using subnets. In this way, address allocation is also made more efficient.

There are five IP addresses per subnet reserved by Azure cloud services, from x.x.x.0 to x.x.x.3 and the last address.

- x.x.x.0 is the network address used by Azure.

- x.x.x.1 is Azure reserves for the default gateway.

- x.x.x.2 and x.x.x.3 to map the Azure DNS IPs to the VNet space.

- x.x.x.255 is a network broadcast address for subnets of size /25 and more prominent. This will be a different address in smaller subnets.

CIDR supports a maximum IPv4 subnet size of /2 and a minimum of /29 (CIDR IPv4 subnet definitions). For IPv6, /64 is the minimum subnet size.

Take in your design and deployment consideration that

- VNets are Layer-3 overlays. The Azure platform does not support Layer-2 semantics.

- Classless inter-domain routing (CIDR) must be used to specify each subnet's address range.

- Azure network engineers can build many subnets and allow a service endpoint for some subnets.

- Azure VNet does not support multicast or broadcast.

- A routing table can be deployed on the Azure and associated with a subnet

- Subnets can be used for traffic management.

- Virtual network service endpoints permit you to regulate access to Azure resources by subnet.

- Azure network engineers can use Network Security Groups to segment your network further based on IP address classification.

- The default limit per virtual network is 3,000 subnets, but that can be scaled up to 10,000 with Microsoft support.

Regions: For all Azure resources, a region is required. In a virtual network, resources can only be created in the same subscription and region as the resource, and it is possible to connect virtual networks across regions and subscriptions. When determining where to deploy your resources, consider the location of your customers (consumers). While Azure engineers can pair VNets with different virtual networks in different regions, they can only be created in one Azure region.

Subscriptions: Subscriptions are scoped for VNets. There is support for multiple virtual networks within Azure subscriptions and Azure regions.

Consider your naming conventions when designing your Azure network during the design and deployment process. Resource names should incorporate information about each resource. Resource types, workloads, deployment environments, and Azure regions that host the resource can all be identified by their proper names. Adding the entire VNet address space to your subnet is not necessary. It is best to plan and reserve address space in advance. Microsoft recommends a few large VNets instead of having multiple small VNets. Network Security Groups (NSGs) can also affect subnets under your VNets.

Now that you have explored VNets, let's further understand how to use Azure native services (such as Azure ExpressRoute, Azure Traffic Manager, and Azure Application Gateway) as critical components of connecting Azure VMware Solution workloads to an on-premises environment as well as to external users.

These critical use cases can be enabled by network connectivity from a design perspective:

- VMware on-premises environments can be extended to Azure.

- You can move VMware workloads from on-premises to Azure.

- You can securely connect Azure VMware Solution workloads to the public internet.

- You can create disaster recovery (DR) processes for an on-premises and an Azure VMware environment, or between two Azure solutions.

Figure 3-15 depicts the network architecture for better understanding.

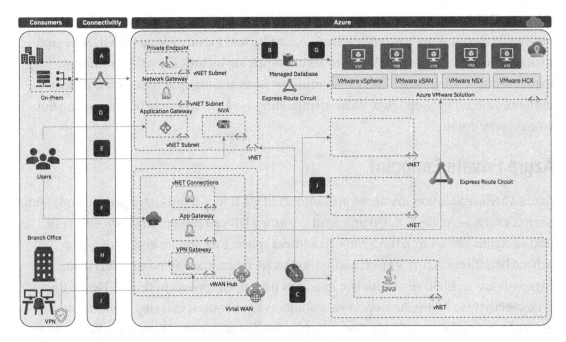

Figure 3-15. *Azure landing zone - networking overview*

In Figure 3-15, the architecture acts as a building block for the following requirements:

- Network connectivity across cloud consumer on-premises and Azure VMware Solution

- Network connectivity across the public internet and Microsoft Azure VMware Solution

- Network connectivity across branch/VPN sites and Microsoft Azure VMware Solution

- Network connectivity across Microsoft Azure and Microsoft Azure VMware Solution

Azure ExpressRoute Global Reach

A diagram of route A illustrates the connection between the Azure VMware Solution environment and the on-premises site. ExpressRoute Global Reach is used to establish the connection. There are two routers involved. MSEE (MS Enterprise Edge) is the first. An on-premises site is connected to Azure via this router. Dedicated Microsoft Enterprise

Edge (D-MSEE) routers are the second type of router. Connectivity is established between Azure and the Azure VMware Solution Virtual Private Cloud (VPC). Microsoft manages both routers. Azure VMware Solution pricing includes D-MSEE router pricing. ExpressRoute Global Reach has a maximum network throughput based on the most miniature circuit between two. VMware migration via HCX can only be done using this connectivity option.

Azure Private Endpoint

Azure VMware Solution instances are connected via Route B through a private endpoint. Services such as Azure SQL DB and Azure Cosmos DB can project a private endpoint into an Azure VNet. From the VNet's IP address space, this private endpoint gets a private IP address. Azure VMware Solution instances are connected to VNets using ExpressRoute, and these instances can access private endpoints in those VNets if there is connectivity to Azure. Azure VMware Solution represents a first step towards the gradual modernization of VMs. For example, this connectivity will enable a Web Server VM in Azure VMware Solution to connect with Azure SQL DB, a managed SQL database service.

Azure VNet Peering

Route C shows connectivity from other Azure regions to an Azure VMware Solution instance. Peering over Azure Virtual Networks enables this connectivity. A VMware solution instance can only be connected to one VNet when provisioning, and this VNet can be peer-to-peer with other VNets that run workloads inside of them. A VMware Solution VM running on Azure can exchange data with multiple workloads in both directions. Azure VMware Solution and other workloads on Azure run smoothly with VNet peering, which provides low-latency, high-throughput connectivity over a Microsoft backbone network.

Azure Application Gateway

Route D shows that Azure services can be integrated with the Azure VMware Solution. This route directs external user requests to Azure Application Gateway, commonly referred to as App Gateway. It exposes a public IP address that can be mapped to a DNS entry, and it is a Layer 7 load balancer. Azure VMware Solution VMs can be used to power App Gateway. Azure VMware Solution VMs combined with App Gateway as a front end ensure that no public IP address is exposed from the Azure VMware Solution environment. App Gateway provides Web Application Firewall (WAF) services that mitigate common vulnerabilities (SQL injection, cross-site request forgery, XSS, etc.) even before requests reach Azure VMware Solution. An Azure VMware Solution environment using App Gateway is excellent for any web-facing workload.

NVA from Azure Marketplace

Network virtual appliances (NVAs) function as network devices that provide services such as connectivity, application delivery, WAN optimization, and security. For example, Azure firewalls and Azure Load Balancers act as NVAs.

Using Azure Marketplace solutions is shown in Route E. Many partner solutions are available on the Azure Marketplace, including firewalls, NVAs, and load balancers. In this flow, customers can choose to accept external requests from their favorite vendor. The request is then forwarded to Azure VMware Solution VMs based on the configured routes and security check, as evaluated by the vendor solution. From an on-premises environment, customers can utilize the license mobility in Azure VMware Solution.

Azure Virtual WAN

An Azure Virtual WAN is a service that combines routing, security, and networking functions into one operational interface. Among these capabilities are the following:

- Virtual private networks based on customer premises equipment (CPE) can automate branch connectivity.

- VPN connectivity between sites is possible.

- Remote users can connect to sites using VPNs.

- Private Azure ExpressRoute connections are available.

- Connectivity within the Azure cloud, such as transitive connectivity

- VPN ExpressRoute interconnectivity

- Routing

- Azure Firewall

- Encryption for private connectivity

Route F demonstrates using a public IP address with Azure virtual WAN (vWAN). Azure vWAN is configured with a public IP address associated with its hub in this route. Firewall rules are then configured with D-NAT rules. Using Azure Firewall Manager, additional firewall rules can also be configured to route requests that arrive at the public IP address to the private IP associated with the Azure VMware Solution VM. With Azure vWAN, cloud consumers can connect any device to any other. Using this feature, multiple on-premises sites/branch locations can gain access to Azure VMware Solution VMs.

Azure PaaS Endpoint

AVS is connected to Azure PaaS services using a public endpoint in route G. AVS and Azure are connected via route 2. It is the Azure PaaS service endpoint that differs between the two routes. Unlike route 2, route 7 uses a public endpoint. Since more and more Azure services offer connectivity over a private endpoint, Microsoft recommends that cloud consumers consume these services over a private endpoint. If the service does not yet have a private endpoint, AVS VMs can connect to their public endpoints to consume it.

Azure ExpressRoute Gateway

Connectivity from branch offices to AVS is shown in Route H. This connection uses a VPN gateway provided by Azure vWAN. Cloud consumers can, however, also switch to ExpressRoute gateway-based connectivity. When multiple branch offices access AVS workloads, this type of connectivity is recommended. As part of this setup, ER or VPN gateway and Azure vWAN establish transitive connectivity between the sites.

Azure VPN Gateway

Route I shows the connectivity between point-to-point VPN sites and site-to-site VPN sites. A VPN gateway is used to provide this connectivity. The VPN topology can be used to make AVS workloads available to VPN sites. VPN gateways in Azure vWAN are built with greater scalability and throughput than VPN gateways in conventional hub networks. AVS workloads can be reached more quickly from multiple VPN sites with this topology.

Azure Virtual Network

Private networks in Azure are built on top of Azure virtual networks. Many Azure resources, including Azure VMs, can communicate securely with each other, the Internet, and on-premises datacenters via Azure VNets. As a virtual network, cloud consumers operate it in their own data center, but Azure network engineers gain the scalability, availability, and isolation of Azure.

From other workloads running in Azure VNets, Route J shows connectivity to AVS workloads. In contrast to the hub-and-spoke topologies that rely on either Azure Firewall or third-party NVAs to establish transitive connectivity, Azure vWAN's VNet-to-VNet connectivity is transitive. It doesn't need either Azure Firewall or a third-party NVA.

AVS Network Topology and Connectivity

Cloud-native and hybrid scenarios present unique challenges when integrating VMware software-defined datacenters with Microsoft Azure Cloud ecosystem. This section examines critical reviews and best practices for networking and connectivity to the Azure Cloud and Azure VMware deployments.

Let's further explore the fundamentals elements prior to designing:

- In a hub-spoke topology, a hub virtual network connects many spoke virtual networks. Data centers on-premises can also be connected to the hub, and they can be used to isolate workloads and peers with the hub.

- A virtual LAN or broadcast domain can be created by stretching (OSI) model Layer 2 across two sites. Datacenter interconnects (DCI), datacenter extensions (DCE), and a Layer 2 VPN are used to describe the L2 extension.

- VXLANs (virtual extension LANs) enable cloud networks to scale. VXLANs extend a local area network using interconnection model Layer 3 technology to create a virtual network.

- In the open systems interconnection (OSI) model, Layer 4 is the fourth layer. L4 facilitates transparent data transfer from one system to another. L4 handles end-to-end error recovery, as well as flow control. In addition to UDP (User Datagram Protocol), UDP-

Lite (UDP-Lite), CUDP (Cyclic UDP), RUDP (Reliable UDP), ATP (AppleTalk Transaction Protocol), MPTCP (Multipath TCP), and SPX (sequential packet exchange), L4 has several other protocols.

- Layer 7 is the seventh layer of the OSI model, referred to as the application layer. The communication parties are identified at Layer 7 and the quality of service between them. L7 handles the privacy and authentication of users and identifies any data syntax constraints. This layer pertains only to applications. It handles API calls and responses. HTTP, HTTPS, and SMTP are some of the most important L7 protocols.

Design thinking around network topology on Azure VMware Solution platforms can use this enterprise-scale design guidance. Foundational design elements include

- Connectivity between on-premises, multi-cloud, edge, and global users via hybrid integration

- Consistent, low-latency performance and scalability for workloads at scale

- Security based on zero-trust for network perimeters and traffic flows

- Extendibility without reworking the design

Best Practices and General Considerations for AVS Network Design

- Consider using an Azure Bastion host in an Azure VNet to access the Azure VMware Solution environment during deployment.

- In the Azure VMware Solution management network, once the routing to the on-premises environment is established, the 0.0.0.0/0 routes from the on-premises networks are not honored, so cloud consumers must advertise more specific routes for the on-premises networks.

- The default gateway remains on-premises with VMware HCX migrations; VMware HCX migrations can use the HCX L2 extension. Migrations requiring Layer 2 extension require ExpressRoute, and

VPN isn't supported. To accommodate the overhead of HCX, a maximum transmission unit size of 1350 should be used.

- Create and configure a firewall on your own premises to ensure that all components of the Azure VMware Solution private cloud are accessible.

- Port mirrored traffic and traffic inspection are both used for network security. To inspect traffic between regions within the SDDC, NSX-T or NVAs are used and bidirectional traffic flows between Azure VMware Solutions and datacenters are inspected using north-south traffic inspection.

- To optimize bandwidth between Azure VMware Solution and an Azure VNet, select an appropriate virtual network gateway SKU (either Standard, HighPerformance, UltraPerformance, ErGw1Az, ErGw2Az, or ErGw3Az) VMware Azure Solutions supports a maximum of four ExpressRoute circuits per region per ExpressRoute gateway.

- For Microsoft Azure VMware Solution, Global Reach is a required ExpressRoute add-on to communicate with on-premises data centers, Azure VNets, and virtual WANs. Azure Route Server can also be used to design cloud users' network connectivity.

- Global Reach provides free peering between the Azure VMware Solution ExpressRoute circuit and other ExpressRoute circuits.

- Cloud consumers can peer ExpressRoute circuits through an ISP and ExpressRoute Direct circuits using Global Reach.

- The Global Reach feature is not available for ExpressRoute Local circuits. With ExpressRoute Local, third-party NVAs in Azure virtual networks enable transit from Azure VMware Solution to on-premises data centers, and Global Reach is not available in all regions.

- Out-of-the-box, Azure VMware Solution provides one free ExpressRoute circuit. It connects Azure VMware Solution and D-MSEE.

- All clusters can communicate in an Azure VMware Solution private cloud since they all share the same /22 address space.

- Connectivity settings for all clusters are the same, including Internet, ExpressRoute, HCX, public IP, and ExpressRoute Global Reach. Basic networking settings can also be shared among application workloads, such as network segments, Dynamic Host Configuration Protocol (DHCP), and domain name systems (DNS).

- VPN and ExpressRoute can be connected using a virtual WAN. However, hub-spoke topologies are not supported.

- There are several options for enabling Internet outbound traffic, filtering it, and inspecting it, including

  - Using Azure Internet Access and Azure Virtual Network, NVA, and Azure Route Server

  - With on-premises Internet access

  - With Azure Firewall or NVA, and Azure Internet Access, a virtual WAN hub can be secured.

- Content and applications can be delivered via inbound Internet methods, including

  - Azure Application Gateway with SSL termination, Azure Application Gateway with L7, and Azure Application Firewall

  - Via DNAT and load balancing

  - Through Azure VNets, Azure Network Virtual Agent, and Azure Route Server

  - Azure Firewall and L4 and DNAT on a virtual WAN hub

  - Multiple scenarios in which a virtual WAN hub is connected to NVA

Networking Deployment Scenarios

Design and deployment of networking capabilities for Azure VMware Solutions is vital. Various Azure networking options are available. A cloud consumer's organization's workload, governance, and requirements determine the architecture and structure of AVS networking services.

A VMware Azure Solution private cloud has no external connectivity when deployed. To establish a connection to an on-premises environment, Azure native services are required. By selecting a low-latency and high-bandwidth connection, Azure ExpressRoute enables a private and secure connection between an on-premises environment and Azure VMware Solution. To establish bidirectional connectivity between an Azure VMware Solution private cloud and on-premises environment, Azure ExpressRoute Global Reach should be used. Figure 3-16 depicts the Azure networking logical architecture.

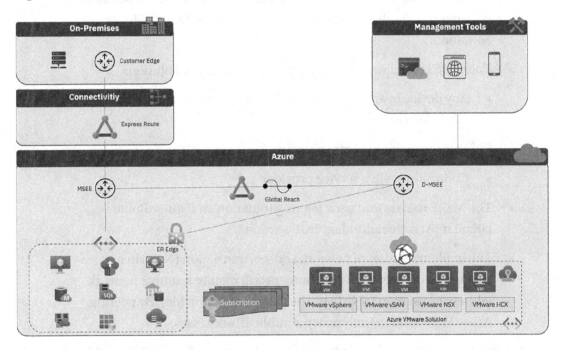

Figure 3-16. *Azure Networking logical architecture*

Connecting Azure VMware Solutions to a customer's data center utilizing Azure ExpressRoute provides a highly available, secure private connection (not on the public Internet) and high bandwidth connections with low latency. Across all regions within a geographic area, this connectivity provides access to Azure native services. To access Azure native services globally, a premium Azure ExpressRoute add-on is required. The ExpressRoutes have built-in Layer 3 redundancy and use the Border Gateway Protocol (BGP) for route exchanges between the Azure VMware Solution and a customer's on-premises data center. Azure ExpressRoute circuits consist of two connections to two MSEEs from the peering provider to the customer's edge network. Each connection goes to an MSEE for highly available, resilient connections Azure VMware Solution.

Microsoft ExpressRoute Global Reach connects Azure VMware Solutions to on-premises environments through ExpressRoute circuits.

Key prerequisites and references influence Azure VMware Solution design and deployment decisions:

- For Microsoft Azure ExpressRoute, a valid and active Azure account is required. An Azure Enterprise Agreement (EA) or a cloud solution provider (CSP) subscription is required to deploy Azure VMware Solution.

- There are several ways to connect to Azure VMware Solution:

  - Any device in an IP VPN network can communicate with any other device.

  - Point-to-point Ethernet network

  - Connections via a service provider

- The MSEE routers and each peering router on an ExpressRoute circuit must have redundant BGP sessions.

- The implementation of network address translation (NAT) in a customer's on-premises environment will require a source network address translation (SNAT) by the customer or provider. By peering, Azure ExpressRoute only accepts public IP addresses.

Key non-functional requirements and references that influence Azure VMware Solution design and deployment decisions are the following:

- Microsoft guarantees that Azure ExpressRoute will be available at least 99.5% of the time.

- There is a range of speeds supported by ExpressRoute circuits, from 50 Mbps to 10Gbps.

- Cloud consumers can choose from three different billing models for Azure ExpressRoute: ExpressRoute Metered Data, ExpressRoute

Unlimited Data, and the Global Reach Add-On. When a service key is provisioned, the ExpressRoute circuit is billed.

- With ExpressRoute with Metered Data, all data transfers ingress (inbound) are free. A predetermined rate is charged for egress (outbound) data transfers, and this rate includes a fixed monthly port fee.

- Unlimited data is available with ExpressRoute and all ingresses (inbounds) and egresses (outbounds) are free. Port fees are included monthly.

- Global Reach Add-On integrates Azure ExpressRoute circuits to create a private network between an on-premises environment and VMware Cloud on Azure.

Using Azure PowerShell, Azure CLI, ARM templates or an Azure portal, cloud consumers/Azure VMware administrators can set up Azure ExpressRoutes.

The following essential requirements and references influence Azure VMware Solution design and deployment decisions:

- Application requirements for HTTP/S or non-HTTP/S Internet ingress into Azure VMware Solutions

- Considerations for the egress path to the Internet

- L2 extension for migrations

- Using NVA in the current architecture

- Virtual WAN or standard hub virtual network connectivity for Azure VMware Solutions

- Connectivity to Azure VMware Solution via a private ExpressRoute from on-premises datacenters, as well as whether Global Reach is enabled

- Requirements for traffic inspection for

  - Ingress from the Internet into Azure VMware Solution applications

  - Egress access to the Internet from Azure VMware Solution

- On-premises datacenter access through Azure VMware Solution

- Enabling an Azure Virtual Network connection

- Between the public and private clouds within Azure VMware Solution

Using Azure VMware Solution traffic inspection requirements, Table 3-1 provides recommendations and considerations for four of the most common networking scenarios.

Table 3-1. *Recommendations and Considerations for Common Networking Scenarios*

Traffic Inspection Needs	Solution	Design Considerations
Scenario 1: Internet ingress and egress	Virtual WAN secured hub with default gateway propagation is recommended. Azure Application Gateway or Azure Firewall can be used for HTTP/HTTPS traffic. In Azure VMware Solution, deploy the secured virtual WAN hub and enable public IP addresses.	On-premises filtering is not possible with this solution. Global Reach bypasses the virtual WAN hub.
Scenario 2: Internet ingress and egress or to on-premises datacenter or to an Azure VNet	Third-party firewalls can be used in the hub virtual network with Azure Route Server. Global Reach must be disabled. For HTTP/HTTPS traffic, use Application Gateway and third-party firewalls for non-HTTP/S traffic.	It's the most popular option for customers who need to centralize all traffic inspection into a hub virtual network while using their existing NVA.

(continued)

Table 3-1. (*continued*)

Traffic Inspection Needs	Solution	Design Considerations
Scenario 3: Internet ingress and egress or to on-premises datacenter or to an Azure VNet or within Azure VMware Solution	NSX-T or an NVA firewall from a third party can be used with Azure VMware Solution. HTTP(s) traffic should go through Application Gateway, while traffic not using HTTP(s) should go through Azure Firewall. The virtual WAN hub should be configured, and public IP enabled in Azure VMware Solution.	Use this option if you need to inspect traffic between two or more Azure VMware Solution private clouds. This option can be used with NSX-T native features or with NVAs running on Azure VMware Solution between L1 and L0.
Scenario 4: Internet ingress or to an Azure VNet	Secure cloud consumers' WANs with virtual WANs. Azure Application Gateway is best for HTTP and HTTPS traffic, and Azure Firewall is best for non-HTTP/S traffic. Ensure a virtual WAN hub is deployed and public IP is enabled in Azure VMware Solution.	0.0.0.0/0 can be advertised from on-premises data centers using this option.

Now let's do deep dive into design elements for each scenario.

Scenario 1: Default Route Propagation for a Secured Virtual WAN Hub

Requirements:

- Cloud consumers of Azure VMware Solution workloads need to inspect traffic between those workloads and the Internet.

Assumption:

- Cloud consumers of Azure VMware Solution and Azure Virtual Network do not require traffic inspection.

- Cloud consumers of the Azure VMware Solution do not need traffic inspection between the cloud and on-premises datacenters.

- PaaS offering for Azure VMware Solutions.

- Cloud consumers of the Azure VMware Solution do not own public IP addresses. If needed, the cloud consumer is expected to add public-facing L4 and L7 inbound services.

- Network connectivity between on-premises data centers and Azure might or might not be provided by ExpressRoute for cloud users.

Design overview:

Figure 3-17 illustrates how the solution could be implemented.

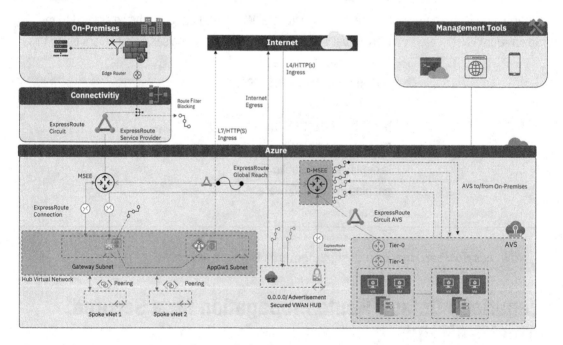

Figure 3-17. *Azure networking - default route propagation for a secured virtual WAN hub*

Azure components to be considered for deployment:

- For firewalls, Azure Firewall is part of the secured virtual WAN hub.

- Load balancing with the Application Gateway

- Translation and filtering of network ingress traffic using L4 DNAT (destination network address translation) and Azure Firewall

- Inbound Internet outbound through Azure Firewall

- Azure network engineers can use ExR, VPN, or SD-WAN to connect Azure VMware Solution to on-premises datacenters.

Design consideration:

Suppose Azure network engineers don't want to receive the default route 0.0.0.0/0 advertisement from Azure VMware Solution because it conflicts with cloud consumers' existing environments. In this case, Azure network engineers need to take more action.

Azure Firewall advertises 0.0.0.0/0 in the secured virtual WAN hub. Also, on-premises, Global Reach advertises 0.0.0.0/0. To prevent route learning from 0.0.0.0/0, implement an on-premises route filter. Cloud consumers will not experience this issue if they use SD-WAN or VPN.

By default, the 0.0.0.0/0 route from a virtual WAN hub propagates to an ExpressRoute gateway instead of directly to the virtual network hub, prioritizing the Internet system route built into the virtual network. 0.0.0.0/0 user-defined routes can be implemented in the virtual network to override the learned default route.

Additionally, VPNs, ExpressRoutes, and virtual network connections to the secure virtual WAN hub that do not require 0.0.0.0/0 advertisements will receive the advertisement. Azure network engineers can implement these strategies:

- With an on-premises edge device, filter out 0.0.0.0/0 traffic.

Alternatively,

- Disconnect the VPN or ExpressRoute.

- Turn on 0.0.0.0/0 propagation.

- Block its propagation on those connections.

- Then reconnect.

Customers of cloud-based services can host Application Gateways on spoke virtual networks connected to hub or hub virtual networks.

Scenario 2: With Global Reach Disabled, Third-Party NVA in Azure Virtual Network with Azure Route Server

Requirements:

- The Azure VMware Solution private cloud customers need fine-grain control over firewalls outside the cloud.

- Consumers will need to use an appliance from their current vendor in Azure and other on-premises environments.

- Cloud consumers usually require public-facing L4 and L7 inbound services for Azure VMware Solutions and outbound Internet connectivity.

Assumption:

- Azure VMware Solution customers want to inspect traffic between on-premises datacenters and Azure VMware Solution, but Global Reach isn't available for geopolitical reasons.

- In Azure, customers require a block of predefined IP addresses for inbound service and a set of public IP addresses for outbound service. Customers do not own public IP addresses in this scenario.

Design overview:

Figure 3-18 illustrates how the solution could be implemented.

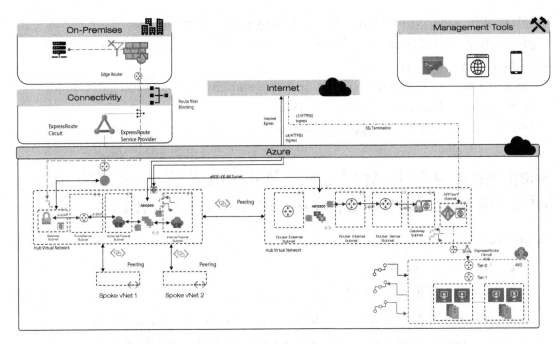

Figure 3-18. *Azure networking with Global Reach disabled, third-party NVA in an Azure virtual network with Azure Route Server*

Azure components to be considered for deployment:

- For firewalls and other network functions, third-party NVAs should be hosted in a virtual network.

- Use the Azure Route Server to route traffic between the Azure VMware Solution, on-premises data centers, and virtual networks.

- L7 HTTP/S load balancing is best achieved through Application Gateway.

- To enable ExpressRoute Global Reach, Azure network engineers must disable it. Azure VMware Solution relies on NVAs to provide outbound Internet access.

Design consideration:

An Azure network engineer needs to disable ExpressRoute Global Reach in the hub virtual network that hosts the NVAs to accomplish this. Microsoft Enterprise Edge ExpressRoute routers direct traffic for Azure VMware Solutions directly between themselves, skipping the hub virtual network.

Make sure traffic is routed through the hub by implementing Azure Route Server. Implementing and managing an NVA solution or utilizing an existing one is the cloud consumer's responsibility.

As a precaution, deploy the NVAs in an active-standby configuration if the cloud consumers need high availability for the NVAs.

The above architectural diagram depicts an NVA with VXLAN support.

Scenario 3: A VMware Egress Without NSX-T or NVA or With VMware Egress from Azure VMware Solution

Requirements:

- NSX is native to Azure VMware Solution, so cloud consumers must use a PaaS deployment.

- NSX tier-0/tier-1 routers or NVAs handle all the traffic between Azure VMware Solution and an Azure virtual network, Azure VMware Solution and the Internet, and Azure VMware Solution on-premises datacenters.

- Cloud consumers require inbound HTTP/S or L4 services.

Assumption:

- Cloud consumers already have ExpressRoute connectivity between their on-premises data centers and Azure.

- For traffic inspection, it would be helpful if cloud consumers had a BYOL (bring your own license) NVA.

Design overview:

Figure 3-19 illustrates how the solution could be implemented.

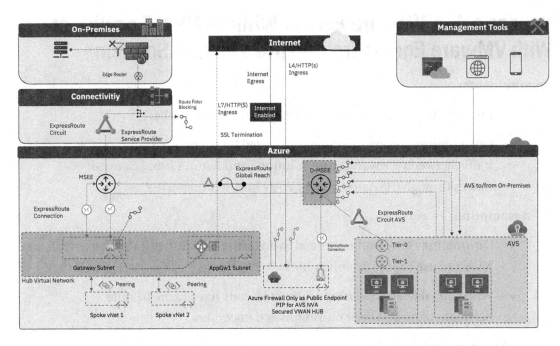

Figure 3-19. *Azure networking - a VMware egress without NSX-T or NVA or with VMware egress from Azure VMware Solution*

Azure components to be considered for deployment:

- In Azure VMware Solution, a NSX Distributed Firewall (DFW) or NVA tier-1 firewall is used.

- For load balancing, use a L7 application gateway.

- L4 DNAT by using Azure Firewall with the VMware Solution for Azure

Design consideration:

Internet access needs to be enabled in the Azure portal for cloud consumers. It's not deterministic, and the outgoing IP address can change. Outside the NVA are public IP addresses, and the NVA in Azure VMware Solution still has private IP addresses and doesn't determine the outgoing public IP address.

Cloud consumers are responsible for bringing the license and implementing high availability for NVAs, a BYOL license.

Scenario 4: A VMware Egress Without NSX-T or NVA or With VMware Egress from Azure VMware Solution

Requirements:

- Inbound services should be available over HTTP/S or L4.

- On-premises traffic inspection is required for outbound traffic. As the traffic between VMware Azure Solutions and Azure Virtual Network moves through the Azure Virtual WAN hub, it is inspected.

Assumption:

- On-premises environments need to advertise 0.0.0.0/0 through the NVA and use the on-premises NVA.

- With Global Reach, cloud consumers already have ExpressRoute between Azure and their on-premises datacenters.

Design overview:

Figure 3-20 illustrates how the solution could be implemented.

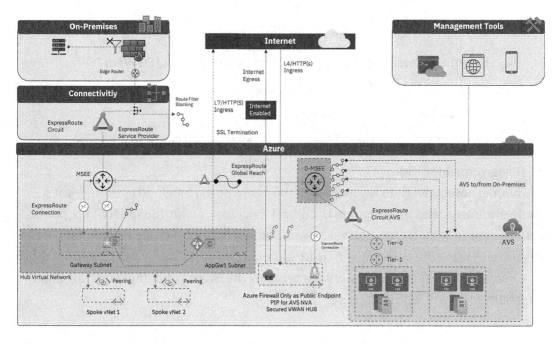

Figure 3-20. Azure networking - a VMware egress without NSX-T or NVA or with VMware egress from Azure VMware Solution

Azure components to be considered for deployment:

- For load balancing, an L7 application gateway

- The L4 DNAT by using Azure Firewall

- On-premises breakout of Internet traffic

- Azure VMware Solution and on-premises datacenters via ExpressRoute

Design consideration:

According to this design, public IP addresses are allocated to the on-premises NVA. The default 0.0.0.0/0 route from the Virtual WAN hub propagates to the ExpressRoute gateway if cloud consumers connect via an ExpressRoute gateway rather than directly to a hub-and-spoke topology, which takes precedence over the Internet system route built into the virtual network. Azure network engineers can overcome this issue by implementing a 0.0.0.0/0 user-defined route in the virtual network to override the learned default route.

AVS Identity and Access Management

The Azure VMware Solution private clouds are equipped with a vCenter Server and NSX-T Manager. A VM workload is managed with vCenter, and the private cloud is managed and extended with NSX-T Manager. As a CloudAdmin, cloud consumers have limited administrator rights for NSX-T Manager and vCenter.

Figure 3-21 depicts AVS identity and access management

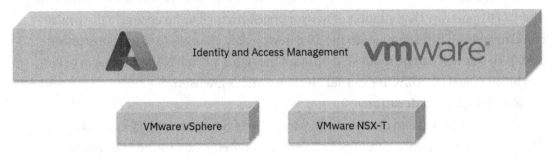

Figure 3-21. Azure identity and access management

VMware vSphere and VMware vSAN (via vCenter):

The CloudAdmin role in vCenter is assigned to a local user, CloudAdmin, in Azure VMware Solution. Cloud consumers can configure users and groups in Active Directory for their private cloud using the CloudAdmin role. CloudAdmins are responsible for managing the workloads of private cloud consumers. Unlike other VMware cloud solutions and on-premises deployments, the CloudAdmin role has privileges related to vCenter in Azure VMware Solution.

The vCenter administrator@vsphere.local account is used in vCenter and ESXi on-premises deployments. Users can be assigned to more AD groups and users as well. The administrator cannot access the administrator account during a VMware Solution deployment on Azure. CloudAdmin users and groups can be assigned to AD within vCenter. The CloudAdmin role does not have permission to add an identity source to vCenter such as an on-premises LDAP or LDAPS server. However, cloud consumers can add an identity source and assign CloudAdmin roles to users and groups using the Run command.

Microsoft does not support and cannot manage specific management components in private clouds. Among them are clusters, hosts, datastores, and virtual switches.

A managed resource for support of platform operations is the vsphere.local SSO domain provided in Azure VMware Solution. Local groups and users can't be created or managed outside of those provided by default with cloud consumers' private clouds.

Custom roles are available on vCenter but not on the Azure VMware Solution portal.

VMware NSX-T:

NSX-T Manager can be accessed using the admin account. Consumers have full privileges and can create and manage Tier-1 (T1) gateways, network segments (logical switches), and all cloud services. Furthermore, cloud consumers can access the NSX-T Tier-0 (T0) gateway. Degradation of network performance or no access to the private cloud may result from changes to the T0 gateway. Any changes to cloud consumers' NSX-T T0 gateway can be requested through the Azure portal. NSX-T manager access can be managed via RBAC if external identity sources are used.

Key design considerations:

Cloud consumers can create a local user called CloudAdmin in vCenter after deploying Azure VMware Solution. The user is assigned to the CloudAdmin role with several permissions in vCenter. Azure VMware Solutions users can also create custom roles based on the principle of least privilege.

Key design best practices:

- Deploy an AD DS domain controller in the identity subscription as part of the identity and access management enterprise-scale landing zone.

- Cloud consumers should be able to assign only a limited number of CloudAdmin roles. Assign Azure VMware Solution users through custom roles and least privileges.

- Microsoft recommends rotating CloudAdmin and NSX admin passwords with caution.

- Azure VMware Solution role-based access control (RBAC) permissions should only be granted to users who need to manage Azure VMware Solution and to the resource group where it's deployed.

- Custom roles can only be configured at the hierarchy level if needed for vSphere permissions. Permissions should be granted at the appropriate VM folder or resource pool, and datacenter permissions should never be applied to vSphere.

- To direct Azure and Azure services from Active Directory, update the Sites and Services.

- AD DS traffic from VMware Solution is directed to appropriate domain controllers.

- Run the following commands in cloud consumers' private clouds:

  - NSX-T and vCenter require an AD DS domain controller as an identity source.

  - Manage the lifecycle of the vSphere. local/CloudAdmin group.

- vCenter and NSX-T can be managed by creating groups in Active Directory and using RBAC. Cloud consumers can create custom roles and can be assigned to Active Directory groups.

AVS Security, Governance, and Compliance

An IT environment that is virtualized has software-based security solutions different from traditional network security, which is hardware-based and runs on devices like firewalls, routers, and switches.

Virtualized security's flexibility and dynamic nature make it different from hardware-based security. The software can be deployed anywhere in the network and is often cloud-based rather than tied to a specific device. As operators create workloads and applications dynamically in virtualized networks, virtualized security allows security services and functions to move with those dynamically created workloads.

For virtualized security, it is crucial to isolate multitenant environments in public cloud environments. Hybrid and multi-cloud environments, where data and workloads move between multiple vendors, can be made more secure by virtualized security.

The functions of traditional hardware security appliances (such as firewalls and antivirus protection) can be virtualized and delivered via software. Additional security functions can also be performed via virtualization. Virtualization offers these features, and they are designed to address the unique security needs of virtualized environments.

This can be accomplished by implementing a virtualized security application directly on bare-metal hypervisors (a position that allows it to provide practical monitoring of applications) or by hosting it as a service on a virtual machine. Physical security, linked to a specific device, cannot be deployed quickly where it is most effective. Figure 3-22 depicts AVS security.

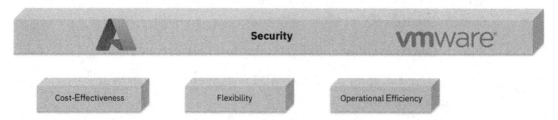

Figure 3-22. *Azure security*

In addition to being more flexible and efficient than traditional physical security, virtualized security is essential to meet the security demands of a virtualized network. Its specific advantages include the following:

- **Cost-effectiveness:** By implementing virtualized security, companies can maintain a secure network without spending money on expensive proprietary hardware. Organizations that use resources efficiently can save more money by purchasing cloud-based virtualized security services. Pricing for virtualized security services is often determined by usage.

- **Flexibility:** Workloads can be followed anywhere with virtualized security, which is very important in a virtualized environment. Multiple data centers and hybrid cloud environments can be protected, enabling companies to benefit from virtualization while keeping their data safe.

- **Operational efficiency:** The setup and configuration of several hardware appliances are not required with virtualized security; it is much faster and easier to deploy than hardware-based security. Instead, they can scale security systems through the centralized software, enabling rapid deployment. Security tasks can also be automated using software, allowing IT teams to spend more time on other tasks.

You can securely implement and holistically govern for Azure VMware Solution throughout its lifecycle. This section covers specific design elements and provides targeted recommendations for Azure VMware Solution security, governance, and compliance.

The following factors should be considered when determining which systems, users, or devices can access Azure VMware Solution and how to secure the platform in general:

1. AVS security

2. AVS governance

3. AVS compliance

AVS Security

When an Azure architect designs the AVS solution from security aspects, four central components need to be considered: identity security, environmental and network security, guest application, and VM security. Figure 3-23 depicts the overall view of AVS security.

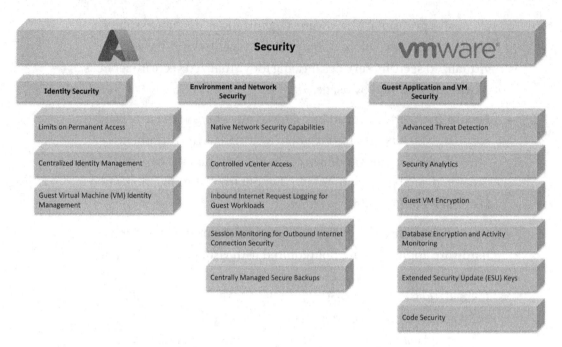

Figure 3-23. *Azure security - logical view*

Let's start with identity security.

Limits on permanent access: In the Azure VMware Solution private cloud, Azure VMware Solution uses the Contributor role. This limit is intended to prevent accidental or intentional misuse of contributor rights. Audit and limit cloud consumers' time on highly privileged accounts by using privileged account management solutions.

Set up a privileged access group for Azure AD within Azure Privileged Identity Management (PIM) to manage Azure AD user and service principal accounts. The Azure VMware Solution Group can be used for creating and managing time-bound, justification-based access to clusters.

Audit history reports from Azure AD PIM can be used to track Azure VMware Solution administrative activities, operations, and assignments. Cloud users can archive the reports in Azure Storage for long-term audit retention.

Centralized identity management: Using the Azure VMware Solution will grant cloud consumers access to the VMware environment as a cloud administrator or network administrator. Azure VMware Solution contributors with role-based access control (RBAC) see these administrative accounts.

The VMware control plane RBAC capabilities can be used to properly manage role and account access to prevent overuse or abuse of CloudAdmin and network administrator users. Use least-privilege principles to create multiple targeted identity objects, such as users and groups. Azure VMware Solution administrators' access should be limited, and accounts should be configured to be break-glass accounts. When all other administrative accounts are unavailable, use the built-in accounts.

With the CloudAdmin account provided by VMware, you can integrate AD DS and Azure AD DS with VMware vCenter and NSX-T control applications and domain services administrative identities. Manage and operate Azure VMware Solutions using domains, services-sourced users and groups, and don't allow account sharing. Create custom vCenter roles and associate them with AD DS groups for fine-grained privileged access control to VMware control surfaces.

With Azure VMware Solution, it is possible to rotate and reset NSX-T and vCenter administrative account passwords. Rotate these accounts regularly whenever cloud consumers use the break-glass configuration.

Guest virtual machine identity management: Manage and protect business processes and data using centralized authentication and authorization for Azure VMware Solution guests. Manage applications and guests within the Azure VMware Solution framework. Set up guest VMs to use a centralized identity management solution for authentication and authorization.

Azure VMware Solution guest VMs and application identity management should be handled by AD DS or Lightweight Directory Access Protocol (LDAP). To ensure continued functionality during outages, domain services architecture accounts for outage scenarios. A seamless guest authentication and authorization experience is provided by connecting AD DS with Azure AD.

Next, let's look at environment and network security.

Native network security capabilities: Implement network security software, such as traffic filtering, Open Web Application Security Project (OWASP) rule compliance, and unified firewall management, as well as distributed denial of service protection (DDoS).

- Segment traffic is controlled by traffic filtering. NSX or Azure NVA capabilities can be used to implement guest network traffic filtering devices to limit access between guest network segments.

- Cloud VMware Solution guest web applications are protected from generic web attacks by compliance with the OWASP Core Rule Set. Protect web applications hosted by Azure VMware Solution guests with the OWASP capabilities of Azure Application Gateway Web

Application Firewall (WAF). Integrate WAF logs into your logging strategy and enable prevention mode using the latest policy.

- It is possible to reduce the risk of unauthorized access by managing firewall rules. For Azure VMware Solution, the firewall architecture contributes to a more comprehensive approach to network management and environmental security. Stateful firewalls are those that allow for traffic flow, inspection, centralized rule management, and event collection.

- Azure VMware Solution workloads are protected from DDoS attacks that could cause financial losses or poor user experiences. Apply DDoS protection on the Azure virtual network that hosts the ExpressRoute termination gateway for the Azure VMware Solution connection. Consider using Azure Policy for automatic enforcement of DDoS protection.

Controlled vCenter access: vCenter can be accessed through uncontrolled access, which increases the attack surface area. NSX Manager and Azure VMware Solution vCenter can be accessed securely using a dedicated privileged access workstation (PAW). Create a group of user accounts and assign them to this group.

Inbound internet request logging for guest workloads: Azure Firewall or an NVA that maintains an audit log of requests made to guest VMs is recommended. Integrate those logs into cloud consumers' security incident and event management (SIEM) solution for appropriate monitoring and alerting. Azure event information and logging can be processed using Microsoft Sentinel before integrating existing SIEM solutions.

Session monitoring for outbound internet connection security: Detect unusual or suspicious outbound Internet activity by using rule control and session auditing from Azure VMware Solution. To ensure maximum security, decide when and where to perform outbound network inspections.

Rather than relying on the default Internet connectivity Azure VMware Solution provides, utilize specialized firewall, NVA, and virtual WAN services for outbound Internet connectivity.

When filtering egress traffic with Azure Firewall, use service tags like virtual networks and fully qualified domain names (FQDNs). Similar capabilities are available for other NVAs.

Secure backups managed centrally: Use RBAC and delayed delete to prevent accidental or intentional deletion of backup data. Protect backup data from being deleted using Azure Key Vault, which manages encryption keys and restricts access to backup storage locations.

Ensure data is encrypted both in transit and at rest using Azure Backup or another backup technology validated for VMware solutions. Use resource locks and the soft-delete feature to protect against accidental or intentional deletion of backups using Azure Recovery Services vaults.

Finally, let's look at the last component: guest application and VM security.

Detection of advanced threats: To prevent various security risks and data breaches, use endpoint security protection, security alert configuration, change control processes, and vulnerability assessments. Cloud consumers can use Microsoft Defender for Cloud to manage threats, protect endpoints, monitor security alerts, patch operating systems, and enforce compliance regulations.

Onboard cloud consumers' guest VMs using Azure Arc for servers. Create dashboards and alerts using Azure Log Analytics, Azure Monitor, and Microsoft Defender for Cloud once cloud consumers are onboarded. To protect and alert on threats associated with VM guests, use Microsoft Defender Security Center.

Before cloud consumers migrate or create new guest VMs, install the Log Analytics agent on VMware VMs. Configure the MMA agent to send metrics and logs to the Azure Log Analytics workspace. Check that the Azure VMware Solution VM reports alerts to Azure Monitor and Microsoft Defender for Cloud after migration.

In addition, an Azure VMware Solution certified partner can assist cloud consumers in assessing VM security postures and providing regulatory compliance against Center for Internet Security (CIS) requirements.

Security analytics: Use security analytics to detect cyber-attacks by collecting, correlating, and analyzing security event data from Azure VMware Solution VMs and other sources. Microsoft Sentinel can access data from Microsoft Defender for Cloud. Install and configure Azure Service Manager, Azure Resource Manager, Domain Name System (DNS), and other Azure services related to Azure VMware Solution deployment. Consider using a partner data connector.

Guest VM Encryption: Azure VMware Solution offers VSAN storage platform data-at-rest encryption as a guest VM feature. Depending on the workload and environment, it may be necessary to encrypt the data more to protect it. Consider encrypting the guest

VM operating system (OS) and data in these situations. Encrypt guest VMs with native guest OS tools. Protect the encryption keys in Azure Key Vault.

Database encryption and activity monitoring: To prevent unauthorized access to SQL and other databases, cloud consumers can encrypt them using Azure VMware Solution. Database workloads should be encrypted at rest using transparent data encryption (TDE) or an equivalent native database feature. Ensure that workloads are on encrypted disks and that sensitive secrets are stored in a key vault dedicated to the resource group.

Cloud consumers can use Azure Key Vault for their keys in bring-your-own-key scenarios, such as BYOK for Azure SQL Database's transparent data encryption. Maintain key and data management separately.

Monitoring for unusual database activity can reduce the risk of insider attacks. Microsoft recommends monitoring native databases with Activity Monitor or an Azure VMware Solution certified partner solution. Cloud consumers should use Azure database services if they want enhanced auditing controls.

Keys for extended security updates: Provide and configure keys for pushing and installing security updates to Azure VMware Solution VMs. Configure ESU keys using the Volume Activation Management Tool.

Code security: Ensure security measures are implemented in DevOps workflows to avoid security vulnerabilities in Azure VMware Solution workloads. Use modern authorization and authentication workflows like Open Authorization (OAuth) and OpenID Connect.

For a versioned repository that ensures the integrity of your codebase, use GitHub Enterprise Server on Azure VMware. Azure VMware Solution or Azure Secure Environment can be used to build and run agents.

AVS Governance

Plan for the AVS environment and workloads governance by designing and deploying the following recommendations. Figure 3-24 depicts the overall view of AVS governance.

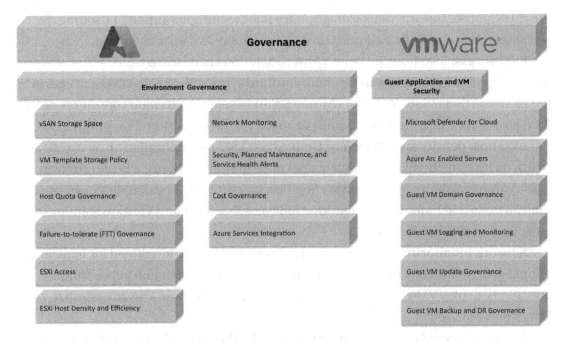

Figure 3-24. *Azure governance - logical view*

Let's start with environmental governance.

vSAN storage space: If vSAN storage space is insufficient, SLA guarantees may be affected. The SLA for Azure VMware Solution outlines customer and partner responsibilities. Percentage Datastore Disk Used alerts should be assigned proper priorities and owners. What percentage 80%?

VM template storage policy: Storage policies that reserve too much vSAN capacity can be problematic. VM templates should have thin-provisioned storage policies, which do not require space reservations. When VMs do not reserve the entire amount of storage up front, storage resources can be used more efficiently.

Host quota governance: When there is insufficient host capacity for growth or disaster recovery (DR) needs, there can be a delay of 5-7 days in getting more host capacity. Consider growth and disaster recovery in the solution design when requesting host quotas and periodically review maximums and growth rates to ensure appropriate lead times for expansion requests. For example, if a cluster of three nodes needs three more for DR, request a six-node host quota. There is no additional charge for host quotas.

Failure-to-tolerate (FTT) governance: Maintain the SLA of Azure VMware Solution by establishing FTT settings proportional to the cluster size. When changing the size of the cluster, make sure the vSAN storage policy is set to the appropriate FTT setting. Be aware that changing FTT can impact storage availability as data is replicated.

ESXi access: ESXi hosts in Azure VMware Solution are restricted. ESXi host access is required for third-party software. Identify any third-party software that needs access to the ESXi host that Microsoft Azure VMware Solution supports. If cloud consumers need ESXi host access, support requests must be made via the Azure portal support request.

ESXi host density and efficiency: Understand ESXi host utilization on an excellent return on investment (ROI). Monitor overall node utilization against a healthy density of guest VMs to maximize Azure VMware Solution investments. Providing sufficient lead time for node additions when monitoring indicates that the Azure VMware Solution environment needs to be resized.

Network monitoring: Make sure internal network traffic is monitored for malicious or unknown traffic. For a detailed insight into Azure VMware Solution networking operations, deploy VMware vRealize Network Insights (vRNI) and VMware vRealize Operations Manager.

Security planned maintenance and service health alerts: Prepare and respond appropriately to issues and outages by understanding and viewing service health. Set up alerts for Azure VMware Solution service issues, planned maintenance, security advisories, and health advisories. Microsoft's recommended maintenance windows do not apply to workload activities in Azure VMware Solution.

Cost governance: Keep track of costs to ensure budget allocation and financial accountability. Implement a cost management solution to track costs, allocate costs, create budgets, monitor costs, and maintain good financial governance. Azure Cost Management and Billing tools make it easy to create a budget, create alerts, allocate costs, and produce reports for financial stakeholders.

Azure services integration: Avoid utilizing the public endpoint of the Azure PaaS, since this can cause traffic to leave cloud consumers network boundaries. Use a private endpoint to access Azure services such as Azure SQL Database and Azure Blob Storage so that traffic stays within a defined virtual network boundary.

Next, let's move forward with guest applications and VM governance. Cloud consumers need to better understand cybersecurity readiness and response with security posture awareness for Azure VMware Solutions guest VMs and applications. The following components are essential.

Microsoft Defender enablement: For Azure services and Azure VMware Solution guest VM workloads, enable Microsoft Defender for Cloud.

Use Azure Arc-enabled servers: Azure Arc-enabled servers can be used to manage Azure VMware Solution guest VMs with tooling that replicates Azure native resource tooling, such as

- Manage, report, and audit guest configurations and settings with Azure Policy

- Configurations and supported extensions that simplify the deployment process

- Using Update Management for managing updates for Azure VMware Solutions guest virtual machines

- Managing guest virtual machines using tags

Guest VM logging and monitoring:

- Debug guest VMs more effectively by enabling diagnostic metrics and logging.

- Enhance debugging and troubleshooting capabilities by implementing logging and querying capabilities.

- Getting VM insight information on guest VMs allows you to detect performance bottlenecks and operational issues.

- VM boundary alerts can be configured to capture VM boundary events.

Cloud consumers need to deploy Log Analytics agents (MMA) on guest VMs before migrating or deploying new guest VMs into the Azure VMware Solution environment. Integrate Azure Log Analytics with the MMA and link the workspace with Azure Automation. Verify the status of any MMA agents deployed on guest VMs before migration with Azure Monitor.

Guest VM domain governance: To enable Azure VMware Solution guest VMs to auto-join an Active Directory domain without error-prone manual processes, use extensions such as the JsonADDomainExtension or equivalent automation options.

Guest VM update governance: The top attack vectors that can expose or compromise Azure VMware Solution guest VMs and applications are delayed or incomplete updates or patches. Make sure updates are promptly installed.

Guest VM backup governance: Plan regular backups to avoid missing backups or relying on old backups that could cause data loss. Schedule backups and monitor backup success with a backup solution. Monitoring and alerting backup events ensure that scheduled backups are successful.

Guest VM DR governance: During business continuity and disaster recovery (BCDR) events, poorly documented recovery point objectives (RPO) and recovery time objectives (RTO) can leave customers unhappy and operational goals unmet. Business continuity can be improved by implementing disaster recovery orchestration.

DR orchestration for Azure VMware solutions detects and reports any issues with continuous replication to disaster recovery sites. Determine the RPOs and RTOs for all Azure and VMware Solutions. Make disaster recovery and business continuity solutions that meet the orchestration's verified RPO and RTO requirements.

AVS Compliance

Plan for the AVS environment and workload compliance by designing and deploying the following recommendations. Figure 3-25 depicts the overall view of AVS Compliance.

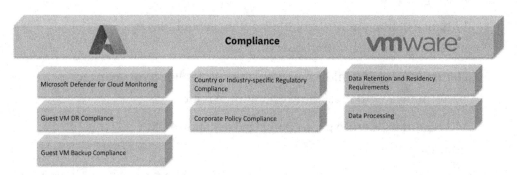

Figure 3-25. *Azure compliance - logical view*

Let's start with Microsoft Defender for Cloud Monitoring.

Microsoft Defender for Cloud monitoring: Monitor security and regulatory compliance with Defender for Cloud's regulatory compliance view. To track deviations from the expected compliance posture, configure Defender for Cloud workflow automation.

Guest VM DR compliance: Track the compliance of Azure VMware Solution guest VMs with DR configurations to ensure their mission-critical applications and workloads remain available during a disaster. Provide at-scale replication provisioning, noncompliance status monitoring, and automatic remediation by using Azure Site Recovery or an Azure VMware Solution-certified BCDR solution.

Guest VM backup compliance: Track and monitor compliance with Azure VMware Solution guest VM backups to ensure that the VMs are backed up. Azure VMware Solution certified partners can provide an at-scale perspective, drill-down analysis, and an actionable interface for tracking and monitoring VM backups.

Country- or industry-specific regulatory compliance: Achieve compliance with country- and industry-specific regulations by ensuring Azure VMware Solution guest workload compliance. Recognize how regulatory compliance is handled in the cloud. Cloud consumers can view or download the Azure VMware Solution and Azure Audit reports from the Service Trust Portal to support the compliance story.

Report firewall audits on HTTP/S and non-HTTP/S endpoints in order to comply with regulatory requirements.

Corporate policy compliance: To prevent company rules and regulations breaches, monitor Azure VMware Solution guest workload compliance. Microsoft recommends using Azure Arc-enabled servers and Azure Policy, or an equivalent third-party solution. Regularly assess and manage compliance with applicable internal and external regulations for Azure VMware Solution guest VMs and applications.

Data retention and residency requirements: Data stored in clusters cannot be retained or extracted by Azure VMware Solution. In addition to terminating all running workloads and components, deleting a cluster also obliterates all cluster data and configuration settings, including public IP addresses. There's no way to recover data from a deleted cluster.

VMware Solution for Azure does not guarantee that all metadata and configuration data for running the service exists only within the deployed geographical region. For assistance with data residency requirements, contact Azure VMware Solution support.

Data processing: Before signing up for a cloud service, cloud consumers should read the terms and conditions. Microsoft Azure VMware Solution customers who have transferred for L3 support need to pay attention to the VMware data processing agreement. Microsoft shares VMware's professional service data and associated personal data when VMware support is needed for a support issue. After that, Microsoft and VMware operate independently.

AVS Management and Monitoring

To achieve operational excellence in the design and deployment of Azure VMware Solution, you need a highly well-designed management and monitoring solution.

Here are the key considerations for Azure VMware Solution platform management and monitoring:

- Create alerts and dashboards on the most critical metrics for the cloud consumer's operations team.

- VMware vRealize Operations Manager and vRealize Network Insight are licensed VMware solutions. Together, they offer a detailed view of VMware solutions for Azure. The NSX-T distributed firewall can be monitored through vCenter events and flow logs. vRealize Log Insight for VMware Solution for Azure currently supports pull logging. Tasks, alerts, and possibilities are captured. Unstructured data from hosts cannot be pushed to vRealize via Syslog.

- VMware vRealize Operations don't support in-guest memory collection via VMware tools. In-guest memory consumption is still supported.

- Azure VMware Solution uses a local identity provider. Utilize a single administrator account for the initial configuration of the Azure VMware Solution. Traceability of actions is facilitated by integrating Azure VMware Solution with Active Directory.

For platform management and monitoring of Azure VMware Solutions, review the following Microsoft recommendations for your design and deployment:

- Through the Azure portal, monitor the baseline performance of the Azure VMware Solution infrastructure.

- vSAN storage has a finite capacity, so managing it is imperative. VM workloads should be stored on vSAN only. Reduce unnecessary storage on vSAN by considering the following design considerations:

  1. VM template storage can be moved off vSAN using Azure Blob Storage content libraries.

  2. Back up to an Azure virtual machine using Microsoft tooling or a partner vendor.

- Azure VMware Solution requires that 25% of vSAN slack space be kept available on the cluster to ensure SLAs.

- Install an existing identity provider with the Azure VMware Solution vCenter.

- Monitoring an ExpressRoute circuit from on-premises into Azure is required in a hybrid environment.

- In Azure Network Watcher, configure two connection monitors to monitor connectivity.

    1. Establish a Connection Monitor between an Azure resource and an Azure VMware Solution-based virtual machine. This monitor offers information about the network connection between Azure and Azure VMware Solution over ExpressRoute.

    2. Connect an on-premises VM to an Azure VMware Solution-based VM by configuring a second Connection Monitor. This monitor displays the availability and performance of network connections between on-premises and Azure VMware Solution over ExpressRoute Global Reach.

- The following KPIs need to be considered:

    1. Monitoring and alerts for vSAN datastore disk usage >70%.

    2. Monitor vSAN% datastore disk use >75% and alert.

    3. The % CPU >80% warning will be monitored and alerted.

    4. Monitoring and alerting on average memory usage >80%.

The following recommendations will help you manage and monitor Azure VMware Solution workloads for your design and deployment:

- Managing and monitoring Azure VMware Solution workloads is worthwhile during workload migration. With Azure native solutions, consider using an Azure Arc server to manage and monitor workloads hosted by VMware Solutions on Azure.

- With Azure VMware Solution, thick provisioning is enabled by default. VMs can be efficiently provisioned using thin provisioning on vSAN. Monitoring vSAN datastore capacity alerts with the above methodology reduces the risk factor.

- Choose between thick- and thin-provisioned disks. Depending on the workload requirements, it's possible to have thick or thin disks in a VM. The two extra components ensure vSAN storage is never over capacity by evaluating the storage configuration.

- If you plan to use a network virtual appliance, consider monitoring trace logs between on-premises and Azure. Monitor the connection between Azure and the VMware Solution.

- Following the hybrid guidance for Windows and Linux, configure guest monitoring for VMs running on Azure VMware Solution. This is true for Windows and Linux integrations for Azure:

  1. **Log Analytics:** This tool aggregates queries and analyzes logs generated by Azure resources.

  2. **Microsoft Defender for Cloud:** An infrastructure security management system that strengthens your security posture by providing advanced threat protection across hybrid and Azure resources. Azure VMware Solution VMs are continually assessed, and vulnerabilities are reported.

  3. **Microsoft Sentinel:** A solution for securing information and events in the cloud. Across cloud and on-premises environments, this Azure resource provides security analytics, alert detection, and automated threat response.

  4. **Azure Update Management:** Updates the operating systems of Windows and Linux machines on-premises and in the cloud.

  5. **Azure Monitor:** This monitoring solution collects, analyzes, and acts upon telemetry from the cloud and on-premises environments.

AVS Business Continuity and Disaster Recovery

Business continuity and disaster recovery are primary factors when planning an SDDC in a datacenter or on a cloud hosting business-critical application. Thanks to the widespread use of virtualization, the availability of datacenters has moved up the priority list. Whenever a new datacenter is planned, or a datacenter is migrated to the cloud, this is an important consideration.

Disaster recovery is the fastest and safest way, with minimal data loss, to get a business up and running after a disaster. A properly planned solution allows for disaster recovery and provides for planned failovers and catastrophe prevention.

Cloud consumers who run VMware on-premises incorporate Azure VMware Solution into their hybrid cloud strategy due to the immense benefits of using the Azure Global Infrastructure.

As organizations plan hybrid cloud strategies, disaster recovery is vital to ensure business continuity in a disaster.

This section discusses the architectural considerations and best practices for implementing disaster recovery using VMware Cloud on Azure. We'll focus mainly on VMware Cloud on Azure and the VMware Site Recovery Manager (SRM) add-on.

When disaster recovery is not designed correctly, it can result in loss of service and failure to meet SLAs. Customers can suffer financial and reputational damage as a result.

Disaster recovery solutions require planning for business continuity. These solutions include

- Risk analysis of current critical applications

- Business impact in the event of a disaster

- Preparedness for disasters

- RTO and RPO

- Virtualization's role in recovery

When recovering a production site, cloud consumers should consider their computing, storage, and networking requirements. In a virtualized recovery site, resources do not have to sit idle all the time so that the recovery site can operate in a distributed fashion. Consumers can run critical or non-critical workloads on the recovery site based on the available resources.

Cloud consumers will need additional storage resources to store the replicated data if they run the recovery site in distributed mode.

Here are the key design considerations and Microsoft recommendations for Azure VMware Solution business continuity:

- Consider a validated backup solution for VMware VMs, such as Microsoft Azure Backup Server (MABS) or from one of Microsoft's backup partners.

- Azure VMware Solution is deployed with VMware vSAN storage policies. With three to five hosts, clusters can tolerate one host failure without data loss. Two host failures are tolerable when the cluster has six and 16 hosts. Each virtual machine can have its own VMware vSAN storage policy. Although these policies are the default, cloud consumers can change the policies used by VMware VMs to meet their needs.

- Azure VMware Solution comes with VMware high availability (HA) enabled by default. A node's memory and compute resources are reserved through the HA admittance policy. This reservation ensures sufficient reserve capacity to restart workloads on another node in an Azure VMware Solution cluster.

- The Azure VMware Solution private cloud can be backed up using Microsoft Azure Backup Server.

- MABS does not currently support backing up to a secondary Azure VMware Solution private cloud.

- As part of the Azure VMware Solution private cloud, install the Azure Backup Server in the Azure region. Using this deployment method, traffic costs can be reduced, administration can be simplified, and the primary/secondary topology can be maintained.

- Azure IaaS or Azure VMware Solution can be used to deploy MABS. It is highly recommended to deploy it in an Azure virtual network outside the Azure VMware Solution private cloud. Due to vSAN's limited capacity within the Azure VMware Solution private cloud, this virtual network is connected to the same ExpressRoute to reduce consumption.

- NSX Manager, HCX Manager, or vCenter can be reinstalled from a backup for Azure VMware Solution platform components.

Here are the key design considerations and Microsoft recommendations for Azure VMware solution disaster recovery:

- For applications and VM tiers, align recovery time, capacity, and point objectives with business requirements. Design replication technologies appropriately to achieve these objectives.

- The availability group can be application-native, such as SQL Always On, or non-native, such as VMware Site Recovery Manager (SRM) or Azure Site Recovery. The Azure VMware Solution private cloud's disaster recovery site should be selected. Choosing the right disaster recovery tool depends on the site.

- Scalable Site Recovery Manager supports migration from third-party locations to Azure VMware Solution.

- VMware Site Recovery Manager offers cloud consumers the ability to back up their Microsoft Azure VMware Solution private cloud to a second Microsoft Azure VMware Solution private cloud.

- Cloud consumers can use Azure Site Recovery to recover their Azure VMware Solution private cloud to Azure IaaS.

- The Azure Site Recovery Deployment Planner can plan disaster recovery to Azure native services.

- Workloads should be started in the correct order in the recovery plan after Azure Site Recovery failover.

- Azure VMware Solution partners like JetStream Software and HCX also support disaster recovery scenarios.

- It determines which Azure VMware Solution workloads should be protected during a disaster recovery event. To reduce costs associated with disaster recovery implementation, consider only protecting those critical workloads to business operations.

- Configure functional domain roles in the secondary environment, such as Active Directory domain controllers.

- Cloud consumers need to enable ExpressRoute Global Reach between both back-end ExpressRoute circuits to disaster recovery between Azure VMware Solution private clouds in distinct Azure regions. When required, the circuits can be used for disaster recovery solutions like VMware SRM and VMware HCX.

- Disaster recovery allows cloud consumers to use the same IP address space on the secondary Azure region as the primary Azure region. The solution foundation will require engineers to add more overhead.

  1. Cloud consumers can keep the same IP addresses for the recovered VM they used for the Azure VMware Solution VMs. In this case, create isolated VLANs or segments in the secondary site and ensure none of them are interconnected with the environment. The subnet moves to the secondary site, and the IP addresses change. Adapt disaster recovery routes for cloud consumers accordingly. This method works when aiming for minimal interaction, but it also adds engineering overhead.

  2. Separate IP addresses can also be used for recovered VMs. Cloud consumers can use different IP addresses for recovered VMs. The VMware Site Recovery Manager's custom IP map will be detailed in the recovery plan if the VM is moved to a secondary site. To change the IP address, select this map. The new IP address allocation is assigned to a defined virtual network using Azure Site Recovery.

- Full and partially recover from disasters:

  1. VMware SRM is available to cloud users for partial and full disaster recovery. Cloud consumers can fail some or all of their VMs from primary to secondary when running Azure VMware Solution in regions one and two.

  2. The requirement determines partial disaster recovery vs. full disaster recovery for VM recovery and IP address retention.

  3. You can maintain the IP address and achieve partial disaster recovery in SRM by moving the subnet's gateway to the secondary Azure VMware solution.

- VMware Site Recovery Manager can be used when working with Azure VMware Solution in primary and secondary sites. Protected and recovery sites are also called primary and secondary sites.

- Microsoft recommends Azure Site Recovery if Azure IaaS is the disaster recovery target.

- Utilize automated recovery plans within each of the solutions to minimize manual input. Disaster recovery plans for the Azure VMware Solution private cloud can be used with VMware Site Recovery Manager or Azure Site Recovery. In recovery plans, machines are grouped into recovery groups for failover, and the recovery process is defined by creating small independent units that can failover.

- Microsoft recommends using the geopolitical region pair as a secondary disaster recovery environment considering the proximity of regions and reducing costs.

- Don't use the same address space twice. If you want to use region 1, use 192.168.0.0/16, and for region 2, use 10.0.0.0/16. In this way, you reduce the chances of IP addresses overlapping.

- ExpressRoute Global Reach can be used to connect the Azure VMware Solution primary and secondary clouds.

Azure Platform Automation and DevOps

A series of best practices for automation and DevOps are implemented in the enterprise-scale landing zone. They can help deploy the VMware Solution Azure private cloud. This section discusses factors to consider when deploying Azure VMware Solution and provides guidelines for operational automation.

The Azure Cloud Adoption Framework architecture and best practices are used here, focusing on designing for scalability. The solution consists of two essential components. The first part is guidance about Azure VMware Solution deployment and automation. The second part consists of open-source components that can be adapted to help consumers build their private clouds. The goal of this solution is to begin an end-to-end automation journey. Still, the organizations can decide which components to deploy manually, based on the considerations in this section.

The enterprise scale for Azure VMware Solution automation repository provides templates and scripts that help cloud consumers deploy Azure VMware Solutions. Before you deploy on the cloud, Microsoft recommends reviewing the templates to understand the deployed resources and the associated costs. Figure 3-26 depicts Azure deployment methods.

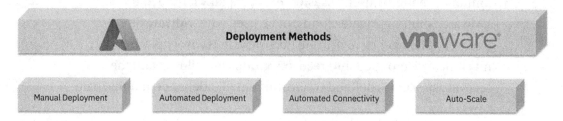

Figure 3-26. *Azure deployment methods*

Manual deployment: Cloud consumers can configure and deploy private clouds running on VMware's Azure platform through the Azure portal. Smaller-scale deployments are best suited to this option. Whenever users repeatedly want to deploy large-scale Azure VMware Solution topologies, they should consider an automated deployment. In addition to configuring connectivity to the private cloud, cloud consumers can use the Azure portal to scale it manually.

Here are the key design considerations and Microsoft recommendations for an Azure VMware Solution manual deployment strategy:

- Manual deployments can be used for initial pilots and small-scale environments in the cloud. They can also be used by cloud consumers who do not have existing automation or infrastructure-as-code practices.

- During the deployment of Azure VMware Solution through the Azure portal, Azure CLI, or Azure PowerShell modules, cloud consumers are shown terms and conditions about data protection in the solution. If they use ARM APIs directly or deploy via ARM or Bicep templates, they need to review these terms and conditions before deploying automation.

- Automate the Azure VMware Solution private cloud creation process to limit the manual intervention required for on-demand environments.

- Within the Azure portal, cloud consumers can monitor the private cloud creation process by using the deployments blade of the target resource group. Before proceeding, cloud consumers should confirm that the private cloud has successfully been deployed. The private cloud might not be able to connect to vCenter if the Failed level is displayed. This might require removing and redeploying the private cloud.

- It's essential for cloud consumers who opt for manual deployment to document the configurations they use to set up the private cloud. Users should download the template they used to document their deployment. There is a parameters file in this template artifact that includes configurations for selected cloud consumers and the ARM template used to deploy the private cloud.

- Microsoft recommends placing a resource lock to restrict resource deletion if cloud consumers interact with the private cloud regularly through the Azure portal. To determine scale operations, Microsoft recommends using read-only resource locks.

Automated deployment: Azure VMware Solution environments can be deployed repeatedly using automated deployments, allowing cloud users to design and deploy the environments on-demand. In this way, multiple domains and regions can be deployed efficiently and at scale. Furthermore, they offer an on-demand, repeatable, and low-risk deployment process.

Here are the key design considerations and Microsoft recommendations for an Azure VMware Solution automated deployment strategy:

- Private cloud deployment of Azure VMware Solution may take several hours. If cloud consumers are using the private cloud, they may monitor this process by viewing the deployment status on ARM. Ensure that appropriate timeout values are selected to accommodate the private cloud provisioning process. Cloud consumers may use a deployment pipeline or deploy with PowerShell or the Azure CLI.

- As recommended in the network topology and connectivity recommendations, private clouds and workload networks can be preallocated address ranges ahead of time. Add these address ranges to the environment configuration. The address overlap isn't validated during deployment. Having two private clouds with the same address range can create issues due to the lack of validation. Additionally, overlapping networks within Azure or on-premises can cause issues.

- Cloud consumers can apply service principles for deployment to provide the least privileged access. Additionally, cloud consumers can restrict access to the deployment process using RBAC in Azure.

- Private cloud users can deploy their applications using a DevOps strategy, using pipelines for automated and repeatable deployments without using local tools.

- Build a minimal private cloud and then scale as needed.

- Request quotas or capacity ahead of time to ensure a successful deployment.

- Ensure the private cloud's deployment process and status are monitored before deploying subresources. No configuration updates can be made once a private cloud is in a Succeeded state. Microsoft recommends that cloud consumers with failed private clouds stop further operations and open a support ticket.

- Include relevant resource locks in the automated deployment or ensure their application through policy.

Automated networking: Connectivity can be set up via ExpressRoute after cloud consumers deploy the Azure VMware Solution private cloud. The following paths are vital for network connectivity:

- A virtual network gateway connects a virtual network or an Azure Virtual WAN to the Internet.

- Using Global Reach, connect Azure VMware Solution and an existing ExpressRoute.

Here are the key design considerations and Microsoft recommendations for Azure VMware Solution automated network connectivity:

- Azure VMware Solution private clouds can be integrated with Azure virtual networks or ExpressRoutes. From the management and workload networks within the private cloud, this connection advertises routes automatically. Consider validating broadcast networks before connecting since there are no overlap checks.

- ExpressRoute authorization keys can be aligned with existing naming schemes for resources consumers connect to. In doing so, associated resources can be easily identified.

- Azure VMware Solution's private cloud may not host ExpressRoute virtual network gateways and ExpressRoute circuits. Decide whether cloud consumers wish to access all of these resources through a single service principle.

- By deploying NSX-T workload networking services through the Azure portal, NSX-T Manager makes it easier to manage NSX-T components. Consumers of the cloud should assess how much control they need over the network segments.

  1. Configure DNS zones for private DNS integration using the NSX-T workload networking in the Azure portal.

  2. Use NSX-T workload networking within the Azure portal for network topologies that only need a single tier-one gateway.

  3. NSX-T Manager can be used directly for advanced configurations.

- Use Azure Key Vault or a similar secret store to pass authorization keys between deployments if cloud consumers use separate service principles for Azure VMware Solution deployment and ExpressRoute configuration.

- Azure VMware Solution private clouds can only carry out a limited number of parallel operations at a given time. Microsoft recommends using dependencies to deploy serially in templates defining many Azure VMware Solution private cloud subresources.

Auto Scaling: The number of hosts in an Azure VMware Solution cluster is determined by its scale. Users can automate scaling in and out of cloud clusters by modifying per-cluster scaling through programmatic means. An Azure Monitor alert may trigger this automation on-demand, on a schedule, or on a regular basis.

Here are the key design considerations and Microsoft recommendations for Azure VMware Solution auto scaling:

- Automatic scaling out can provide more capacity on-demand, but the cost of adding more hosts must be considered. There should be a limit on this cost depending on the subscription quota, but manual limits should also be in place.

- Consider the impact of the scale-in on running workloads and storage policies applied within the cluster before cloud consumers automate the process. RAID 5 workloads, for example, cannot be scaled into a three-node cluster. Additionally, memory and storage use should be considered since they could interfere with scaling up.

- There can only be one single-scale operation at a time, so orchestrating scale operations between multiple clusters is necessary.

- Adding a new node to an existing cluster is not instantaneous when using the Azure VMware Solution scale operation. Integrations and third-party solutions may not be able to handle host removal and addition in a continuous fashion. Make sure all third-party solutions are performing as expected. The validation ensures that removing or adding hosts will not require additional steps when the product is refreshed or reconfigured.

- Put hard limits for both scale-in and scale-out operations outside of a quota.

- Request a quota ahead of time so that it won't affect scaling. Rather than guaranteeing capacity, quotas allow for deployment up to a specific limit. Keep an eye on the quota limit regularly to ensure there's always room.

- If cloud consumers use an automated scaling system, ensure it is monitored and alerts cloud consumers when it is done. This will prevent unexpected scales from occurring.

- Make sure there is adequate headroom before scaling-in operations using Azure Monitor Metrics. During and after scaling operations, pay attention to CPU, memory, and storage. With this attention to capacity, you ensure that it does not affect SLAs.

Azure VMware Solution private clouds exist as resources within the ARM accessible through several automation tools. First-party Microsoft tooling usually supports ARM specifications within a few weeks of release. In this section, the considerations are presented in a way that can be applied to different toolkits from an automation perspective.

Here are the key design considerations and Microsoft recommendations for Azure VMware Solution automated tooling:

- To define configuration as a single artifact, use declarative toolings like ARM and Bicep templates. Compared to manual deployment, command-line and script-based toolings like Azure CLI and PowerShell require a more step-by-step approach.

- Third-party automation tools, such as Terraform, can be used to deploy Azure VMware Solution and Azure native services. Ensure that the Azure VMware Solution currently provides the features you wish to use.

- Be mindful of failure-to-deploy implications when using script-based deployment and monitor appropriately. Assume monitoring both the deployment and the private cloud status of the Azure VMware Solution.

- Automate the deployment of Azure VMware Solutions using Azure CLI, PowerShell, ARM, or Bicep declarative templates.

- When possible, consider what-if scenarios before executing changes, pausing on resource deletion for verification.

- Cloud consumers can use Azure Blueprints to deploy Infrastructure as Code for a single deployment operation. In Azure Blueprints, deployments are stamped and repeatable, so there is no need for automation pipelines.

Creating resources within vCenter and NSX-T Manager can also be automated as part of an Azure VMware Solution private cloud. Here are some considerations for designing automation at the VMware level:

- PowerCLI for VMware vSphere automation

- PowerCLI for VMware NSX-T automation

- Providers such as Terraform for VMware NSX-T and VMware vSphere

- vRealize Automation and vRealize Operations

Here are the key design considerations and Microsoft recommendations for Azure VMware Solution PowerCLI/VMware vSphere automation:

- VMware vCenter can be completely controlled programmatically using PowerCLI to create VMs, resource pools, and templates.

- Since VMware vCenter is only accessible through private connectivity or a private IP address, cloud consumers must install PowerCLI on a machine connected to the Azure VMware Solution management network. If possible, use a self-hosted pipeline execution agent. A virtual machine within a virtual network or NSX-T segment can run PowerCLI with this agent.

- Cloud consumers might not be able to access certain cloud operations due to the CloudAdmin role's limitations. Validate the permissions required for the automation you plan to implement with CloudAdmin permissions.

- Consider using a service account for VMware vCenter level automation via Active Directory integration for least privilege access.

Here are the key design considerations and Microsoft recommendations for Azure VMware Solution PowerCLI/VMware NSX-T automation:

- NSX-T is accessible to the admin user by default in an Azure VMware Solution private cloud. Changes made via PowerCLI or the NSX-T APIs will impact this default access. Modifying Microsoft-managed components like transport zones and tier-zero gateways is not permitted.

- To communicate with NSX-T, the VM running PowerCLI needs to be connected to the Azure VMware Solution private cloud.

- The workload network can be controlled by ARM. This control allows Azure CLI and PowerShell operations using Azure RBAC rather than NSX-T identity to be performed using ARM API.

Here are the key design considerations and Microsoft recommendations for Azure VMware Solution Terraform for VMware NSX-T and VMware vSphere:

- Resources can be deployed to the cloud using vSphere and NSX-T providers for Terraform. A declarative approach is used to deploy these resources in the private cloud.

- Terraform needs a private connection to the private cloud management network to communicate with vCenter and NSX-T Manager API endpoints. Think about deploying from a virtual machine on Azure that can route traffic to the private cloud.

Here are the key design considerations and Microsoft recommendations for Azure VMware Solution Terraform for vRealize Automation and vRealize Operations:

- Cloud consumers can deploy virtual machines within Azure VMware Solution using vRealize Automation as in an on-premises environment.

- Azure VMware Solution supports a limited number of deployment models. It is possible to host the vRealize Automation appliances on-premises or utilize vRealize Cloud Management.

- vRealize Automation and vRealize Operations appliances require private connectivity to Azure VMware Solution, just as PowerCLI does.

Cloud consumers can set up automation at the VM level within Azure VMware Solution workloads. Ansible, Chef, and Puppet are examples of automation. On-premises agents are also available for Azure Automation for VM-level configuration in the cloud.

Summary

In this chapter, you read about Azure's well-architected framework; the AVS Solution building blocks; AVS network topology and connectivity; AVS identity and access management; AVS security, governance, and compliance; AVS management and monitoring; AVS business continuity and disaster recovery; and AVS platform automation.

In the next chapter of the book, you will read about the planning methodology of AVS Solution and the assessment and deployment of Azure VMware Solution.

CHAPTER 4

Plan and Prepare AVS

Microsoft Azure is one of the most prominent cloud service providers, offering options for IaaS, PaaS, and SaaS that cater to modern enterprises' rapidly changing business requirements.

As part of the design and deployment of the AVS solution, determining the number of resources, naming the resources, sizing the cluster, registering the AVS providers, and allocating the network are vital factors.

Developing a production-ready environment for creating VMs and migration is critical to the success of a cloud consumer's Azure VMware deployment. AVS administrators should identify and gather the necessary information for cloud consumers to deploy their services during the planning process. Document the information cloud consumers collect as the deployment plans proceed; a successful deployment results in a production-ready environment for creating VMs and migrating data.

This chapter provides the planning and assessment essential,

By the end of this chapter, you should understand the following:

- AVS Azure Cloud enablement

- AVS compute planning and preparing

- AVS storage planning and preparing

- AVS network planning and preparing

- AVS management and monitoring planning and preparing

AVS Azure Cloud Enablement

A VMware-based private cloud is provided in Azure by Azure VMware Solution. Dedicated, bare-metal Azure hosts power private clouds. Azure PowerShell and the Azure Portal are used to deploying and managing hosts. Azure VMware Solution includes VMware vSphere, VMware vCenter, VMware vSAN, VMware HCX, and NSX software.

© Puthiyavan Udayakumar 2022
P. Udayakumar, *Design and Deploy Azure VMware Solutions*, https://doi.org/10.1007/978-1-4842-8312-7_4

The Microsoft Azure Cloud Adoption Framework's plan methodology assists cloud consumers in establishing an overall cloud adoption plan for cloud-based digital transformation. Cloud consumers can use VMware planning guidance to create backlogs and plans for building necessary skills for their teams, all based on what they intend to do in the cloud.

High-level adoption approach:

Cloud adoption plans convert aspirational goals into actionable plans. Cloud consumers' collective cloud teams can use the cloud adoption plan to guide their technical efforts and align them with the organization's business strategies. Figure 4-1 depicts the high-level adoption approach.

Figure 4-1. *High-level adoption approach*

Scoping: Cloud consumers will have finalized the objectives and success criteria for the Azure VMware Solution project during the scoping stage. The following should be translated into the business and technical requirements for the scope of work:

- Needs of the business

  - Migration schedule

  - Migration of an application successfully

- Technical requirements

  - Migration of a set number of virtual machines from one data center to another

  - Estimated number of Azure VMware Solution nodes in each Azure region

Architectural design: The architectural design will be constructed in conjunction and with the support of Microsoft and a partner after the scoping and requirements have been described. The following items will be discussed and evaluated as part of "discovery" and "technical review" as part of this process.

Core AVS overview:

- License requirements on Azure Reserved VM Instances

- Instances, private clouds, and clusters

- Storage

- High-level connectivity

- Identity and access

- Monitoring and maintenance

Networking and security:

- Connectivity over WAN and ExpressRoute

- WAN security (options available)

- Layer 2 scalability

- Firewall

- Integration for Azure

Migration and management:

- An example of a migration toolchain, including typical processes and runbooks

- Describing the capabilities and limitations of the HCX cluster

- High availability and disaster recovery

- Backup

The administrator of a cloud organization should make sure all domain owners know the plan's scope and success criteria. Microsoft recommends that domain owners in various fields, such as network, security, and operations, participate in this phase.

Pilot deployment: Microsoft recommends starting the project with a pilot or proof of concept once the scope of work has been agreed upon and in place. Microsoft recommends VMware for Azure to be deployed for production.

- Install and configure the Azure VMware Solution cloud service and nodes

- Networking configuration

- HCX configuration if necessary

- Add additional Azure services and applications if needed

Pilot validation: Analyze the pilot against established technical and business requirements for the Azure VMware Solution and confirm that success criteria have been met.

Production: Start transitioning production VMware workloads to the new Azure VMware Solution environment. Develop a migration ramp-up plan for Azure VMware Solution's private cloud node capacity requirements. Use the resources and guidance for Azure migrations to estimate the number of nodes the environment will require. (is there a link to these or a reference?)

Extend and modernize: Once cloud consumers have established their Azure VMware Solution environment, the hub-and-spoke network connection ensures that extension to other Azure public cloud services is seamless.

To modernize an application in the current infrastructure design, cloud consumers often optimize through resource management, monitoring, and security.

As a starting point in this section, let's talk about planning AVS services.

High-level planning approach: Plan methodology rationalizes cloud consumers' digital estate by following the five Rs(which are?). Migration and modernization processes tend to be streamlined, efficient, and repeatable in the most common path to the cloud. The planning process prioritizes rehost options with limited architecture support and rebuild options from the five Rs.

Cloud consumers must consider many business and technical factors to scope, design, evaluate, and deploy Azure VMware Solution. Establishing the right solution for business needs requires defining cloud consumers' objectives and success criteria at the start of any successful project.

Azure VMware Solution has objectives that align with business goals and initial motivations.

- When evacuating a data center, cloud consumers usually define a timeline that meets the fixed date for closing the data center. For instance, "the migration must be completed from the datacenter by x date."

- Cloud consumers will need to know how to burst capacity on Azure VMware Solution and where disaster recovery sites are located to increase infrastructure scale, capacity, and disaster recovery. This might include objectives such as increasing capacity by x number of nodes (or integrating storage) or establishing disaster recovery sites within a particular region.

- The hardware/software end of support requires you to establish how many licenses cloud consumers have and what is the license mobility between current on-premises environments and the cloud. For example, in Azure VMware Solution, cloud consumers could receive extended security updates for several Windows Server virtual machines and SQL Server virtual machines. (is there any guidance for this to determine what licensing you need? Approach MS Account team?

Similarly, the success criteria of the Azure VMware Solution project are aligned with the outcomes the cloud consumers organization is looking for:

- Reduce TCO and realize cost savings. Through cloud economics and Azure Reservations, it is often measured to lower the footprint of the datacenter and optimize costs. Cloud consumers should develop precise success measures for reducing the TCO for VMware workloads, whether at a macro level or specific to the Azure VMware Solution project.

- Understand the ease of implementation and change management. With VMware skills and processes using Azure VMware Solution, success measures related to resources are defined in hours. Identify any in-house project support requirements, any retraining of IT professionals, or new skills to be acquired.

- Minimize business interruptions and downtime. Provides success measures related to acceptable downtime, if any, and other factors that may affect business continuity, including system communication latency and processes reengineering.

IT managers and IT leaders are both responsible for driving the AVS services initiative. Although there are many benefits to implementing AVS, it requires proper planning, an assessment, well-defined requirements, and strategic investments.

An AVS business case is the first step in planning the service. A business case is required to justify an IT project's time, cost, and effort. It is increasingly essential for the business board and senior management to focus on investments that produce original business value. The business board and senior management must approve a business case. The business case should demonstrate the project's benefits and why it is wanted.

It can be vital in getting approval and funding for the AVS project to enhance end user experiences if a well-developed business case stands out among competing preferences within the organization.

As a result of the AVS business case, it is possible to critically examine the possibilities, options, project steps, and financial investment to determine what activities will yield the most significant business value.

The following is critical to define the scope of the business case:

- Recognize a business problem.

- Craft a business problem statement.

- Classify business aspirations in pursuing the opportunity.

- Prioritize business objectives.

- Designate metrics to business objectives.

The first step in developing a business case is identifying the problem that needs to be solved. The following is an example.

Company XYZ wants to evaluate either SDDC on-premises or consume AVS from a public cloud service provider. All business requirements are unique, so there is no one-stop solution for everyone's business. To recognize a business problem and perform an initial evaluation, making SDDC on-premises or AVS a business-wide decision depends on various elements. Identifying the answers to the following questions helps define the business problem statement:

- Is the company seeking a shift from complete IT services to cloud-based services or happy to stay on-premises?

- Is the company comfortable with CapEx or OpEx?

- Does the company have a refreshed infrastructure currently in the business budget for the future?

- Does the company have on-premises expertise? Is there a cost and headcount to hire someone with VMware skills?

- Does the company wants to go global with resiliency and end users need service available on the move with better performance?

After evaluation, company XYZ wants AVS based on the following. In terms of perks, overcoming infrastructure requirements is appealing, but it depends on how the business deploys the SDDC. SDDC solutions on-premises can be expensive since they require specialized infrastructure, staff expertise, and ongoing support and administration. In addition, on-premises infrastructure typically needs to be refreshed every 3 to 5 years and turns obsolete as soon as it starts working.

SDDC and AVS increase the ability to scale up/down to address the above business challenge. Going global should consume the service closest to the end users to deliver better performance.

Following is crucial for defining the review and developing each choice:

- Produce a list of choices, a minimum of three options wherever possible.

- Collect input from business-wide vital stakeholders.

To develop a business case, the second step is to determine the options for seizing that opportunity, and the following is an example.

Company XYZ wants to evaluate either SDDC on-premises or consume AVS from a public cloud service provider. The answer depends. Company XYZ wants to move forward with AVS based on business requirements and the choices of solutions that comply with its regulation demands. As well, company XYZ wants to build an agile, long-term remote workplace, using cloud-based apps to optimize the end user experience and offer better performance, security, and compliance. This addresses various challenging use cases, including streaming audio and video and graphics.

Now company XYZ's business case should reflect the AVS Services. When deciding on AVS, four significant areas need consideration: infrastructure, features, cost, and an operational model fit the organization's demands. Identifying the answer to the following questions helps to develop each choice. While it's easy to be persuaded by a low cost, choosing the most economical AVS provider could set the AVS initiative up for collapse because of cheap cloud IaaS, features, or fumbling support. Alternatively, take cost as one factor while accomplishing AVS due diligence and consider all components, including modern infrastructure, agile features, and aligning to the business operational model.

The following factors must be considered to evaluate each choice:

- Combine any choices that can be implemented logically together.

- Exclude extensive, high-risk decisions.

- Pick the easy-to-implement solution over the complex and challenging.

In evaluating a business case, the third step is to seize that opportunity. The comprehensive list of alternatives is narrowed down to three options that best meet organizational business objectives and stakeholders' needs due to multiple inputs from vendors and internal key stakeholders.

Create an actual project based on business requirements and ideas and shape it into a project endeavor that leads to business results.

The key to a successful project is careful planning and a purposeful approach. Finding the right solution and completing it correctly will be difficult, time-consuming, and frustrating without a clear understanding of what an organization is trying to achieve. Setting expectations and preparing for the project is vital. AVS can deliver cloud experiences without managing the underlying server infrastructure, but proper planning is still required.

Convert ideas into a project that leads to business results. Achieving a clear definition of an AVS project is critical. Three factors define an AVS project: objective, scope, and requirements.

Defining objectives:

- Why is the AVS project?

- When will you finish it?

- What business is achieved with it?

Defining scope:

- How broad are the boundaries of the project?

- How narrow are the edges of the project?

- How do you measure the success of the project?

Defining business requirements:

- Time, scope, and cost involved

- Value proposition

- TCO and ROI view

As a next step, let's move forward with the technical viewpoints to consider.

Cloud consumers can deploy hardware and software for their private cloud in an Azure integrated and automated manner with VMware.

The Azure VMware Solution makes it possible to run VMware workloads on Azure. Azure VMware Solution supports direct migration of virtual machines from VMware environments on-premises, and cloud VMs work exactly as they do on-premises.

AVS administrators/architects need to plan and implement Azure VMware Solution before it can be deployed to cloud consumers. Here are some critical components to consider:

- Plan and prepare the required Azure components.

- Plan and prepare the subscription-eligibility criteria.

- Open a support ticket and register the resource provider.

Plan and prepare the required Azure components: In an AVS resource group, a private cloud must be created. Subscriptions and regions are each associated with a resource group. Decide which subscription will be used for AVS first. Microsoft Enterprise Agreement (EA) or Cloud Solution Provider (CSP) Azure plans must use this subscription. Resource groups can contain resources in more than one region. To maintain consistency and simplicity, the resource group is recommended to be hosted in the same region as the AVS private cloud.

Before deploying an Azure VMware solution, consider the components listed in Table 4-1.

Table 4-1. *Azure Core Components and Definitions*

Component	Notes
Subscription	Build a new subscription or reuse an existing one.
Azure Region	Choose from the AVS service available region.
Resource group	Build a new resource group or reuse an existing one.

Subscription: Azure subscriptions provide organizations with a structure to organize and manage their assets.

Decide which subscription to use to deploy Azure VMware solutions. Subscriptions can be created or used from existing subscriptions.

Azure management groups are designed to be flexible because every organization is different. An AVS cloud estate can, for example, be modeled based on the organizational hierarchy of the cloud consumer. Cloud consumers can use this method to define and apply policies at higher levels of the hierarchy. Thanks to inheritance, the policy will automatically apply to management groups lower in the hierarchy. It is helpful to create an initial hierarchy of management groups that reflects the organizational needs.

Consider the following subscription design strategies to address cloud consumers' business priorities.

Management workload separation strategy: Adding new workloads to the cloud is common for organizations. In groups responsible for production and nonproduction management, different ownership of subscriptions may result in multiple subscriptions. This approach allows for the separation of work. The inheritance model is not fully utilized to apply policies automatically across a subset of cloud consumer subscriptions.

Application workload category strategy: Cloud subscriptions typically grow as a company's cloud footprint expands. The applications differ fundamentally in terms of business criticality, compliance requirements, access controls, or data protection requirements. Subscriptions for these application categories are built from the production subscriptions, and subscriptions for nonproduction applications are organized under the management teams for production and nonproduction. The operations staff of a central IT department typically owns and manages these subscriptions.

It is common for organizations to categorize their applications differently and separate subscriptions based on specific applications, services, or application archetypes. Workloads within this category are designed to consume most of a subscription's resource limit. Additionally, mission-critical workloads might be separated from other workloads to avoid conflicts under these limits. Examples of such workloads include the following:

- Workloads that are critical to mission success

- Cloud consumers' organizations include applications in their cost of goods sold (COGS). A company's widgets contain an Azure IoT module that sends telemetry. COGS may require a dedicated subscription for accounting or governance purposes to be part of this process.

- To comply with regulatory requirements, applications must comply with PCI-DSS, HIPAA, and FedRAMP.

Functional strategy: The functional strategy divides subscriptions and accounts according to functional areas such as finance, sales, and IT support. Hierarchical management groups are used to achieve this.

Business unit strategy: With the business unit strategy, subscriptions and accounts are organized based on profit and loss category, division, or a similar business structure.

Geographic strategy: Organizations with global operations use a management group hierarchy to group subscriptions and accounts based on geographic regions.

Azure Region

The Microsoft Azure datacenters are located all over the world. When leveraging or creating cloud resources, the cloud consumers use physical equipment in one or more of these locations, such as AVS or virtual machines.

Azure does not expose individual datacenters to end users; instead, it organizes them by regions. At least one, and possibly more, nearby datacenter is located in a region connected with a low-latency network.

To balance workloads appropriately within each region, Azure intelligently assigns and controls resources. In addition, it provides better scalability and redundancy and preserves cloud consumers' data residency. Azure has specialized regions where cloud consumers can build out their applications for compliance and legal purposes.

Among all cloud providers, Azure has the most global regions. This gives cloud consumers the flexibility to bring applications closer to cloud consumers users no matter where they are. This also means better scalability redundancy and preserves data residency for cloud consumers' services.

Cloud consumers should be aware of two other terms: geographies and availability zones. When cloud consumers identify AVS resources, AVS uses Azure regions.

Geopolitical boundaries or country borders define Azure's geographical division of the world. Azure geographies typically contain two or more regions that preserve data residency and compliance boundaries. Several benefits can be derived from this approach:

- Customers who have specific requirements for data residency and compliance can keep their data and applications close to home.

- Data residency, sovereignty, compliance, and resilience requirements are respected in a geographically defined area.

- Because they are connected to a dedicated high-capacity networking infrastructure, geographical systems are fault-tolerant.

AVS service was available in the Azure regions listed in Table 4-2 as of the writing of this book.

Table 4-2. *AVS Availability Across Azure Regions*

Region	Products	AVS
Africa	South Africa North	Loading
Asia	East Asia	Yes
	Southeast Asia	Yes
Australia	Australia East	Yes
	Australia Southeast	Yes
Brazil	Brazil South	Yes
Canada	Canada Central	Yes
	Canada East	Yes
Europe	North Europe	Yes
	West Europe	Yes
France	France Central	Yes
Germany	Germany West Central	Yes
Japan	Japan East	Yes
	Japan West	Yes
Sweden	Sweden Central	Loading
UK	UK South	Yes
	UK West	Yes
USA	Central US	Yes
	East US	Yes
	East US 2	Yes
	North Central US	Yes
	South Central US	Yes
	West US	Yes
	West US 2	Loading
	West US 3	Loading

There are many Azure regions around the world. Choosing the right Azure region is incredibly important because every region has different characteristics. Among them are the services available, capacity, restrictions, and sovereignty.

The availability of Azure services differs depending on the region. A cloud consumers' workload region containing the desired service should be selected.

The maximum capacity is different for each region. There is a possibility that this can affect what kinds of subscriptions can deploy what types of services and under what conditions. Subscription quotas are not affected by this. If you're planning to migrate a large datacenter to Azure, you might want to consult the Azure field team or account manager to confirm that you can deploy at the scale you require.

In certain regions, certain restrictions apply to the deployment of services. Some regions can only be used as a backup or failover target. Other considerations include data sovereignty.

The government of that country determines the sovereignty of a particular region. Although all Azure regions are sovereign, they are isolated from the rest of Azure. Microsoft may not manage these services, and they might be restricted to certain customers. The following sovereign regions are affected:

- Microsoft Azure China 21Vianet

- Azure Germany will be deprecated in favor of nonsovereign Azure regions in Germany.

- Azure, the US government

- Microsoft manages two regions in Australia for the Australian government, its customers, and contractors. As a result, these regions are also subject to client constraints.

When cloud consumers operate in multiple geographic regions, which is essential for resilience, this adds complexity in the following ways:

- Asset distribution

- User access profiles

- Compliance requirements

- Regional resiliency

For cloud consumers to adopt the cloud effectively, regional selection is essential.

Azure Resource Group

The Azure platform is based on resource groups. A resource group encapsulates resources on Azure. A cloud consumer creates virtual machines, application gateways, and CosmosDB instances using Azure subscriptions. A resource can belong to only one resource group, and all resources must have a resource group. Resource groups cannot be nested, and resources can be moved between them. Each resource has to be placed in a resource group before it can be provisioned.

Manage and track workload costs by organizing the cloud-based resources. To define a hierarchy of management groups, represent a naming convention, and apply resource tagging to cloud resources, define a hierarchy of management groups.

- **Resource:** Azure manageable items are available through the Azure portal. A resource can be a virtual machine, a storage account, a web app, a database, and a virtual network. A resource can be a group of resources, a subscription, a management group, or a tag.

- **Resource group:** A container for Azure solutions that holds related resources. Resources that need to be managed together are included in a resource group. Cloud consumers define resource groups based on what makes the most sense to them.

  - Managing and organizing Azure resources is made easier by resource groups. Cloud consumers can provide some organization to resources they create in Azure by placing resources that have similar usage, type, or location. There's a lot of disorder among resources, so consider a logical grouping.

  - Resource groups can also be applied to RBAC permissions and RBAC groups. With RBAC permissions to a resource group, cloud consumers can restrict access to what is needed.

  - All resources are deleted if cloud consumers delete a resource group. In non-production environments, where cloud consumers might try an experiment but dispose of it once they're done, organizing resources by life cycle can be useful. Resources can be removed in groups.

- **Azure Resource Manager:** Azure Resource Manager provides deployment and management services for Azure. Cloud consumers can create, update, and delete resources within their Azure accounts using the management layer. Cloud consumers use access control, locks, and tags to organize and secure their resources after deployment.

The Resource Manager receives requests sent by users, administrators, and developers from tools, APIs, and SDKs. These requests are authenticated and authorized. The Resource Manager submits the request to Azure service, which takes the requested action. Cloud consumers reap the benefits of consistent results and capabilities in various tools because the same API handles all requests.

PowerShell, Azure CLI, REST APIs, and client SDKs are also available to access all capabilities available in the portal. Within 180 days of the initial release, API functionality will be available in the Azure portal.

With Azure Resource Manager, cloud consumers can do the following:

- Use declarative templates instead of scripts to manage their infrastructure.

- All of their solution resources should be deployed, managed, and monitored as a group rather than individually.

- Maintain consistent deployment of their solutions throughout the development lifecycle.

- Make sure that resources are deployed in the proper order by specifying their dependencies.

- Use the native integration of Azure role-based access control (Azure RBAC) into the management platform.

- Organize their subscriptions logically by assigning tags to resources.

- See the costs for a group of resources sharing the same tag to understand how their organizations are billed.

AVS Compute Plan and Prepare

A VMware vSphere cluster is planned for cloud consumers based on the Azure location and the cloud consumers' workload capacity needs. VMware vSphere includes both ESXi (the evolution of ESX Server) and vCenter Server for the virtualization layer.

AVS Compute Host

Figure 4-2 depicts the AVS compute host.

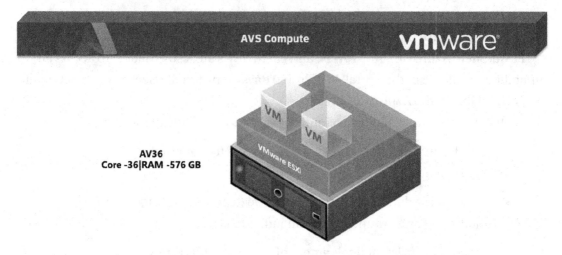

Figure 4-2. *AVS compute host*

- Azure bare metal serves as the foundation of the AVS (Azure VMware Solution). The AV 36 servers have dual 18 core 2.3GHz Intel CPUs and 576GB of RAM.

- A hyperconverged, bare-metal infrastructure is the foundation for Azure VMware Solution clusters. The storage is 3.2TB NVMe cache tier- Raw and 15.20 SSD capacity RAW.

- For an Azure VMware Solutions private cloud to be deployed, there must be at least three nodes.

- Clusters are built and scaled from isolated pools of hosts. Each of these hosts has passed hardware tests and has had its data securely deleted.

Before you take a deep dive into the AVS vSphere solution, let's get started with the foundation of VMware vSphere. Cloud users can use VMware vSphere to virtualize enterprise data centers and build private clouds.

VMware vSphere

VMware vSphere extends beyond basic host partitioning and provides additional services like dynamic resource scheduling while aggregating infrastructure resources. vSphere is VMware's virtualization platform that enables datacenters to become aggregate computing infrastructures with computing, storage, and networking resources combined. With vSphere, cloud consumers can manage AVS infrastructures as a single operating environment and operate the datacenters that participate in it.

The two core components of VMware vSphere are listed in Table 4-3.

Table 4-3. *The Building Blocks of VMware vSphere*

VMware ESXi	A physical host on which virtual machines run (including the hypervisor)
VMware vCenter Server Appliance	vSphere's main management component. There are also services associated with the controller of prior versions, including vCenter Server, vSphere Web Client, vSphere Auto Deploy, and vSphere ESXi Dump Collector, as well as vCenter Single Sign-on, License Service, Lookup Service, and VMware Certificate Authority.

The architecture of vCenter 7.0 has been dramatically simplified. There is now only one architecture permitted, the embedded architecture. VMware vCenter Server provides all services, including VMware vCenter Single Sign-On, VMware vCenter License Service, VMware Directory Services, VMware Certificate Authority, VMware vSphere Client (HTML5), VMware vSphere Auto Deploy, VMware vSphere ESXi Dump Collector, VMware vSphere Syslog Service, and VMware vSphere Update Manager.

VMware ESXi

A virtual infrastructure is built on VMware ESXi, a hypervisor. In addition to improved security, reliability, and simplified management, with the compact architecture, rapid installation, configuration, and deployment are all possible on virtualization-optimized server hardware.

VMware ESXi is a bare-metal hypervisor for VMware vSphere, As ESXi runs directly on the physical server. It provides direct access to all server resources, A single instance of ESXi controls all CPU, memory, network, and storage resources and provides near-native performance for virtual machines, unlike hosted hypervisors. Both ESXi and vCenter Server form the core of vSphere. Cloud consumers create and run virtual machines and appliances using ESXi, the virtualization platform. The vCenter Server is the service that allows cloud users to manage multiple hosts in a network and pool host resources.

VMkernel

The VMware VMkernel operating system is a POSIX counterpart. Its features are process creation and control, signals, a file system, and process threads similar to those found in other operating systems. ESXi hosts serve as the intermediary between VMs and the physical hardware they are supported by. For VMs to interact with ESXi servers, they need VMkernel. Multiple VMs can be run simultaneously using this program, and it provides such functionalities as

- Scheduling resources

- Stacks of I/O

- Drivers for devices

Virtual Machine Kernel (VMkernel) is the underlying operating system for VMware ESXi, whereas processes run on top of VMkernel. With the VMkernel, all processes on the system can run, including agents and management applications. It manages resources for the applications and controls all hardware devices on the server. Processes running on top of the VMkernel include the following:

- Direct Console User Interface (DCUI) is a console-based, low-level configuration and management interface that is primarily used for initial configuration.

- VMX is a helper process that provides the execution environment for a virtual machine via the virtual machine monitor process. There is a separate VMM and VMX process for each virtual machine.

- Standard APIs enable hardware-level management from remote applications through the Common Information Model (CIM) system.

- Remote management of VMware infrastructure is enabled through the use of various agents.

Figure 4-3, depicts the AVS ESXi host logical architecture.

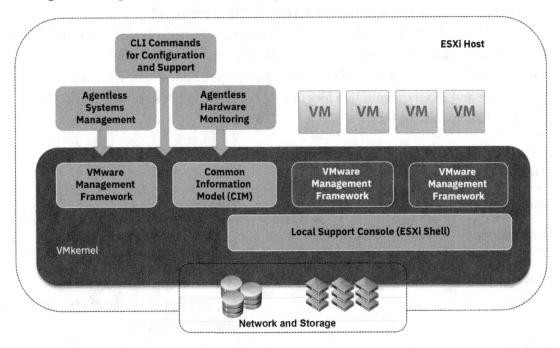

Figure 4-3. *AVS ESXi host logical architecture*

Resource allocation, scheduling, hardware abstraction, and other OS services are handled. It allocates memory, storage, and CPU resources from the host to the VM. Other functions controlled by the VMkernel include

- Management

- vMotion

- vSphere replication

- vSphere high-availability heartbeat

- Fault tolerance

- IP storage

- VMs (typically divided by application or other factors, such as production and testing)

Network segmentation is recommended in vSphere environments to separate VM kernel traffic and virtual machine traffic. Using unique VLANs and IP subnets, cloud consumers can create network segments. (HOw does AVS do this?

To hold ESXi configuration files, log files, and staged patches, the VMkernel uses a simple in-memory file system. To make the file system familiar, it is designed to be similar to the service console of ESX. Log files for VMware ESXi can be found in /var/log/vmware and ESXi configuration files in /etc/vmware. Updates are staged into /tmp. Table 4-4 lists various log files.

Table 4-4. *Log Name and Location*

Component	Location	Purpose
Authentication	/var/log/auth.log	Contains all authentication events for the local system
ESXi host agent log	/var/log/hostd.log	Provides information about the agent that manages and configures ESXi hosts and virtual machines
Shell log	/var/log/shell.log	Keeps a record of all commands entered into the ESXi shell and shell events (for example, when the shell was enabled)
System messages	/var/log/syslog.log	Provides a comprehensive list of general log messages for troubleshooting. These messages used to be located in the message log.
vCenter Server agent log	/var/log/vpxa.log	If vCenter Server manages the host, this table contains information about the agent communicating with it.

(continued)

Table 4-4. (*continued*)

Component	Location	Purpose
Virtual machines	The same directory as the affected virtual machine's configuration files, named `vmware.log` and `vmware*.log`. For example, `/vmfs/volumes/datastore/virtual machine/vwmare.log`	Contains power events for virtual machines, system failure information, tools status and activities, virtual hardware changes, vMotion migrations, machine clones, and so on
VMkernel	`/var/log/vmkernel.log`	Contains information about activities related to virtual machines and ESXi
VMkernel summary	`/var/log/vmksummary.log`	Contains information about uptime and availability statistics for ESXi (comma separated)
VMkernel warnings	`/var/log/vmkwarning.log`	Contains information about virtual machines
Quick boot	`/var/log/loadESX.log`	Each event pertaining to a quick boot restart of an ESXi host is included.
Trusted infrastructure agent	`/var/run/log/kmxa.log`	Contains activity records for the client service on ESXi Trusted Host
Key provider service	`/var/run/log/kmxd.log`	Contains activities related to the vSphere Trust Authority key provider service
Attestation service	`/var/run/log/attestd.log`	Contains activities related to the vSphere Trust Authority attestation service
ESX token service	`/var/run/log/esxtokend.log`	Contains information about vSphere Trust Authority ESX token service activities
ESX API forwarder	`/var/run/log/esxapiadapter.log`	Contains information about the vSphere Trust Authority API forwarder

VMware VMFS, which is used to store virtual machines, is not required to use this file system. Virtual machine file system datastores may be created on a local disk on the host system or a shared storage device. ESXi does not require a local hard drive when only external shared storage is used for VMFS datastores. Diskless setups reduce power and cooling consumption and reduce hard drive failures, increasing reliability for VMware administrators.

Both the in-memory file system and VMFS datastores can be managed through remote command-line interfaces. The file system is accessible via HTTPS. Authentication occurs via users and groups configured locally on the server, and local privileges control access.

Log files do not survive power failures since the in-memory file system does not persist. VMware administrators can configure ESXi to work with a remote Syslog server, storing all log information on a separate system.

ESXi allows the creation of local users and groups. As in other operating systems, groups can combine multiple users and can be used, for example, to set privileges for many users at once. They can also distinguish users gaining access via the virtual infrastructure client, remote command-line interfaces, or the virtual infrastructure API. The VMkernel comes with a handful of system users and groups that can be assigned to identify specific processes. Each user or group can be given its own administrative rights.

User and group definitions are located on the file system in the files /etc/passwd, /etc/shadow, and /etc/group. As in other operating systems, passwords are generated using standard crypt functions.

"User world" is the term used to describe a process in the VMkernel operating system. A POSIX-compliant general-purpose operating system like Linux offers a more general environment than what is offered by user worlds.

VMware ESXi Deployment Preparation Aspects

An 8GB boot device is required for ESXi 7.0 installation. A minimum 4GB boot device is required for upgrading to ESXi 7.0. To create the boot partition, boot banks, and the VMFS_L ESX=OSData volume on local disks, SANs, or iSCSI LUNs, a 32GB disk is required. The ESX-OSData volume, the /scratch partition, the VM tools, and the core dump location are replaced. Without a local disk, ESXi 7.0 operates in degraded mode, placing the scratch partition on the RAM disk of the ESXi host and linking it to `scratch/tmp`. `/scratch` can be configured to use a different disk or LUN by a VMware administrator. Do not run the ESXi host in a degraded mode for best performance and memory optimization. ESXi 7.0's installer also attempts to allocate a scratch region on a local disk when it installs from USB or SD devices; otherwise, it places `/scratch` on the RAM disk. See Table 4-5.

Table 4-5. *Required Network Ports for ESXi Deployment*

Service	Protocol/Port	Direction	Description
CIM server	TCP 5988	Inbound	Server for Common Information Model (CIM)
CIM secure server	TCP 5989	Inbound	Secure Server for CIM
DVSSync	UDP 8301, 8302	Inbound, outbound	Used for synchronizing states of distributed virtual ports between hosts that have VMware FT record/replay enabled
NFC	TCP 902	Inbound, outbound	ESXi uses Network File Copy (NFC) for operations such as copying and moving data between datastores
vSAN clustering	UDP 12345, 23451	Inbound, outbound	Used by vSAN nodes for multicast to establish cluster members and distribute vSAN metadata
DHCP	UDP 68	Inbound, outbound	DHCP client for IPv4
DNS	UDP 53	Inbound	DNS client
DNS	TCP/UDP 53	Outbound	DNS client
Fault tolerance	TCP/UDP 8200, 8100, 8300	Inbound	Traffic between hosts for vSphere fault tolerance (FT)
Fault tolerance	TCP/UDP 80, 8200, 8100, 8300	Outbound	Supports vSphere FT
vSAN transport	TCP 2233	Inbound	vSAN reliable datagram transport for vSAN storage I/O

(*continued*)

Table 4-5. (*continued*)

Service	Protocol/Port	Direction	Description
SSH	TCP 22	Inbound	SSH server
vSphere web Client	TCP 902, 443	Inbound	Allows user connections from vSphere web client
DHCPv6	TCP/UDP 547	Outbound	DHCP client for IPv6
WOL	UDP 9	Outbound	Wake-on-LAN
iSCSI	TCP 3260	Outbound	Supports software iSCSI
vMotion	TCP 8000	Outbound	Supports vMotion
vCenter Agent	UDP 902	Outbound	Used by the vCenter Agent

VMware vCenter

The virtualization platform vCenter manages vSphere environments. vSphere 6.X supports multiple vCenter Server topologies and configurations, including the vCenter Server Appliance, vCenter Server for Windows, embedded database (PostgreSQL), external database (SQL Server or Oracle), external platform services controller (PSC), embedded PSC, Enhanced Linked Mode, and Embedded Linked Mode. In vSphere 7.0, the configuration and topology of VMware vCenter Server are much more straightforward.

It provides many of the features of vSphere, such as vSphere high availability and SDK access to the environment for solutions such as VMware vRealize Automation. vCenter Server is only available as an appliance with vSphere 7.0; a single vCenter Server running version 7.0 can manage 2,000 hosts and 25,000 virtual machines.

Embedded architecture from earlier releases is supported in vSphere 7.0 and vSphere 7.0 vCenter architecture. vSphere 7.0 does not support external platform services controllers.

The appliance form factor is also the only way to access vCenter. The Windows version of vCenter has been retired.

Figure 4-4 depicts the method of communication of vCenter Server components and ESXi hosts.

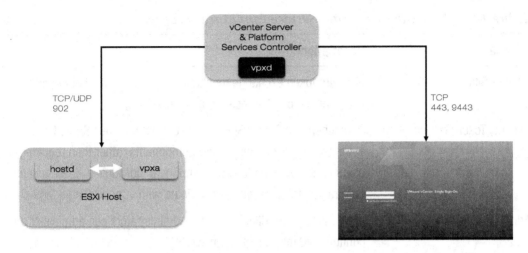

Figure 4-4. *AVS vCenter logical connectivity*

As soon as a VMware Administrator logs in to the vCenter Server through the vSphere Web Client, commands are passed to the ESXi host via the vpxa process on the vCenter Server. In ESXi, vpxa communicates with a host agent named hostd. By using the vSphere Client directly to communicate with an ESXi host, communications are sent directly to the hostd process, and the vCenter Server database is not updated.

For communication with vCenter Server and ESXi hosts, the vSphere Client uses ports 80 and 443.

A daemon running on ESXi host is hostd. The main communication channel between ESXi hosts and VMkernel serves as a management service. The hostd service must be running on the ESXi host for you to communicate directly or from the vCenter.

Among other things, it keeps track of all the virtual machines registered on a host, the storage volumes visible to the host, and the status of all virtual machines. Virtual machines typically transmit most of their commands and operations over it, such as VM power-up, VM vMotion, and VM creation.

The vCenter Server's vpxd is a daemon. In the absence of this service, the VMware administrator will be unable to access the vCenter Server.

vpxa is an agent that runs on the ESXi host. ESXi hosts get installed on vCenter Server when they are added to it. vpxa relays tasks to ESXi from vpxd (service running in vCenter) and hostd (service running on ESXi).

Table 4-6 describes the main services in vCenter Server appliance and related services in the ESXi host.

Table 4-6. The VMware vCenter Service Appliance Services

Service	Description
vCenter Single Sign-On	A secure token exchange mechanism is used instead of requiring components to authenticate users individually.
Security Token Service (STS)	Component of vCenter Single Sign-On that provides SAML token authentication for other vCenter components rather than requiring users to authenticate to each component individually. SAML tokens are granted to users who authenticate with vCenter Single Sign-On.
Administration server	From the vSphere Client, VMware Administrators can administer and configure vCenter Single Sign-On.
vCenter lookup service	The topology of the vSphere infrastructure is stored in this service, enabling secure communication between vSphere components.
VMware directory service	Directory service for the vCenter Single Sign-On domain (vsphere.local).
vCenter Server plug-ins	vCenter applications that add functionality. They usually include both server and client components.
vCenter Server database	All ESXi hosts, virtual machines, and users are stored in the database. vCenter Server is deployed through the wizard.
tcServer	The Storage Policy Based Service of vCenter is used by services such as ICIM/hardware status, performance charts, WebAccess, and vCenter Service status.
License service	It is used to store the available licenses and assign licenses across the entire vSphere environment.
vCenter Server Agent	When an ESXi host is added to vCenter's inventory, a service is installed on that host. Using this service, actions initiated by the vSphere Client are collected, communicated, and executed.
Host agent	With the installation of ESXi, an administrative agent is installed. vSphere Host Client collects, communicates, and runs actions initiated by the host.

vCenter Single Sign-On

vCenter Servers are each associated with a vCenter Single Sign-On (SSO) domain, whose default name is vsphere.local. During deployment, administrators can change this domain name. In vCenter Server and other VMware products, such as vRealize Operations, the SSO domain is considered the local domain.

During the VMware vCenter Server Appliance deployment, (vCenter is automatically deployed in AVS, be careful describing basic functions adn the services in AVS) administrators need to create or join an SSO domain. For LDAP (Lightweight Directory Access Protocol) internal structuring, the VMware Directory Service (vmdir) uses the domain name. Administrators of VMware clouds should give cloud consumers' domains a unique name that cannot be used by OpenLDAP, Microsoft Active Directory, or other directory services.

The SSO domain allows cloud consumers to add users and groups. VMware administrators can authenticate users and groups in the Active Directory or LDAP identity source.

vCenter High Availability

vCenter HA clusters consist of three vCenter Server instances. Initially, the first instance is the Active node, and it is cloned twice to a Passive node and a Witness node. These three nodes act as a failover solution, both active and passive.

Using different ESXi instances for each node helps prevent hardware failures. Protecting the VMware environment of cloud consumers can be accomplished by adding three ESXi hosts to a DRS cluster.

According to the following diagram, only the Active node has the active management interface (public IP address) after vCenter HA is configured. In this configuration, three nodes communicate via a private network called the vCenter HA network, and data is continuously replicated from the Active to the Passive node. (When is vCenter HA configured in AVS, needs to be specific)

VMware vCenter Deployment Preparation Aspects

Cloud customers should plan to address their storage needs before deploying the vCenter Server Appliance. vCenter Server Appliance storage requirements are listed in Table 4-7. As a result, vCenter Server Appliance can run Lifecycle Manager as a service.

Table 4-7. *Predefined sizes for VMware vCenter Server Appliances*

Deployment Type	Storage Default Size	Storage Large Size	Storage X- Large Size
Tiny	415GB	1490GB	3245GB
Small	480GB	1535GB	3295GB
Medium	700GB	1700GB	3460GB
Large	1065GB	1765GB	3525GB
X-Large	1805GB	1905GB	3665GB

VMware vCenter Server network connectivity requirements are described in Table 4-8. Administrators should ensure that cloud consumers' networks and firewalls permit the described connectivity for each applicable connection.

Table 4-8. *Network Ports Required for VMware vCenter Server Appliances*

Required	Protocol/Port	Description
vCenter Server	TCP 22	System port for SSHD
vCenter Server	TCP 80	Port for direct HTTP connections; redirects requests to HTTPS port 443
vCenter Server	TCP 88	Required to be open to join Active Directory
vCenter Server to vCenter Server	TCP/UDP 389	LDAP port for directory services for the vCenter Server group
vCenter Server to vCenter Server	TCP 443	Default port used by vCenter Server to listen for connections from the vSphere web client and SDK clients
vCenter Server	TCP/UDP 514	vSphere Syslog Collector port for vCenter Server and vSphere Syslog Service port for vCenter Server Appliance
vCenter Server	TCP/UDP 902	Default port that the vCenter Server system uses to send data to managed hosts
vCenter Server	TCP 1514	vSphere Syslog Collector TLS port for vCenter Server
vCenter Server	TCP 2012	Control interface RPC for SSO
VMCA	TCP 2014	RPC port for VMware Certificate Authority (VMCA) APIs

(continued)

Table 4-8. (*continued*)

Required	Protocol/Port	Description
vCenter Server	TCP/UDP 2020	Authentication framework management
vCenter Server	TCP 5480	vCenter Server Appliance Management Interface (VAMI)
vCenter Server	TCP/UDP 6500	ESXi Dump Collector port
vCenter Server	TCP 7080, 12721	Secure Token Service (internal ports)
vCenter Server	TCP 7081	vSphere Client (internal ports)
vCenter Server	TCP 7475, 7476	VMware vSphere Authentication Proxy
vSphere Lifecycle Manager	TCP 8084	vSphere Lifecycle Manager SOAP port used by vSphere Lifecycle Manager client plug-in
vSphere Lifecycle Manager	TCP 9084	vSphere Lifecycle Manager web server Port used by ESXi hosts to access host patch files from vSphere Lifecycle Manager server
vSphere Lifecycle Manager	TCP 9087	vSphere Lifecycle Manager Web SSL port used by vSphere Lifecycle Manager client plug-in for uploading host upgrade files to vSphere Lifecycle Manager server
vCenter Server	TCP 9443	vSphere Web Client HTTPS

Cloud consumers should provide computing, storage, and network infrastructure in addition to providing supporting infrastructure, such as Active Directory (AD), Domain Name System (DNS), and Network Time Protocol (NTP).

Authentication Services

Several vSphere environments integrate vCenter SSO with directory services, such as Microsoft AD. In addition to authenticating users from internal groups and users, SSO can connect to trusted external directory services like AD. For example, say a cloud consumer plans to use AD as the identity provider. In such cases, they should ensure that they have access to the appropriate network connectivity, service account credentials, and AD services.

Suppose cloud consumers intend to use AD identity sources and install vCenter Server for Windows. In that case, they should ensure that the Windows server belongs to the AD domain but is not a domain controller.

Domain Name Services

VMware vCenter Server and ESXi hosts and static IP addresses and fully qualified domain names (FQDNs) for cloud consumers. The cloud consumer should ensure that the proper IP address and FQDN entries are registered in their DNS server before installing these components. They should configure forward and reverse DNS records.

In the DNS, they should assign a static IP address and hostname to vCenter Server Appliance before deploying it. DNS registration for the IP address must be valid (internal). During vCenter Server installation, the cloud consumer must provide the FQDN or static IP address. According to VMware, the FQDN is recommended. When a DNS reverse lookup is performed using the IP address of the vCenter appliance, cloud consumers should ensure the correct FQDN is returned. Unless the Web Server component is installed, the web client will fail to support the vSphere web.

In cloud deployments of vCenter Server Appliances, a client fails if the installer cannot find the appliance's FQDN from its IP address. Installers can only locate the appliance's FQDN from the appliance's IP address, and reverse lookup is implemented through PTR records. Cloud consumers must verify that a DNS server can resolve the FQDN they use for the appliance system name before using it.

From vSphere 6.5 onwards, vCenter Server can support mixed IPv4 and IPv6 environments. Cloud consumers may set up vCenter Server Appliances to use IPv6 addresses by using the FQDN or hostname of the appliance.

ESXi host management interfaces must have a valid DNS response from the vCenter Server and all vSphere Web Client instances to resolve the vCenter Server FQDN successfully. Secondly, all ESXi hosts and vSphere web clients must resolve DNS to the vCenter Server.

NTP

Timing needs to be synchronized between the nodes. To support vSphere HA, all vCenter Server instances must be time-synchronized, and all ESXi hosts should be time-synchronized. In most cloud environments, time synchronization is provided by NTP servers. Ensure that NTP servers are running and available before implementing vSphere.

Installing vSphere components such as vCenter Server and ESXi requires providing names or IP addresses for NTP servers. Cloud consumers, for example, can choose to sync time with NTP time servers during deployment of the vCenter Server Appliance and provide a list of NTP servers, separated by commas. In addition, they can allow the appliance to synchronize with the ESXi host.

VMware vSphere Features

The critical principle followed throughout the planning is to achieve high availability and reliability. Maintaining a high-availability position for compute, storage, and network resources is vital to AVS private cloud, datacenter, and virtual machines. The following section illustrate various features that must be turned on as per the requirement.

Clusters

VMware ESXi clusters consist of a group of hosts with a shared network and storage. A cluster consists of four main components: vMotion, HA, Distributed Resource Scheduler (DRS), and FT.

VMware vMotion Feature

Virtual machines can be moved from one physical host, cluster, or datacenter to another with no interruption of service to the guest operating system or applications. With vSphere vMotion, end users can migrate workloads from one server to another without downtime to continue to access their systems. Figure 4-5 depicts the vMotion workflow.

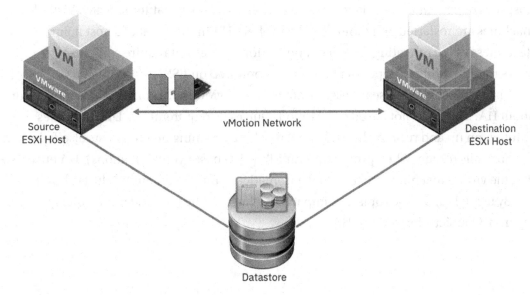

Figure 4-5. *vMotion workflow*

With vSphere 7.0, vMotion migration can occur between clusters, datastores, networks, vCenter Servers, and over long distances with an RTT of 150ms.

With vSphere vMotion, the execution state of the virtual machine is transferred from the source host to the destination host, primarily over high-speed networks. These components make up the execution state.

- A virtual device's state, including the CPU, network and disk adapters, the SVGA, and so on

- Network connections and SCSI connections

- The physical memory of the virtual machine

- Most users are unaware that a VM has changed hosts because they lose a single ping

VMware HA Feature

vSphere HA allows virtual machines to be accessed from a cluster of ESXi hosts to provide higher levels of availability than each ESXi host can provide. When an ESXi host fails, vSphere HA will automatically restart VM(s) on another ESXi host in the same cluster. In as little as 60 seconds, HA will begin to restore VMs.

Virtual machines can be automatically recovered through HA when a physical host goes down. All virtual machines in a cluster are restarted automatically. Virtual machines are restarted and monitored by vSphere HA in the event of a host failure. Regardless of the operating system or application, it does not require complex configuration. Multiple types of failures are monitored on ESXi hosts by agents.

Virtual machines are seamlessly available using vMotion, a common misconception about HA. The HA is not based on vMotion. Due to its requirements, DRS only uses vMotion on up and running hosts. Virtual machines running on ESXi hosts also fail when the host fails (except when protected with FT, which has severe limitations). HA ensures that the virtual machines are restarted automatically on the remaining cluster hosts.

By using HA, outages or issues impacting a host can be resolved more quickly. Figure 4-6 depicts the vSphere HA workflow.

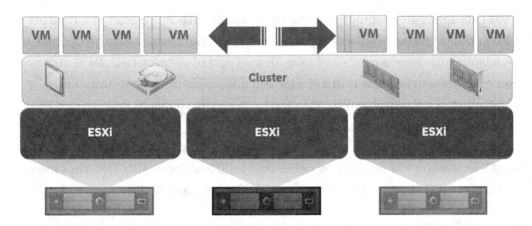

Figure 4-6. *vSphere HA workflow*

VMware Distributed Resource Scheduler Feature

In a cluster, Virtual Machine Distributed Resource Scheduler (DRS) monitors and balances virtual machines across hosts via vSphere vMotion. DRS also includes VMware Distributed Power Management (DPM), which enables the evacuation and powering off of hosts when low utilization is observed. Figure 4-7 depicts the vSphere DRS workflow.

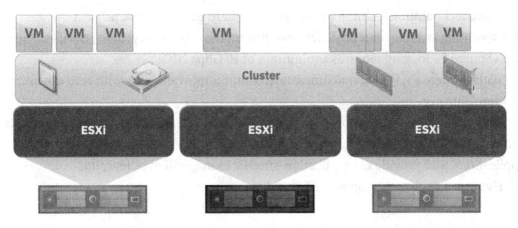

Figure 4-7. *vSphere DRS workflow*

VM DRS aggregates computing capacity across all hosts in a cluster to form a pool of CPU and RAM resources. It intelligently allocates resources based on predefined rules adapted to business needs and priorities. As part of VMware DRS, DPM automates power management for servers in a cluster and minimizes power consumption.

DRS clusters extensively utilize vMotion to move virtual machines from one ESXi host to another for load balancing.

DRS in vSphere 7 has been greatly improved and changed. The main difference is that DRS focuses on VM satisfaction rather than ESXi host load. Also, DRS runs more frequently on the cluster, every minute instead of every five minutes.

VMware Fault Tolerance Feature

When VMware Administrator enables FT on one virtual machine, it creates a second virtual machine to operate alongside it. In virtual lockstep with the primary virtual machine, this virtual machine resides on a different host in the cluster. In a failure, the second virtual machine takes over with the minor service interruption possible. VM instances share FT legacy storage.

Legacy FT does not protect VMDK problems (corruption, access, etc.). vSphere 6 introduced support for storage redundancy and multiprocessors.

Fast checkpointing technology is used in vSphere FT in vSphere 6.7; fast checkpointing is a snapshot of all data, not just memory (memory, disks, devices, and so on). vSphere FT logging requires a minimum of 10 Gbps NIC.

With vSphere FT, virtual machines have continuous availability with zero downtime and zero data loss.

VMs with vSphere 7.0 support up to 8 vCPUs and 128GB of RAM with no loss of TCP connections, are entirely transparent to guest software, are not dependent on guest OS or applications, and provide no application-specific management or learning.

Figure 4-8 depicts the vSphere FT workflow.

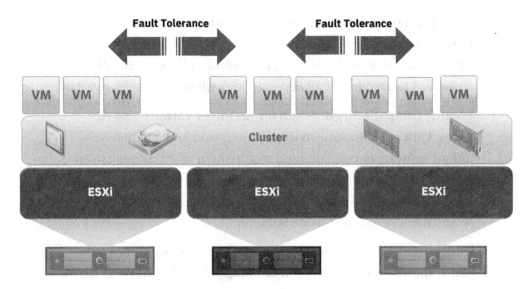

Figure 4-8. *vSphere fault tolerance workflow*

Now you have the overview of the VMware vSphere product, which is associated with primary elements. Azure VMware Solution provides a unified VMware Software-Defined Datacenter (SDDC) integrating with Microsoft Azure. Microsoft manages full deployment.

As the next step on AVS compute planning, capacity planning is a crucial task for host planning.

Cloud consumers can run VMware applications on Azure's infrastructure using Azure VMware Solution. Azure VMware Solution allows on-premises VMware environments to be extended to the cloud. A VMware environment on-premises can also be migrated to Azure VMware Solution. Customers can connect their on-premises environment to the Azure VMware Solution through various network options.

Cloud consumers must plan the overall capacity before deploying Azure VMware Solutions, which will assist them in making technical and business decisions.

The following use cases require capacity planning or sizing:

- **Analyze an existing VMware IT environment:** On-premises VMware environments tend to grow organically. On-premises VMware customers would like to know how good their VMware environment is. Make an objective assessment to eliminate any guesswork in the decision-making process.

- **Identify relationships between application components:**
  Customers may wish to consider Azure VMware Solution for only
  some of their workloads. Viewing a subset of workloads will allow
  customers to account for all dependencies when calculating capacity.

- **Identify compatibility between on-premises VMware and the
  Azure VMware Solution environment:** A workload might have a
  unique software or configuration requirement when running in an
  on-premises VMware environment. To make appropriate decisions
  ahead of time, cloud consumers should explore meeting that
  requirement in Azure VMware Solution.

- **Understand monthly and yearly costs:** Ideally, customers would
  like to know how much they will be charged monthly and annually.
  A capacity planning exercise can help provide customers with
  potential costs.

VMware Azure Solution capacity planning includes the phases depicted in
Figure 4-9.

Figure 4-9. *Azure AVS capacity planning*

- **Discovery:** Inventory will be collected from a VMware on-premises
  environment during this phase.

- **Grouping:** Cloud users can group logically related virtual machines
  (such as applications and databases).

- **Assessment:** This phase evaluates clusters of virtual machines to determine their suitability for VMware's Azure solutions.

- **Reporting:** This phase provides a cost estimate based on the assessment results.

Discovery

Azure Migrate is available in two modes. Azure Migrate creates OVA (Open Virtualization Appliance) templates in the first mode. An on-premises VMware site can use this template to bootstrap an Azure Migrate VM. Once Azure Migrate is configured, the on-premises inventory data will be sent to Azure. The second mode involves uploading the data from on-premises inventory using a CSV file with a predefined format. The CSV file must contain four mandatory fields (VM/Server Name, Number of Cores, Memory, and Eligible OS Name). Other optional fields can be added to improve accuracy (such as Number of disks, Disk IOPS, Throughput, etc.). The output of VMware utilities can be used to create a CSV file.

Grouping

VMware inventory details can be grouped once they have been gathered. Consumers can easily manage many VMs in the cloud after discovery by grouping them together. Among the possibilities for grouping are workload (HR, eCommerce, and so on), environment (Production versus non-Production), location (such as US, EU, and so on), and criticality (mission-critical, small-scale, and so on). Azure Migrate provides dependency analysis in VMware environments. You can also group related VMs based on the information obtained via dependency analysis.

Assessment

VMs that are part of a group can be assessed. An assessment can be configured with parameters that will help determine an appropriate size and capacity. They can include details about the target Azure VMware Solution site, such as the location, node type, and so on. Azure VMware Solution VMs require important parameters (including FTT and RAID settings and CPU oversubscription). Assessments can be made using two metrics. Using on-premises VMware VM performance profiles, the first metric is a performance-based assessment. You can capture a performance profile going back as far as one month. By selecting a specific percentile (such as 50th, 90th, 99th, and so on) of the assessment, the evaluation can be further fine-tuned. By multiplying the capacity with a comfort factor, you can provide an additional capacity margin. On-premises is a second metric. It determines how well a VM performs based on its existing specifications (such as CPU, memory, etc.). Additional capacity can be added as needed.

Reporting

A report provides the final results after an assessment has been completed. Among the results are cost and readiness. This report summarizes the number of VMware VMs assessed, the average cost per VM, and the total cost of all VMware VMs. Reporting also provides insight into Azure VMware Solution readiness with a clear breakdown of VM numbers across various readiness statuses, such as Ready, Not Ready, Ready with Conditions, etc. For specific reasons, VMs that might need remediation before migration are listed. This simplifies the management and orchestration of the migration. In addition to reporting, Azure VMware Solution nodes are also required to run assessed VMs. The Azure VMware Solution shows projected CPU, memory, and storage utilization.

Capacity Planning with VMware Native Tools

To determine the number of hosts and clusters in the AVS private cloud, it's necessary to conduct an infrastructure assessment of the existing environment. Currently, only one host type is available, offering a fixed compute, storage, and networking unit. Based on the aggregate workload requirements, customers need to determine how much compute power they will need to deploy in AVS's private cloud. To remain eligible for AVS SLA, consumers must not consume more than 75% of their available storage space. Depending on the storage policy (RAID-1, RAID-5, RAID-6), the functional storage calculation will consider the number of hosts required.

Growth expectations are important to consider. Administrators should allocate enough hosts to accommodate near-term growth expectations and provide a reasonable amount of excess capacity for failures. There is the option to grow and shrink the cluster.

With tools such as vRealize Operations Manager and vRealize Operations Cloud, you can analyze your current resource allocation and demand, make resizing recommendations, and forecast the number of AVS hosts required for migration.

A minimum of three hosts are required for each cluster, and 16 hosts are supported. Consider this when calculating cloud sizing and creating multiple clusters to account for scalability if cloud consumers plan to use the maximum number of hosts.

Other Key Elements to Consider When Planning Compute

- Currently, provisioning takes roughly three to four hours. The process of adding a single node in an existing cluster can take 30-45 minutes.

- There is only one AV36 type of VMware solution available in Azure.

- Deployment and management operations are performed through the Azure portal. The vSphere and NSX-T resources are managed with vCenter and NSX Manager.

- AVS and Azure VMware Solution will not have a single management interface at launch. Cloud consumers manage private cloud clusters with vCenter and NSX Manager locally installed on a private cloud.

- AVS private cloud hosts and clusters are dedicated and securely erased before and after usage.

- ESxi clusters can scale up to 16 ESXi hosts (maximum).

- An AVS private cloud can have a maximum of 12 clusters and 96 hosts.

- Each AVS private cloud can have a single vCenter.

AVS Storage Plan and Prepare

In this section, you'll explore how virtual machines access storage and what types of datastores are available in vSphere, before you move precisely to Azure VMware Solution.

SCSI commands are used to communicate with a virtual disk on a datastore. According to Figure 4-10, SCSI commands are encapsulated into other forms depending on how the ESXi host connects to the storage device on which the datastore resides. Figure 4-10 depicts AVS storage.

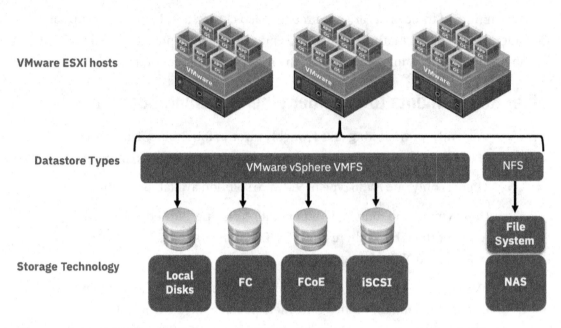

VMware ESXi hosts

Datastore Types

Storage Technology

Figure 4-10. *vSphere VMware storage logical view*

Datastores provide a uniform model for storing the files of virtual machines and hiding each storage device's specifics. A datastore can be formatted with the VMware vSphere VMFS or based on a file system native to the storage device shared via the NFS protocol depending on the type of storage use.

ESXi hosts support several storage technologies in the VMware vSphere environment:

- **Local or direct-attached storage:** Direct connections are used instead of network connections to connect internal or external storage disks.

- **Fiber channel:** A high-speed transport protocol is used in SANs, and SCSI commands are transmitted via a fiber channel (FC) between fiber channel nodes. A fiber channel node may be a server, a storage system, or a tape drive. Fiber channel switches interconnect multiple nodes, forming a "fabric" in a fiber channel network.

- **FCoE:** Fiber channel over Ethernet (FCoE) frames encapsulate fiber channel traffic, and FCoE frames are converged with networking traffic. The FCoE technology allows the same Ethernet link to carry fiber channel and Ethernet traffic, thus maximizing the use of physical infrastructure. In addition, FCoE reduces cabling and network ports.

- **iSCSI:** With this SCSI transport protocol, access to storage devices and cabling is possible over standard TCP/IP networks. Through TCP/IP, iSCSI maps SCSI block-oriented storage. ESXi hosts send SCSI commands to targets within iSCSI storage systems using initiators such as iSCSI host bus adapters (HBAs).

- **NAS:** Storage shared over TCP/IP networks at the file system level. NAS storage is used for NFS datastores. SCSI commands are incompatible with NFS.

Storage Virtualization Model

Virtualization of storage refers to a logical abstraction of physical storage resources and capacities of virtual machines. ESXi provides storage virtualization. Traditional vSphere environments are built around the storage technologies and ESXi virtualization features discussed in the following sections.

Storage devices: LUNs and storage devices are often used interchangeably in ESXi jargon. LUNs are storage volumes that are presented to ESXi from block storage systems for formatting.

Virtual disk: Virtual disks are collections of files that live on a datastore that is deployed on physical storage. Virtual disks appear to the virtual machine as SCSI drives attached to SCSI controllers. Guest operating systems and applications don't see physical storage.

Local storage: An ESXi host can have local storage on its hard drive and external storage connected directly to the host through protocols such as SAS or nVME. A storage network is not required to communicate with local storage.

Fiber channel: FC is a storage protocol used by storage area networks (SAN) to transfer data traffic between ESXi hosts and shared storage. FC frames are composed of SCSI commands. VMware administrators have to use FC switches to route storage traffic unless they are using FC storage directly. VMware administrators can connect to shared FC devices using an Ethernet network if a host contains FCoE adapters.

iSCSI: The Internet SCSI (iSCSI) transport protocol can be used by ESXi hosts to connect to storage systems via Ethernet. Hosts running ESXi connect to storage systems with hardware or software iSCSI adapters, iSCSI initiators, and standard network adapters.

Hardware iSCSI HBAs rely on hardware adapters to connect to storage systems, offloading iSCSI and network processing. There can be independent and dependent hardware iSCSI adapters. Software iSCSI adapters connect to storage through a software-based iSCSI initiator in the VMkernel and a network adapter.

FCoE: An ESXi host can connect to shared FC devices using an Ethernet network if it contains FCoE adapters.

NAS/NFS: The virtual machine files are stored on remote file servers using NFS over a standard TCP/IP network. To communicate with NAS/NFS servers, ESXi 7.0 utilizes NFS Versions 3 and 4.1. NFS datastores can store and manage virtual machines in the same way that VMware administrators use VMFS datastores.

VMFS" VMware Administrators deploy VMFS datastores on block storage devices. A VMFS is an optimized file system format for storing virtual machines.

Raw device mappings: In a VMFS datastore, a raw device mapping (RDM) file contains metadata that allows a virtual machine to directly access a physical storage device (LUN). VMware administrators can access physical devices directly while still enjoying some of the management benefits of using VMFS-based virtual disks.

VMware administrators can view an RDM as a symbolic link from a VMFS volume to a storage device. A mapping makes a storage device appear as a file in a VMFS volume. It is the RDM that is referenced, not the storage device. There are two compatibility modes.

Virtual compatibility mode: In many ways, the RDM performs the same function as a virtual disk file, allowing additional features, such as virtual machine snapshots and disk modes (dependent, independent-persistent, and separate-nonpersistent).

Physical compatibility mode: Supporting applications that require lower-level control, the RDM provides direct access to the SCSI device.

RDMs are less manageable than virtual disk files, and virtual disk files should only be used when necessary. There are several uses for RDMs.

Administrators will install software that requires SAN-specific features in a VMware virtual machine, such as SAN management, storage-based snapshots, or storage-based replication. Virtual machines can access the storage device via the RDM.

The administrator can configure a Microsoft Custer Server (MSCS) cluster that spans virtual hosts and physical hosts. Rather than virtual disk files, the VMware administrator should configure the data and quorum disks as RDMs.

The benefits of RDMs include the following:

- Like naming a VMFS datastore, VMware administrators can choose a familiar name for mapped devices rather than using the device's name.

- The RDM is automatically updated if physical changes (such as changes in adapter hardware, path changes, or device relocation) occur. Virtual machines do not need to be updated since they refer to RDM.

- Spread locking allows two virtual machines to safely access the same LUN on different servers.

- Permissions are set on the mapping file to be applied to the mapped file, just as they are on virtual disks.

- Almost any file system operation that can be applied to an ordinary file can be used to a mapping file.

Snapshots: When the RDM is used in physical compatibility mode, snapshots cannot be applied to the mapped volume.

vMotion: Virtual machines can be migrated using vMotion, since vCenter Server uses the RDM as a proxy, allowing the exact migration mechanism for virtual disk files.

SAN management agents: Through RDM, SAN management agents (SCSI-based software) can be managed inside a virtual machine. RDMs require hardware-specific SCSI commands and physical compatibility mode.

N-Port ID Virtualization (NPIV): By using multiple worldwide port names (WWPNs), various FC HBA ports can register with the fabric. With this ability, the HBA port appears as multiple virtual ports, each with its ID and virtual port name. Virtual machines can claim these virtual ports and use them for all RDM traffic, and NPIV requires the use of virtual machines with RDMs.

Software-Defined Storage Models

Unlike traditional storage models, software-defined storage abstracts storage capabilities and underlying storage capacities. A virtual machine can be controlled and managed as a unit of storage provisioning with software-defined storage. As described in the following sections, software-defined storage involves vSphere technologies.

VMware vSAN: A virtual storage area network runs natively on each hypervisor in a cluster. The vSAN cluster gathers local and direct-attached storage capacity into a single pool that all hosts can access.

Hyperconverged storage software, vSAN, is fully integrated with the hypervisor. In vSAN, local hard disks and solid state drives are clustered together to create a flash-optimized, highly resilient, shared storage datastore. Using vSAN storage policies, VMware administrators can control each virtual machine's performance, capacity, and availability.

I/O filters are software components installed on ESXi hosts that provide additional data services to virtual machines. Replication, encryption, caching, and more may be benefits depending on the implementation.

The Hyperconverged Infrastructure (HCI) market leader continues to be VMware vSAN. VMware vSAN is proven to be an excellent solution for all workloads. vSAN customers run traditional applications such as Microsoft SQL Server and SAP HANA, next-generation applications like Cassandra, Splunk, and MongoDB, and container-based services orchestrated through Kubernetes. vSAN's success can be attributed to many factors, including performance, flexibility, ease of use, robustness, and the pace at which it is being developed.

Disaggregated tools and specialized skill sets are standard in traditional infrastructure deployment, operations, and maintenance paradigms. Utilizing vSphere and vSAN, hyper-converged infrastructure deployment, management, and operation are simplified using familiar tools. It is the cornerstone of the VMware Cloud Foundation and accelerates customers' Azure VMware Solutions with best-in-class enterprise storage.

The VMware HCI platform, powered by vSAN, is the cornerstone of modern data centers, whether on-premises or in the cloud. More than 18 OEMs support vSAN on standard x86 servers. With VMware Compatibility List hardware, VMware administrators can choose from over 500 vSAN ReadyNode options, integrate with Dell EMC VxRail systems, or build their own using validated hardware. It's an excellent choice for both large and small deployments, with options ranging from a 2-node cluster for small implementations to multiple clusters with up to 64 nodes, each managed by vCenter Server.

It is the best HCI solution today, regardless of whether administrators deploy monolithic or microservices-based applications. vSAN provides developer-ready infrastructure, scales without compromise, and simplifies operations and management tasks.

Features such as vMotion, HA, DRS, and many others are integrated with vSAN. It is possible to set and modify on-the-fly VM-level policies that control VM storage provisioning and storage SLAs. Storage for virtual machines can benefit from vSAN's enterprise-class features, scale, and performance.

An OEM and VMware have validated a vSAN ReadyNode server configuration in a tested, certified hardware form factor for vSAN deployment.

For vSAN caching in hybrid deployments and for vSAN capacity in all-flash deployments, solid-state disks (SSDs) are used. Administrators choose the best SSD devices according to the requirements for the consumer environment based on endurance parameters such as drive writes per day (DWPD) and terabytes written (TBW) of a specific SSD class.

According to the vSAN configuration, consider the following endurance criteria: SSDs serve as both a nonvolatile write cache (approximately 30%) and a read buffer (about 70%) in a hybrid deployment. Consequently, SSD endurance and the number of I/O operations per second are crucial performance factors.

The endurance and performance criteria for an all-flash model are the same. There are more write operations in the caching tier. As a result, SSD capacity tiers can be extended by service.

VMware vVols: Virtual volumes (vVols) encapsulate virtual disks and virtual machine files natively inside a storage system. VMware administrators do not provision virtual volumes directly. Instead, they are automatically created when VMware administrators create, clone, or snapshot a virtual machine. Each virtual machine can be associated with one or more virtual volumes.

vVols enable storage managers to manage abstract storage objects by SAN arrays instead of storage space inside datastores. Virtual machines (instead of datastores) are storage management units with vVols. Instead of using a LUN or datastore, VMware administrators can apply storage policies per virtual machine.

Storage policy-based management: SPBM provides a centralized control panel for vSAN, vVols, and other data services and storage solutions. Through storage policies, the framework aligns application requirements with storage capabilities.

AVS Storage: Azure VMware Solution private clouds offer native, cluster-wide storage with VMware vSAN. Local storage from each host in the cluster is used in the vSAN datastore, and data-at-rest encryption is available and enabled by default. Users of Azure Storage resources can extend their private clouds' storage capabilities.

In a vSAN datastore, local storage is used on each cluster host. The raw, SSD-based capacity of each disk group is 15.4TB, with an NVMe cache tier of 1.6TB.

A cluster's raw capacity tier is equal to its per-host capacity times its number of hosts. For example, in the vSAN tier, a cluster with four hosts can provide 61.6TB of raw capacity. Figure 4-11 depicts AVS vSAN.

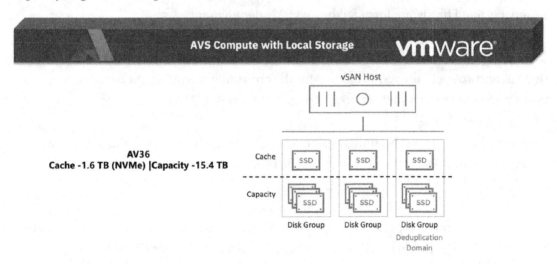

Figure 4-11. *AVS vSAN*

Azure storage services are available to cloud consumers running workloads in AVS private clouds. Microsoft Azure offers Storage Accounts, Table Storage, and Blob Storage, and Azure storage services don't traverse the Internet to access workloads. Cloud consumers can use SLA-based Azure storage services in their AVS private cloud workloads with this connectivity, which improves security.

The most crucial step in preparing and planning for the vSAN cluster is that the capacity of a vSAN datastore can be sized to accommodate the VM files in a cluster and handle failures and maintenance operations.

VMware recommendations to get the raw capacity: To determine the raw capacity of a vSAN datastore, use this formula: multiply the total number of disk groups in the cluster by the size of the capacity devices in each disk group and subtract the overhead caused by the vSAN on-disk format.

Cloud consumers must consider the failures to tolerate the virtual machine storage policies for the cluster when planning the capacity of the vSAN datastore, not just the number of virtual machines and the size of their VMDK files.

When planning and sizing vSAN storage capacity, failures to tolerate is an important consideration. The setting might result in a doubled or more consumption compared to the consumption of a virtual machine and its devices, depending on the availability requirements of the virtual machine.

By setting the failure tolerance method to RAID-1 (mirroring) and the failures to tolerate (FTT) setting to 1, virtual machines can use up to 50 percent of the raw capacity. The usable capacity is about 33% if the FTT is set to 2, and 25% if the FTT is set to 3.

If, however, the failure tolerance method is set to RAID-5/6 (erasure coding) and the FTT to 1, virtual machines can use approximately 75% of the raw capacity. If the FTT is set to 2, approximately 67% of the bandwidth is usable.

To calculate the storage space:

Forecasted overall consumption = Number of VMs in the cluster * Forecasted percentage of consumption per VMDK

To calculate the FTT:

vSAN Datastore capacity = Expected overall consumption * (FTT + 1)

To estimate the overhead:

Versions 3 and later of the on-disk format add an extra overhead, typically 1-2% capacity per device. When software checksum is enabled, deduplication and compression add approximately 6.2% to device capacity.

In Azure VMware Solution, default storage policies include RAID-1 (mirroring), FTT-1, and thick provisioning. In Azure, the cluster grows with the configuration unless cloud consumers want to adjust the storage policy or apply a new policy.

FTT-1 accommodates a single host's failure in a cluster of three hosts. Using an architecture perspective, Microsoft governs failures and replaces the hardware when it detects an event.

Azure Key Vault keys can be planned and used by default for data-at-rest encryption in vSAN datastores. The encryption solution utilizes KMS and supports vCenter operations for key management. The data on SSDs is invalidated immediately on the removal of a host from a cluster.

As soon as capacity consumption reaches 75%, Microsoft provides alerts. Azure Monitor also provides cloud consumers with the ability to monitor capacity consumption metrics.

AVS Network Plan and Prepare

With Microsoft Azure VMware Solution, cloud consumers can use both on-premises and Azure-based resources in a private cloud environment. To deploy the Azure VMware Solution, a plan for the network topology must be developed.

Azure VMware Solution environments need to transfer network traffic to Azure services and on-premises VMware environments. The Azure VMware Solution connects Azure resources and services using a dedicated Azure ExpressRoute circuit. Connectivity to VMware environments on-premises is provided via a separate Azure ExpressRoute circuit. Network connectivity can only be achieved by enabling specific IP address ranges and firewall ports. Private networks are created for the following vSphere components when Azure VMware Solution is deployed:

- Management

- Provisioning

- vMotion

Private networks are used by cloud consumers to access vCenter, vMotion and NSX-T Manager, or to deploy VMs.

Let's read more about NSX-T before planning and preparing the AVS environment.

NSX-T network virtualization creates, deletes, and restores software-based virtual networks, similarly to how server virtualization programmatically creates, snapshots, deletes, and restores VMs.

As a result of network virtualization, the functional equivalent of a network hypervisor replicates all Layer 2 through Layer 7 networking services (e.g., switching, routing, access control, firewalling, QoS) in software. Due to this, these services can be combined in arbitrary ways in seconds to create unique, isolated virtual networks.

Management, control, and data constitute three separate but integrated planes of NSX-T. Processes, modules, and agents implement the three planes.

- Management plane agents reside on every node.

- NSX-T Manager nodes run API services and the cluster management daemons. For each NSX-T installation, a single NSX-T Manager cluster is supported.

NSX-T Manager provides multiple roles that were previously handled by separate appliances. The roles of the policy plane, the management plane, and the central control plane are included here. The NSX-T Controller appliance played a major role in control planes in the past. Transport nodes host daemons and forwarding engines. Figure 4-12 depicts AVS NSX-T.

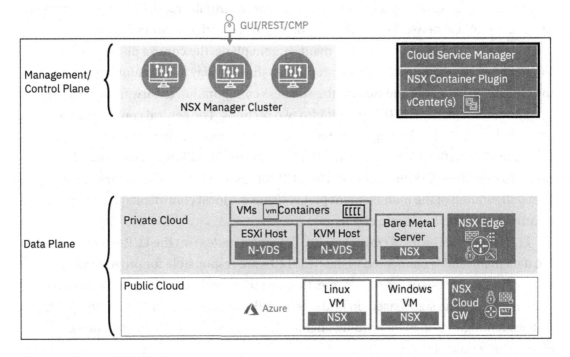

Figure 4-12. *AVS NSX-T*

In addition to providing a single API entry point to the system, the management plane persists user configurations, handles user queries, and performs operational tasks on all system management, control, and data plane nodes.

The management plane is responsible for querying, modifying, and persisting user configuration. Alternatively, the data plane elements are responsible for disseminating that configuration to the control plane. There may be some data belonging to more than one plane. Administrators can also query current status and statistics either from the control plane or directly from the data plane from the management plane.

As configured by the user via configuration, the management plane is the only source of truth for the logical (configured) system. Either NSX-T's UI or a RESTful API is used to make changes.

It is now possible to create a cluster of managers for the user interface and API of NSX-T Data Center. NSX provides both an external load balancer and a virtual IP address provided by NSX for redundancy. Also, the management plane and the central control plane functions have been merged into this new management cluster to reduce the number of virtual appliances deployed and managed by the NSX administrator.

It also contains messages for controlling network virtualization. Cloud customers set up secure physical networks (VLANs) to communicate with the control plane.

Using the configuration from the management plane, the control plane calculates the runtime state. The control plane propagates the topology information reported by the data plane elements and pushes the stateless configuration to forwarding engines.

The control plane in NSX-T is split into two sections. The central control planes are called CCPs. NSX-T Manager cluster nodes provide redundancy and scalability. Logically, CCP traffic is separate from all data plane traffic; failures in the control plane do not affect data plane traffic. The CCP computes some runtime states from the configuration of the management plane. Using the local control plane distributes information about data plane elements.

LCP stands for the local control plane. Transport nodes run the LCP, which controls the data plane and is connected to the CCP. LCPs are responsible for programming the forwarding entries of the data plane: they monitor local link status, compute most ephemeral runtime state based on updates from the data planes and CCPs, and push stateless configuration to forwarding engines. It shares its fate with the data plane element that hosts it.

The data plane performs stateless packet forwarding or transformations based on the control plane's tables, reports topology information to it, and maintains packet-level statistics.

The data plane has the following traffic:

- Workload data

- Also, N-VDS, distributed routing, and NSX-T's firewall. The data is carried over the physical network's designated transport networks.

As part of next step, let's take quick review of Azure networking terminology.

- Subnets are logical divisions of IP networks within Azure. They can be either private or public.

- VNets describe logically isolated cloud sections where Azure resources can be launched.

- Subnetwork gateways and subnets are directed using Azure Virtual Network Routing.

- With Azure Virtual Network Service Endpoints, you can privately connect your private cloud to other clouds or endpoints.

- Azure VPN Gateway Private is a connection to the Azure Virtual Private Cloud.

- Peering between two Azure Virtual Private Clouds enables traffic to be routed using private IP addresses.

- A Network Security Group describes security rules for allowing or blocking network traffic to Azure resources.

- Azure NAT Gateways enable outbound Internet traffic from Azure instances on private subnets.

- Azure Firewall is a cloud-based network security service that protects your Azure Virtual Network resources managed by Microsoft.

- An Azure Content Delivery Network (CDN) is a globally distributed network that caches content to ensure high-bandwidth delivery.

- It is a DNS-based traffic load balancer. You can spread traffic to your public-facing applications across Azure's global regions.

- Microsoft Azure Front Door Service enables enterprises to define, manage, and monitor the global routing and failover of all web traffic to their websites and optimize their performance.

- Azure Web Application Firewall (WAF) offers protection against exploits and vulnerabilities such as SQL injection, cross-site scripting, and other standard attacks.

- Azure Load Balancer distributes traffic evenly among multiple targets in multiple Azure availability zones. Furthermore, it offers Layer 4 load balancing for all UDP and TCP protocols with high performance and low latency. The service handles all incoming and outgoing connections.

- An Application Gateway manages traffic between your web applications and Application Delivery Controllers (ADCs).

- Azure Network Watcher helps to monitor, diagnose, and view metrics and logs of Azure resources in Azure virtual networks.

- Azure Monitor for Networks provides a comprehensive overview of the health and metrics of all installed network resources without requiring any configuration. As well as maximizing the availability and performance of your apps, Azure Monitor provides a complete solution for gathering, analyzing, and executing on telemetry from Azure virtual networks and on-premises environments.

- Azure virtual network terminal access points collect network data continuously from virtual machines and stream it to packet collectors.

Microsoft Azure is a cloud platform with a global network of data centers managed by the company.

Users of Azure services can host their business presence in the cloud and run their own custom software applications on fully virtualized computers. In addition to remote storage, database hosting, and account management, the Microsoft Azure cloud platform also offers other cloud services. Azure also offers artificial intelligence and the Internet of Things (IoT) capabilities.

An ever-expanding set of Azure cloud services enables cloud consumers organizations to meet their current and future business challenges. Azure lets users manage, deploy, and build applications using anything they choose on a global network.

Azure Networking provides zero-trust and low-latency networking services with integrated hybrid networks and cloud-native apps.

Azure Networking connects compute resources and provides access to applications. Azure customers can access the features and services of Azure's global datacenters via its networking capabilities.

Microsoft supports cloud consumers with a vast network of highly available, scalable, performant, and secure public and private fiber infrastructure, spanning 60+ regions and 170+ points of presence around the globe. With services that can be accessed from on-premises, multiple clouds, and edge locations, cloud customers can enjoy a consistent, low-latency experience.

Because all traffic is routed through the Microsoft global network by default (cold potato routing), cloud consumers can deliver predictable, low-latency performance for their applications by utilizing Microsoft Azure's optimal routing. Utilize a vast network spanning multiple regions with a 1ms latency for resilient cloud deployments across multiple availability zones, Azure ExpressRoute enables Azure network engineers to deliver up to 100 GBPS performance in a reliable manner, optimized SaaS and SDWAN connectivity via Azure Peering, and robust security. With routing preferences, Azure network engineers can set up organization traffic routes between Azure and the Internet with more choices. Through Azure Load Balancer, application performance is optimized with ultra-low latency.

There are two types of IP addresses that Azure uses and allocates: public IP addresses and private IP addresses.

- Communication of resources within an Azure resource group is made possible via private IP addresses. Resources cannot access an external IP address through the network. In addition to the VM Network Interface and Internal Load Balancer, Application Gateway can also be connected using a private address.

- Azure resources can communicate over the Internet with Azure services that are available for public viewing. Thus, resources can be accessed from outside the network through public IP addresses. In addition to VM Network Interface and a public facing, Internet-facing load balancer, Application Gateway, VPN Gateway, and Azure Firewall tools can use public addresses.

There are two types of IP allocation in Azure Networking. The default selection method by which Azure can assign IP addresses from a subnet's address range is based on available and unreserved addresses. A dynamic IP changes over time and is not fixed.

The static IP allocation method uses a custom allocation method to assign the unreserved open addresses in a subnet range. A static IP address is fixed in time and does not change.

Azure subnets are a small network of IP addresses that covers a range of addresses. VNets can be split into subnets for organizations in Azure. An Azure VNet must have a subnet range and topology specified. Subnets are subparts of big blocks of IP addresses that are used in VNets. Each VM and resource in a network will receive an IP address based on the subnets assigned.

Azure network architects and engineers enable organizations to extend their existing network to Azure and deliver their apps to end users worldwide. They can connect on-premises, multi-cloud, and edge deployments while managing the entire network from a central location.

Azure Virtual WAN's capabilities enable on-premises, multi-cloud, and branch deployments. It enhances edge and 5G scenarios by enabling Azure Edge Zones, Azure Edge Zones with the carrier, and Azure Private Edge Zones.

Azure VMware engineers and architects can utilize services that support the Zero Trust approach to security to safeguard workloads and virtual networks running on Azure. They utilize micro-segmentation to secure virtual network infrastructure, AWS WAF and Azure Bastion to protect applications, and Azure DDoS Protection to detect threats intelligently. Figure 4-13 depicts the AVS network offerings.

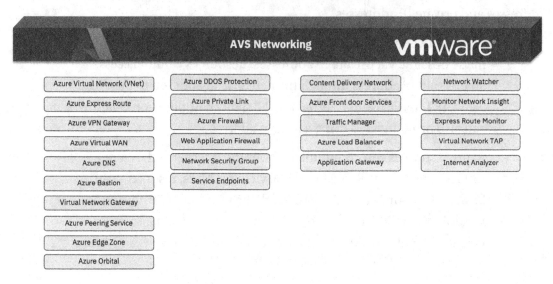

Figure 4-13. *AVS network offerings*

Organizations focus on their apps with easy-to-use scalable services and tools. Azure Networking as a service enables the connectivity and scale you need without requiring Azure network engineers to build or manage down to the fiber. It helps the Azure engineer to manage traffic for applications using Azure App Gateway and protect using Azure WAF, establish and monitor global routing with Azure Front Door, offer turnkey firewall abilities with Azure Firewall, and use VNet NAT to guarantee reliable outbound connectivity from a predictable IP space.

As a cloud computing platform service created by Microsoft, Azure hosts your existing applications, allows you to develop new applications faster, and enhances on-premises applications. Microsoft-managed data centers are ideal for developing, testing, deploying, and managing applications and services.

During every phase of IT transformation, networks used to be an essential part of every IT ecosystem to have a well-functioning infrastructure. It is no wonder that networking is a necessary part of the cloud from various looks, beginning from the remote connection to your Azure VMs, to traversing your data in your environment across on-premises and Azure.

Azure virtual networks help Azure resources, such as virtual machines, web applications, and databases, interact with each other, with cloud consumers users on the Internet, and with your on-premises cloud consumer computers. Azure networks are web-based connections that link resources in Azure.

The following key networking capabilities are available through Azure virtual networks:

- Internet communication

- Isolation and micro-segmentation

- Connectivity among Azure resources

- Connectivity with on-premises resources

- Route and filter network traffic

- Attach virtual networks

In addition to Virtual Network Services and Azure Content Delivery Network, Azure Network Services also provide tools to connect network engineers and cloud and on-premises resources.

With Azure, Azure engineers/architects can access a range of networking services that can be used individually or in combination. Four different vital groups of services are offered in Azure: network connectivity services, application protection services, application protection services, and network monitoring.

Network connectivity services provide connectivity between Azure resources and on-premises resources by using any or all the following networking services as VNet, ExpressRoute, VPN Gateway, Virtual WAN, Virtual Network NAT Gateway, Azure DNS, Azure Bastion, Virtual Network Gateway, Peering Service, Edge Zone, and Orbital.

Application protection services can be used to protect applications with DDoS protection, Private Link, Firewall, Web Application Firewall, Network Security Groups, and Service Endpoints.

Application delivery services deliver applications using any combination of networking services such as Content Delivery Network (CDN), Azure Front Door Service, Traffic Manager, Application Load Balancer, and Application Gateway.

Network monitoring is done via services such as Network Watcher, ExpressRoute Monitor, Azure Monitor, Internet Analyzer, and Terminal Access Point (TAP).

Let's move to network planning and preparing the AVS environment. Let's get started with IP segments planning. Figure 4-14 depicts the key elements involved in AVS planning and preparing.

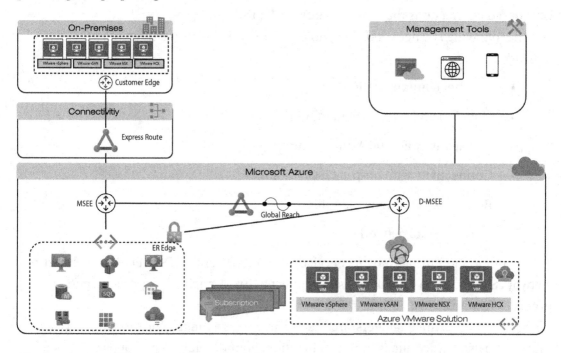

Figure 4-14. *AVS network connectivity*

A /22 CIDR networking model is required by Azure VMware Solution, for example, 10.0.0.0/22. The address space is divided into smaller network segments (subnets) used to manage Azure VMware Solution components such as vCenter, VMware HCX, NSX-T, and vMotion. If cloud consumers already have any existing network segments on-premises or in Azure, the /22 CIDR network address block shouldn't overlap. See Table 4-9.

Table 4-9. *Network-Recommended IP Segments*

Network IP Required Components	IP Segments	Example
Private cloud management	/26	10.50.0.0/26
HCX migrations	/26	10.50.0.64/26
Global Reach reserved	/26	10.50.0.128/26
ExpressRoute reserved	/27	10.50.0.192/27
ExpressRoute peering	/27	10.50.0.224/27
ESXi management	/25	10.50.1.0/25
vMotion network	/25	10.50.1.128/25
Replication network	/25	10.50.2.0/25
vSAN	/25	10.50.2.128/25
HCX uplink	/26	10.50.3.0/26
Reserved	3 /26 blocks	10.50.3.64/26, 10.50.3.128/26, 10.50.3.192/26

As per Microsoft recommendation, before deploying Azure VMware Solution, IP addresses must be determined. The service ingests a/22 CIDR network address block provided by cloud consumers. Consumers can segment the address space within NSX-T Manager into smaller segments. These IP segments are used by VMware HCX, VMware NSX-T, and VMware vMotion. To migrate VMs into Azure, the Azure VMware Solution, the cloud consumer's existing Azure environment and on-premises domain will need to exchange routes. Cloud consumers should not use network address blocks configured on-premises or Azure that overlap with the /22 CIDR block.

To create the first NSX-T segment within the Azure VMware Solution private cloud, a VM IP segment must be built. Azure VMware Solution supports the deployment of VMs via the VM IP segment. An on-premises VMware environment can be extended to Azure VMware Solution through the addition of network segments. vSphere Distributed Switches (vDS) must be used for on-premises networks because they cannot be extended.

Cloud consumers can choose an existing virtual network, create a new one, or leave the field blank.

The Gateway Subnet for the Azure VMware Solution ExpressRoute circuit must be designated if cloud consumers choose an existing virtual network. In addition, if they create a brand-new virtual network, they must create a gateway subnet for the Azure VMware Solution ExpressRoute circuit. They can either choose an existing virtual network or create a new one, and all ExpressRoute configurations to peer the circuit into Azure will be handled by cloud consumers. In addition, the Azure environment will be provisioned.

After Azure VMware Solution has completed deployment, cloud consumers need to create a virtual network gateway and peer the ExpressRoute circuit to Azure if the virtual network is blank.

Cloud consumers will need an ExpressRoute circuit and Azure Virtual Network for Azure VMware Solution. Select either an existing ExpressRoute virtual network gateway or a new one. After creating the private clouds, they will have to create a new virtual network gateway if they decide to use one. Cloud consumers can use an existing ExpressRoute virtual network gateway. For planning purposes, note which cloud consumers use ExpressRoute virtual network gateways.

In Azure VMware Solution, there are two types of connectivity:

- **Basic connectivity:** An ExpressRoute connection is deployed with the Azure VMware Solution to connect to an Azure virtual network. Azure VMware Solution's ExpressRoute circuit provides connectivity to and from the Azure VMware Solution private cloud for other Azure services, such as Azure Monitor and Microsoft Defender for Cloud.

- **Fully interconnected:** This connectivity model extends the basic interconnectivity implementation to include interconnectivity between on-premises and Azure VMware Solution private clouds. ExpressRoute circuits are used to configure this connection. Cloud consumers can purchase existing circuits or new ones.

ExpressRoute Global Reach must be enabled to route traffic between the Azure VMware Solution private cloud and the on-premises environment. Azure VMware Solution's private cloud deployment does not include a customer-provided ExpressRoute circuit. An ASN of 4 bytes must be supported by all gateways involved with the deployment. As an ASN, a system can exchange routing information with other systems and has a unique identifier that is globally available. BGP is used for advertising all routes between the on-premises environment and Azure.

To configure ExpressRoute Global Reach, a few prerequisites need to be met:

- Azure VMware Solution ExpressRoute circuits require connectivity within the private cloud of Azure VMware Solution to and from Azure.

- The customer must provide a separate ExpressRoute circuit. On-premises environments are connected to Azure via this circuit.

- For ExpressRoute Global Reach peering, a /29 non-overlapping address block is required.

- All gateways, including ExpressRoute, should support ASN 4-bytes. The Azure VMware Solution uses 4-byte public ASNs to advertise network routes.

The ports listed in Table 4-10 must be allowed if the on-premises network infrastructure is restrictive.

Table 4-10. *Minimum Connectivity Between On-Premises and AVS*

Source	Destination	Protocol	Port
Azure VMware Solution private-cloud DNS server	On-premises DNS server	UDP	53
On-premises DNS server	Azure VMware Solution DNS server	UDP	53
On-premises network	Azure VMware Solution vCenter	TCP (HTTP/HTTPS)	80, 443
Azure VMware Solution private-cloud management network	On-premises Active Directory	TCP	389
On-premises vCenter	Azure VMware Solution management network	TCP	8000
Web browser	Hybrid Cloud Manager (HCM)	TCP (HTTPS)	9443
Admin network	HCM	SSH	22
HCM	Cloud gateway	TCP (HTTPS)	8123, 9443
Cloud gateway	Layer 2 connectivity	TCP (HTTPS)	443
Cloud gateway	ESXi hosts	TCP	80, 902
Cloud gateway (local)	Cloud gateway (remote)	UDP	4500, 500

Virtual machines running in the Azure VMware Solution require name resolution and DHCP services for IP address lookup and allocation. On-premises and Azure VMs can use name resolution. Azure VMware Solution cloud consumers can use NSX's DHCP service or a local DHCP server. In Azure VMware Solution, cloud consumers do not have to route DHCP traffic over the WAN back to their on-premises environment when configuring DHCP.

Consider the following as you prepare and plan:

- Cloud consumers can extend network segments from on-premises to Azure VMware solutions. A vSphere Standard (vSS) Switch network cannot be extended in a cloud consumer's on-premises VMware environment.

AVS Management and Monitoring Planning and Preparing

In a hybrid environment (Azure, Azure VMware Solution, and on-premises), Microsoft Azure native services allow users to monitor, manage, and protect their VMs. Figure 4-15 depicts AVS management and monitoring.

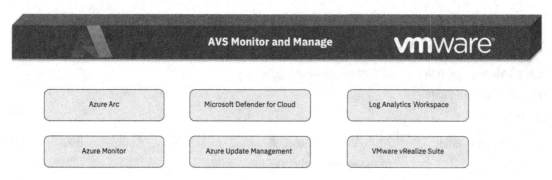

Figure 4-15. *AVS management and monitoring*

Azure native services can manage cloud consumers' VMs in a hybrid environment (Azure, Azure VMware Solution, and on-premises).

Azure Arc enables the management of any infrastructure, including Azure VMware Solution, on-premises infrastructure, or any other cloud platform. Customers can manage Windows and Linux servers and virtual machines hosted outside of Azure, on their corporate network, or another cloud provider with Azure Arc-enabled servers. By using Azure Arc-enabled Kubernetes, cloud consumers can attach Kubernetes clusters hosted in their Azure VMware Solution environments.

Use Azure Arc-enabled servers VM extension support for new and existing VMs to deploy the Log Analytics agent quickly.

Monitoring and visibility for cloud consumers Azure, Azure VMware Solutions, and on-premises virtual machines.

Azure Monitor collects, scrutinizes, and works on telemetry from cloud consumers' AVS cloud and on-premises environments. It does not require installation. Consumers can monitor the performance of their guest operating systems to discover and map application dependencies for Azure VMware Solution or on-premises VMs. Cloud consumers can collect logs and performance counters using Log Analytics agents and extensions in the Log Analytics workspace in Azure Monitor.

Azure Monitor allows cloud consumers to gather data from different sources to monitor and analyze other data types for analysis, visualization, and alerting. Azure Monitor can also create alert rules to detect issues in cloud consumers' environments, such as high resource usage, missing patches, low disk space, and unhealthy VMs. ITSM (IT Service Management) tools can be configured to send alerts when VMware administrators detect an event. Email notifications can also be sent when events are detected.

Azure Monitor has the following additional benefits:

- Monitoring in real-time

- Better visibility into the infrastructure

- Instant notifications

- Resolves problems automatically

- Cost efficiency

Azure Update Management in Azure Automation lets cloud consumers update their Windows and Linux machines.

With Azure Update Management, AVS administrators can manage operating system updates for cloud consumers' Windows and Linux computers in a hybrid environment. It monitors patch compliance and alerts Azure Monitor about deviations from patching compliance. Azure Update Management needs access to cloud consumers' Log Analytics workspace to determine the update status of cloud consumers' VMs.

Microsoft Defender for Cloud enhances data center security by protecting hybrid workloads in the cloud and on-premises from advanced threats. Azure VMware Solution evaluates VM vulnerabilities, raises alerts when necessary, and forwards them to Azure Monitor for resolution. By way of example, it considers the status of operating system patches, security configurations, and endpoint security. Security policies can also be configured in Microsoft Defender for Cloud.

Microsoft Defender for Cloud protects against advanced threats including

- File integrity monitoring

- Fileless security alerts

- Operating system patch assessment

- Security misconfigurations assessment

- Endpoint protection assessment

Azure Monitor's Log Analytics workspace uses the Log Analytics agent or extensions to enable log collection and performance counter collection. It provides data and logs to multiple Azure native services from a single collection point.

Review the following planning considerations for platform management and monitoring of Azure VMware Solution:

- AVS operations teams should be able to create alerts and dashboards on the metrics that matter most.

- License solutions from VMware's eco-system include vRealize Operations Manager and vRealize Network Insight. With these solutions, you gain an in-depth understanding of VMware's Azure platform. Monitoring data like vCenter events and flow logs are available for the NSX-T distributed firewall. Pull logging is currently supported by vRealize Log Insight for VMware Solution for Azure. Tasks, alarms, and events can be captured. Syslog pushing from hosts to vRealize is now not supported.

- VMware tools do not support in-guest memory collection in vRealize Operations. In-guest memory collection will continue to work as before.

- Cloud consumers need to manage vSAN storage capacity since it is a finite resource. VM workloads should only be stored in vSAN. Consider these design considerations for reducing unnecessary vSAN storage.

- Configure content libraries on Azure Blob Storage to move VM template storage off vSAN.

- Choose a partner vendor or Microsoft tool to store Azure virtual machine backups.

- VMware Azure uses a local identity provider. Utilize one administrative account for the initial configuration of the Azure VMware Solution. Integrating Azure VMware Solution with Active Directory enables users to track actions.

From a migration management planning perspective, cloud and data center apps can be migrated, workloads rebalanced, and business continuity is assured with VMware HCX. VMware workloads can be migrated to Azure VMware Solution and other connected sites through various migration options.

HCX Connector deploys virtual appliances (automatically) requiring multiple IP segments. Consumers use the IP segments when they create their network profiles. Identify the following for a VMware HCX deployment, which supports a small product pilot or use case. Depending on how cloud consumers migrate, this can change accordingly.

Management network: To deploy VMware HCX on-premises, you will need to identify a management network for VMware HCX. Typically, it will be the same management network cloud consumers use for their on-premises VMware cluster. Identify at least two IP addresses on this network segment for VMware HCX. Cloud consumers might need more IP addresses depending on their deployment beyond a pilot or small use case.

Specifically, to prepare for large environments, create a new /26 and present it to the cloud consumer's on-premises VMware cluster instead of the management network. Cloud consumers can create up to 10 service meshes and 60 network extenders (one per service mesh). Azure VMware Solution private clouds can extend eight networks per network extender.

Uplink network: On-premises deployments of VMware HCX require cloud consumers to identify an uplink network. The same network is used for VMware HCX's management.

vMotion network: On-premises VMware Cluster HCX deployments require cloud consumers to identify a network they can use for vMotion. This is typically the same network for vMotion with their on-premises VMware cluster. Provide at least two IPs on this network segment for VMware HCX. Cloud consumers may require more IPs, depending on the scope and scale of their deployment. It would help if cloud consumers exposed the vMotion network on a distributed virtual switch or vSwitch0. If it's not, modify the environment to accommodate it.

Replication network: A replication network is required when VMware HCX is deployed on-premises. Cloud consumers' management and uplink networks should use the same network as their consumers. Use the dedicated replication VMkernel network of the on-premises cluster hosts for the replication network if the hosts are connected via a dedicated replication VMkernel network.

Summary

In this chapter, you read about the preparing and planning methodology for AVS Solution including AVS Azure Cloud enablement, AVS compute planning and preparing, AVS storage planning and preparing, AVS network planning and preparing, and AVS management and monitoring planning and preparing.

In the next chapter of the book, you will read about the deployment methodology of AVS Solution.

CHAPTER 5

Deployment Essentials of AVS

Businesses always want cloud migrations to be low risk, low cost, and of low complexity. Cloud consumers' on-premises environment and all of their existing investments, skills, and tools can be extended to a public cloud platform in a simple, secure manner. A VMware solution from Azure enables this.

It is excellent news for cloud consumers who use VMware vSphere, NSX, vSAN or vCenter that they can all be seamlessly extended to the cloud. Azure VMware Solution was developed in partnership with VMware. As a VMware Cloud Verified solution, you can access the same VMware Cloud infrastructure capabilities that you use on-premises, using an Azure bare metal infrastructure built on Microsoft Azure.

This chapter provides the deployment essentials. By the end of this chapter, you should understand the following:

- AVS deployment overview

- AVS essential deployment and connectivity information

- AVS essential post deployment information

- Configuring NSX-T Data Center network components

- Deploying a disaster recovery solution using VMware HCX

- Deploying a disaster recovery solution using VMware SRM

- Deploying a monitoring solution using VMware vROPS

- Deploying a virtual desktop infrastructure solution using VMware Horizon

© Puthiyavan Udayakumar 2022
P. Udayakumar, *Design and Deploy Azure VMware Solutions*, https://doi.org/10.1007/978-1-4842-8312-7_5

AVS Deployment Essentials Overview

In this chapter, you'll learn about the Azure VMware solution deployment essentials, including computing, storage, networking, workload management, application mobility with VMware HCX management and operations, and VMware solutions that integrate directly with AVS. Then you'll explore availability maintenance and remediation.

AVS is an integrated offering from VMware and Microsoft that combines VMware's enterprise-class computing, networking, and storage capabilities with the speed, elasticity, and geographic reach of the Azure Cloud.

Because of the consistent infrastructure between on-premises and the cloud, customers don't have to change their applications during migration. If you have VMware expertise, you can move your applications live without a hitch.

For day-to-day administration, this brings consistency between on-premises and the cloud. With AVS, consumers can use the same tools and processes as traditional on-premises infrastructure such as vSphere, but with non-converged compute, storage, and networking.

The latest hardware of AVS improves price performance. With AVS hyperconverged infrastructure, compute storage and networking can be combined for lower pricing. At the same time, vSphere in the cloud drives up consolidation ratios and highly qualified Microsoft operations and security teams.

AVS administrators/architects can use this chapter to understand the fundamentals of AVS deployment, identify prerequisites, plan for the initial deployment, build the first AVS private cloud, and connect the on-premises datacenter with the AVS private cloud. Figure 5-1 depicts the deployment considerations.

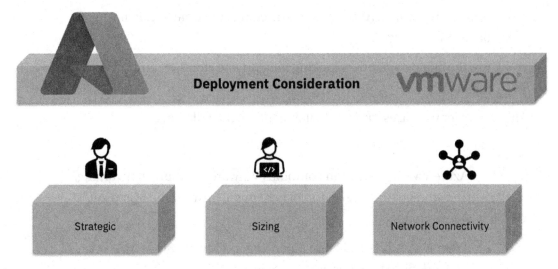

Figure 5-1. *Azure VMware Solution deployment considerations*

Strategic Deployment Considerations

This section covers strategic deployment considerations for implementing cloud consumers' AVS private clouds. Five dimensions should be taken into consideration as AVS architect/administrators prepare:

- How do we intend to accomplish business requirements?

- When and where will we accomplish them within the Azure landscape?

- What time, effort, and cost are required?

- What is the plan of action?

- What steps are required to accomplish the objective?

Once you've answers these questions, next you need to make placement decisions. You may have to ask yourself several questions, such as

- Is AVS supported in the regions where the cloud consumers use Azure?

- Do the cloud consumers have an existing Azure footprint?

- Do the cloud consumers have an existing Azure connectivity?

- What is the nearest AVS region to the cloud consumers' existing datacenter or users?

- Are the cloud consumers looking for a private cloud in multiple AZ regions?

The five major use cases for AVS deployment are the following:

- Data center expansion

  - Azure VMware Solution combines VMware compute, networking, and storage running on top of bare metal hosts in the Microsoft Azure cloud.

  - From NSX Advanced Load Balancing to VMware SD-WAN, networking extensions are available.

  - The vRealize portfolio products allow AVS to be managed, monitored, and automated.

- Disaster recovery

  - vSphere, vCenter, NSX-T, vSAN, and HCX provide the core capabilities of AVS. VMware products that have been certified with AVS provide VMware services that extend the capabilities of these core capabilities.

  - VMware Site Recovery Manager primarily handles disaster recovery in the Azure Cloud.

  - VMware HCX also handles disaster recovery in the Azure Cloud.

  - JetStream also handles disaster recovery to the Azure Cloud. JetStream DR is cloud-native and minimizes downtime for VMs in the event of a disaster. Both the protected sites as well as the recovery sites are equipped with JetStream DR.

- Cloud migration

  - The migration of virtual machines to Azure VMware Solution is made possible through VMware HCX.

- Virtual desktops

  - Virtual desktops Infrastructure/Desktop as a Service on AVS are supported by VMware Horizon.

- Application modernization

  - Tanzu Kubernetes Grid is VMware's consistent Kubernetes runtime, while Tanzu Mission Control is VMware's centralized management platform.

It is essential to analyze how these use cases will determine the sizing placement connectivity requirements based on their quirks, caveats, and needs.

Sizing Deployment Consideration

- An AVS architect must figure out how many hosts cloud consumers need.

- Where they're going to go, use

- How many hosts do the cloud consumers need per region?

- How can cloud consumers limit the blast radius by using multiple clusters?

Customers may need more hosts than might fit in one cluster, which is among other traditional VMware vSphere reasons for deploying multiple clusters.

The maximum number of hosts must be considered. By default, cloud subscribers are limited to a single private cloud. The limit can be raised by working with Microsoft support, but one private cloud is allowed by default.

Private clouds can have a maximum of 12 clusters. Cloud consumers can have up to 16 nodes per cluster and up to 96 nodes per private cloud.

Additionally, suppose the AVS deployment model uses VMware vCenter NSX manager, HCX appliances, and VC replication appliances. In that case, all of this will reside in the Management or First cluster and consume resources from that cluster.

The aggregate resource allocation or demand of the existing VM footprint in the data center that you are trying to extend or migrate needs to be considered when sizing data center extensions, cloud migrations, or disaster recovery scenarios. Microsoft tends to lead the way with Azure Migrate, one of the tools that does modeling well.

Azure Migrate is a Microsoft tool and it is free. Azure Migrate works in two different ways. A lightweight appliance can be deployed into the VMware vCenter environments of cloud consumers. Cloud consumers' VMs will be discovered, and performance data will be collected using that appliance without an agent.

As part of Azure Migrate, cloud consumers can discover, assess, and migrate on-premises workloads and apps. It also tracks instances in private and public clouds. Azure Migrate tools and independent software vendors offerings are also offered through the hub.

With Azure Migrate, cloud consumers can assess on-premises servers for migration to Azure virtual machines and Azure VMware Solution.

VMware administrators can also create a CSV file with inventory information. The RV tool's output can be easily manipulated to fit Microsoft's format using a specific template.

The appliance or CSV file data is imported into an Azure migrate project, and some parameters are set. Based on the observed VM performance or the actual allocation of resources, some sizing can be projected.

Azure administrators can set targets for CPU oversubscription and memory overcommit, set deduplication and compression factors, and then Azure Migrate will generate a report. It will show cloud consumers the number of AVS hosts needed and their project utilization after migration and estimate the monthly cost.

VMware vRealize Operations Manager is also a good tool, and VMware administrators may already have this deployed in cloud consumers' environments. This deployment is more accessible by a built-in what-if analysis report that does all the heavy lifting for cloud consumers. It's called the VMware migration planning cloud report. AVS administrators can select AVS as the target cloud, select the region they wish to play in, and then choose the number of VMs to link to a model based on their names, application tags, custom groups, or vCenter objects.

They can adjust for reserved capacity, steady-state headroom, and vSAN fault tolerance. They can do compression and set an assumed annual growth rate to take that into account; it builds the model, and then they run the scenario that generates a report.

Furthermore, all historical performance data will be migrated to vRealize Operations Manager operations on the AVS side if cloud consumers migrate these VMs down the road.

VMware vRealize Operations Manager and Azure Migrate provides cloud consumers with the monthly cost estimate and the resource usage after migration.

VMware vRealize Operations Manager offers a few more settings, which can be helpful if cloud consumers want to experiment with different overprovisioning scenarios. Azure Migrate adds a few more knobs to the total. Still, it's using the vRealize model engine's past historical performance data, and it doesn't feel the need to expose all those options to cloud consumers.

Cloud users can then decide how many hosts they need, and everything will be fine. The two options return a projected number of AVS required monthly costs and resource utilization estimates post-migration. Cloud consumers may choose either tool if they have VMware vRealize Operations Manager, and both work once initial sizing is determined.

Before deploying a VMware Azure private cloud, AVS administrators need to ensure that the following things are in place:

- Build an Azure account.

- The subscription fee is applied to the quota in the form of a quota.

- Ensure that the subscription conforms to the Microsoft enterprise agreement.

- Check the subscription quota.

- It is essential to determine whether you will use an existing or new Azure ExpressRoute virtual network gateway for connectivity. This is detailed in the next section.

- Validate administrative rights and permission to create a private cloud. A minimum contributor level is required for cloud subscribers.

Build an Azure Account

To use Azure VMware Solution, you must first register the resource provider with your subscription.

Step 1: Log into the Azure portal at `https://portal.azure.com/`.

Step 2: On the Azure portal menu, Choose All services.

Step 3: In the All services box, type subscription, and then choose Subscriptions.

Step 4: Choose the subscription from the subscription list to view.

Step 5: Choose Resource providers and type Microsoft.AVS into the search bar, as depicted in Figure 5-2.

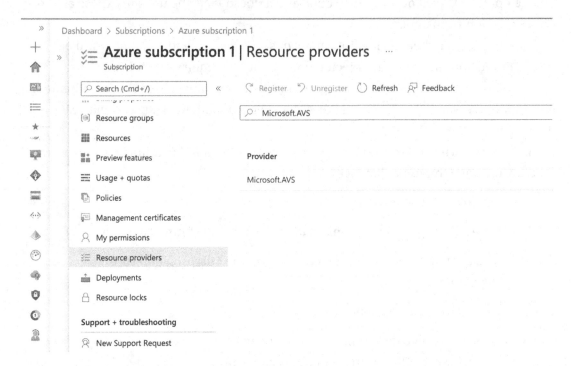

Figure 5-2. *Microsoft.AVS register*

Step 6: If the resource provider is not registered, choose Register.

Network Connectivity Deployment Considerations

Connectivity deployment is based on the following key parameters. Cloud consumers need to come back to their organization's current Azure state:

- AVS is the cloud consumers' first time being introduced to Azure.

- Cloud consumers already have an existing Azure environment.

Scenario 1: AVS is the cloud consumers' first time being introduced to Azure. The following example is a proof of concept for non-production workloads or getting set up.

For the first time in Azure, consumers might use a VPN. As shown in Figure 5-3, AVS is connected to a dedicated Microsoft Edge server. Figure 5-3 depicts site-to-site VPN to AVS.

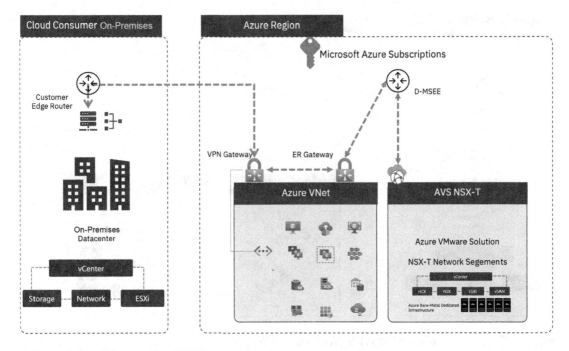

Figure 5-3. *Site-to-site VPN to AVS*

This deployment consists of a single Azure region with a virtual hub that connects to AVS via a VPN gateway and cloud consumers via an ExpressRoute gateway.

Neither VMware nor Microsoft recommends this for POCs since some add-ons don't work well over VPNs.

Also, VMware says this isn't the case anymore, so HCX migrations were not supported previously. A site-to-site VPN now supports the cloud, provided the cloud consumer has a network connection and meets the minimum underlay requirements.

AVS administrators deploy AVS to utilize this as a target site for disaster recovery. However, if cloud consumers want to deploy the VMware site recovery manager, an ExpressRoute is still mandatory as of the writing of this book.

Scenario 2: Cloud consumers have an existing Azure environment. Many cloud consumers connect their on-premises data centers to Azure regions using Express Global Reach.

Connectivity between cloud customers' on-premises resources can be achieved by peering that ExpressRoute circuit with the private ExpressRoute circuit that supports AVS. Figure 5-4 depicts ExpressRoute to AVS.

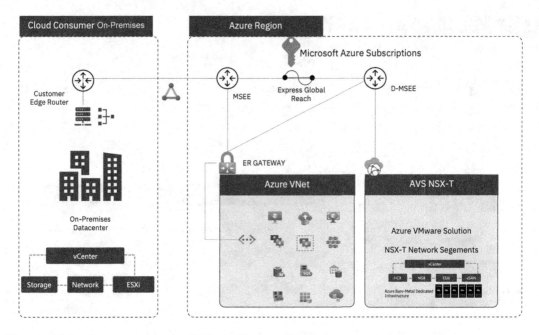

Figure 5-4. *On-premises to AVS via ExpressRoute*

One of the standard deployment patterns for network connectivity is the hub-and-spoke model. The hub VNet serves as a primary connection point in this model. Figure 5-5 depicts the hub-and-spoke model.

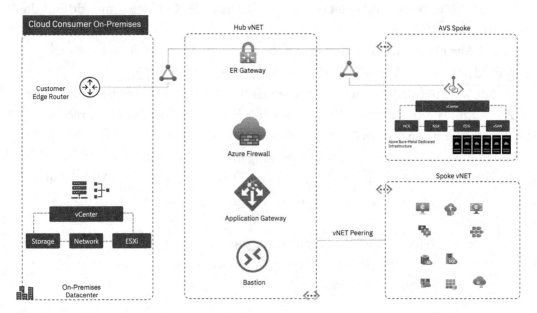

Figure 5-5. *Hub-and-spoke model*

Azure network engineers might have a separate VNet supporting different teams' projects or use cases. The hub VNet appears to be used to express connections back to the on-premises datacenter.

AVS becomes just another spoke that connects to that hub through an ExpressRoute gateway, and ExpressRoute Global Reach is responsible for transitive connectivity between AVS and on-premises.

The enterprise landing zone multi-subscription approach is similar for AVS administrators/architects. Consumers of cloud services have a child subscription containing AVS and connect that child subscription to a gateway in a connectivity subscription.

Another supported network deployment is the virtual WAN, a hub-and-spoke configuration. Cloud consumers can configure a virtual WAN hub in a region for on-premises data centers and branch offices.

Network IP Addressing Deployment Considerations

Once again, AVS becomes another spoke when linked to the virtual LAN hub gateway. In addition to non-overlapping network and IP allocations, Azure network engineers also need to plan.

AVS administrators need to assign the AVS private cloud a /22 block. The private cloud provisioning system will automatically divide it into private cloud networks, HCX, vSAN, VMotion, ExpressRoute peering, and some reserved ranges for future flexibility.

AVS consumers need a new VNet into which to connect AVS. To assign new IP space to the virtual network, Azure network engineers need to define a new subnet called a gateway subnet, which will host the virtual network gateway connecting to AVS ExpressRoutes. They may also need to define additional subnets in that unit. They must create network segments within the private cloud to host VMs.

As well as allocating IP space for those subnets, Azure network engineers/AVS architects should consider how the cloud consumers will provide DNS and DHCP services for them. It may be necessary to create additional on-premises segments for HCX management, HCX uplink, HCX VMotion, and HCX replication if they intend to use HCX for extending on-prem networks.

Overall, users and applications can access VMware private cloud environments from on-premises or Azure-based environments. Specific network address ranges and firewall ports are required to make the services available, such as "Azure ExpressRoute" and "VPN connections."

The following is a summary of elements to consider for network planning:

- Virtual network and ExpressRoute circuits

- Subnetwork and routing requirements

- Network ports are needed to communicate with services.

Your Azure virtual network is connected to the Azure VMware Solution private cloud via an Azure ExpressRoute connection. You can access services running in your Azure subscription from your private cloud environment through this high-bandwidth, low-latency connection. For each private cloud deployment, BGP-based routing is automatically enabled and provisioned.

For Azure VMware Solution private clouds, a /22 CIDR network address block is required, as shown in Table 5-1. The network complements existing on-premises networks. Consequently, the address block should not overlap with other virtual networks in your subscription or on-premises network. Management, provisioning, and vMotion networks within this address block get provisioned automatically.

Table 5-1. *Network Plan*

Network Usage	Subnet	Example
Private cloud management	/26	10.50.0.0/26
HCX management migrations	/26	10.50.0.64/26
Global Reach Reserved	/26	10.50.0.128/26
NSX-T DNS service	/32	10.50.0.192/32
Reserved	/32	10.50.0.193/32
Reserved	/32	10.50.0.194/32
Reserved	/32	10.50.0.195/32
Reserved	/30	10.50.0.196/30
Reserved	/29	10.50.0.200/29
Reserved	/28	10.50.0.208/28
ExpressRoute peering	/27	10.50.0.224/27
ESXi management	/25	10.50.1.0/25

(*continued*)

Table 5-1. (*continued*)

Network Usage	Subnet	Example
vMotion network	/25	10.50.1.128/25
Replication network	/25	10.50.2.0/25
vSAN	/25	10.50.2.128/25
HCX uplink	/26	10.50.3.0/26
Reserved	/26	10.50.3.64/26
Reserved	/26	10.50.3.128/26
Reserved	/26	10.50.3.192/26

DHCP and name resolution are required by applications and workloads running on a private cloud. The infrastructure needed to provide these services is DHCP and DNS. Your private cloud environment can be configured to deliver these services via virtual machines.

Essential Deployment Considerations for the Azure VMware Solution

The following are essential deployment points that should be taken into consideration:

- Network providers must support 4-byte Autonomous System Numbers (ASN) for all gateways, including ExpressRoute. Azure VMware Solution uses 4-byte public ASNs to advertise routes.

- AVS resources are not enabled for public internet access by default.

- /22 CIDR networks that do not overlap with any existing network segments deployed on-premises or in Azure are required for AVS.

- Microsoft Azure is the service provider of AVS, which has been engineered jointly by VMware and Microsoft. Azure provides periodic updates and fixes, remediation of failures, and general support.

- Following compute configuration, maximums need to be considered while deploying AVS.

  - The maximum number of hosts per cluster is 16.

  - The maximum number of hosts per private cloud is 96.

  - Clusters per private cloud: 12

  - vCenter per private cloud: 1

  - vSAN capacity limit is 75% of total usable space

- The VMware vSphere virtualization platform runs on all-flash vSAN on bare metal.

- Azure VMware Solution requires a minimum of three hosts. Hourly charges are applied per host, and prepaying for one or three years will reduce this cost.

- Azure VMware Solution may impose egress charges on VM traffic communicating with on-premises environments through extended networks.

- Additionally, additional monthly cost may be incurred by VNet gateways, ExpressRoute circuits, Azure Bastion services, Azure VMs, Azure VM disks, and public IP addresses.

AVS Essential Deployment and Connectivity

Let's explore how to deploy a new AVS object. This section uses an environment deployed in the UK West region and connected to an administrative jump box behind Azure Bastion and connected to an on-premises data center via ExpressRoute Global Reach. Figure 5-6 shows the step-by-step overview of what every AVS administrators/ architect must deploy.

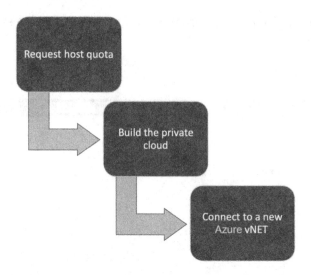

Figure 5-6. *AVS-phased deployment approach*

Stage 1: Request Host Quota

The following step-by-step walkthrough shows how to request a host quota for EA customers.

> **Step 1:** Log into a personal or business account in the Azure portal at `https://portal.azure.com/`. Figure 5-7 depicts the Azure portal.

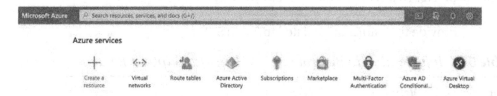

Figure 5-7. *Azure portal*

Step 2: Under Help + Support, build a New Support Request. See Figure 5-8.

Figure 5-8.   *Azure portal – help and support*

Provide the information listed in Table 5-2.

Table 5-2.   *Information to Be Provided in Help and Support Request Creation*

Filed	Value
Issue Type	Technical
Subscription	Choose your subscription An Azure subscription needs to adhere to one of the following for cloud users: • Subscribe to an Azure Enterprise Agreement (EA) with Microsoft. • An Azure plan or Azure subscription is managed by a cloud solution provider (CSP). • A Microsoft Customer Agreement with Microsoft

(continued)

Table 5-2. (*continued*)

Filed	Value
Service	All services ➤ Azure VMware Solution
Resource	General question
Summary	Required capacity
Problem type	Capacity management issues
Problem Subtype	Customer request for additional host quota/capacity

Step 3: Under the Details tab, provide information about the support ticket, as depicted in Figure 5-9.

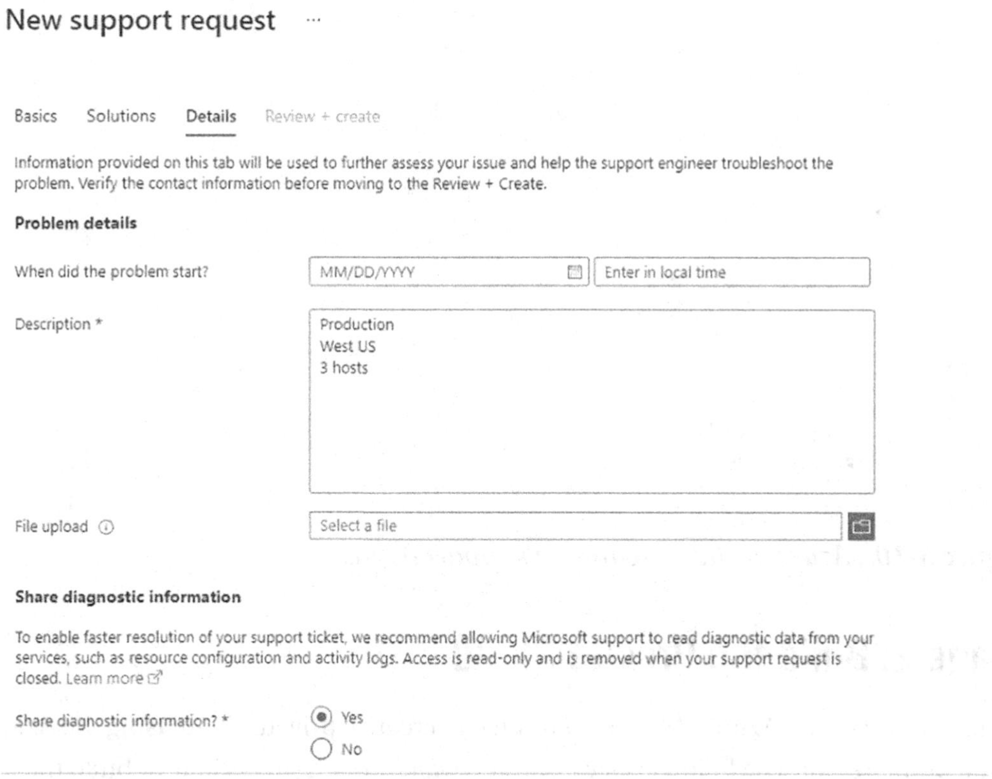

New support request ⋯

Basics   Solutions   Details   Review + create

Information provided on this tab will be used to further assess your issue and help the support engineer troubleshoot the problem. Verify the contact information before moving to the Review + Create.

Problem details

When did the problem start?   MM/DD/YYYY   Enter in local time

Description *   Production
                                   West US
                                   3 hosts

File upload ⓘ   Select a file

Share diagnostic information

To enable faster resolution of your support ticket, we recommend allowing Microsoft support to read diagnostic data from your services, such as resource configuration and activity logs. Access is read-only and is removed when your support request is closed. Learn more ⎘

Share diagnostic information? *   ⦿ Yes
                                   ○ No

Figure 5-9. *Azure portal – new support request*

Step 4: Once finished, select Review + create, as depicted in Figure 5-10.

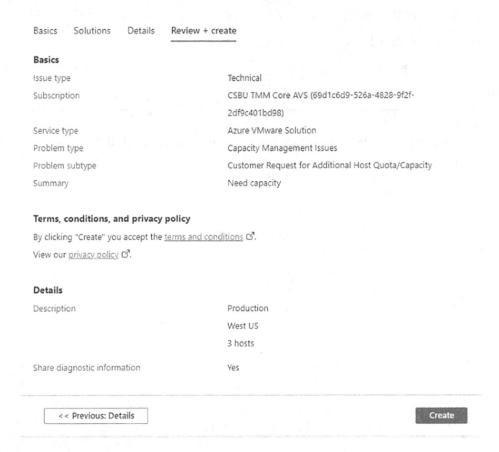

Figure 5-10. *Azure portal – creating a support request*

Stage 2: Build the Private Cloud

Administrators of an Azure VMware Solution can create a private cloud using the Azure portal or Azure CLI. The following step-by-step walkthrough shows how to build the private cloud using Azure portal.

Step 1: Log into a personal or business account on the Azure portal at `https://portal.azure.com/`. Figure 5-11 depicts the Azure portal.

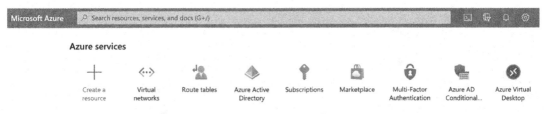

Figure 5-11. *Azure portal*

Step 2: Select Create a new Azure resource.

Step 3: In the Search the Marketplace text box, type AVS and select AVS from the list.

Step 4: In the AVS window, select Create, as depicted in Figure 5-12.

Figure 5-12. *Azure portal – create a private cloud*

Step 5: Fill in the Basics tab as depicted in Figure 5-13.

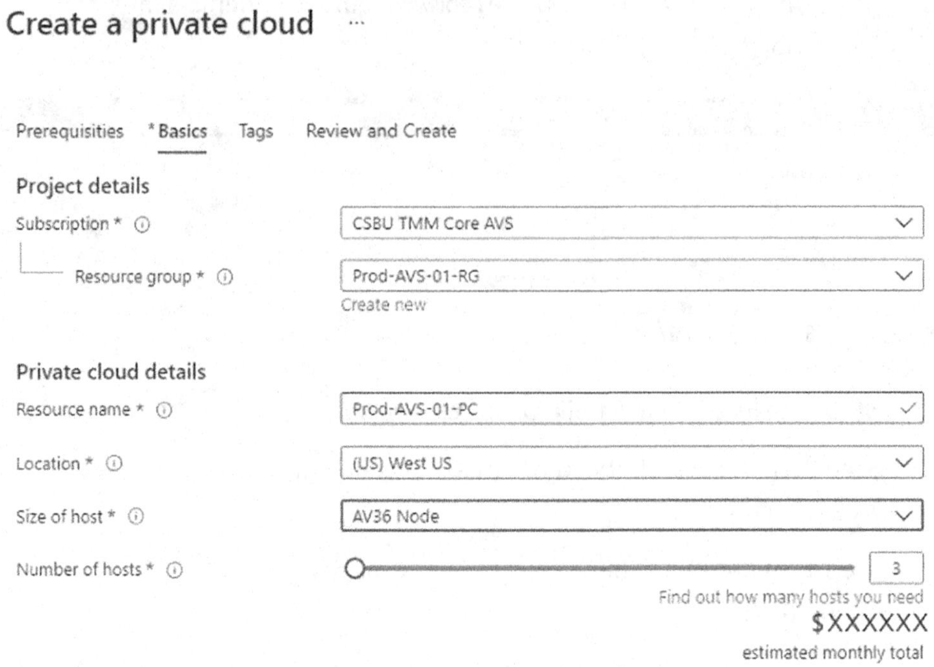

Create a private cloud ...

Prerequisities   *Basics   Tags   Review and Create

Project details

Subscription * ⓘ   CSBU TMM Core AVS ⌄

⌐
    Resource group * ⓘ   Prod-AVS-01-RG ⌄
                  Create new

Private cloud details

Resource name * ⓘ   Prod-AVS-01-PC ✓

Location * ⓘ   (US) West US ⌄

Size of host * ⓘ   AV36 Node ⌄

Number of hosts * ⓘ   ◯————————————————— 3

                                  Find out how many hosts you need

                                      $XXXXXX
                                   estimated monthly total

Figure 5-13. *Create a private cloud - basics*

Enter values for the fields as listed in Table 5-3

Table 5-3. *Basic Information to Create a Private Cloud*

Field	Value
Subscription	Choose the subscription you plan to use for the deployment.
	An Azure subscription needs to adhere to one of the following options for cloud users:
	• Subscribe to an Azure Enterprise Agreement with Microsoft.
	• An Azure plan or Azure subscription is managed by a cloud solution provider.
	• A Microsoft Customer Agreement with Microsoft
Resource group	Choose the resource group for your private cloud resources.
Resource name	Provide the name of your Azure VMware Solution private cloud.
Location	Choose a location, such as east us. This is the region you defined during the planning phase.

(continued)

Table 5-3. (*continued*)

Field	Value
Size of host	Configure your cloud with the right specifications. Choose AV36.
Number of hosts	This number of ESXi hosts will make up your default private cloud cluster. It shows the number of hosts allocated for the private cloud cluster. The default value is 3, which can be raised or lowered after deployment.
Address block for private cloud	Provide a block of IP addresses for the private cloud. This network is used by vCenter Server and NSX-T Manager for cluster management. For example, 10.170.0.0/22 is the /22 address space. An Azure VNet address should be unique and not overlap with an on-premises or another Azure VNet.

Step 6: Once finished, select Review + create. On the next screen, verify the information entered. If the information is all correct, select Create, as depicted in Figure 5-14.

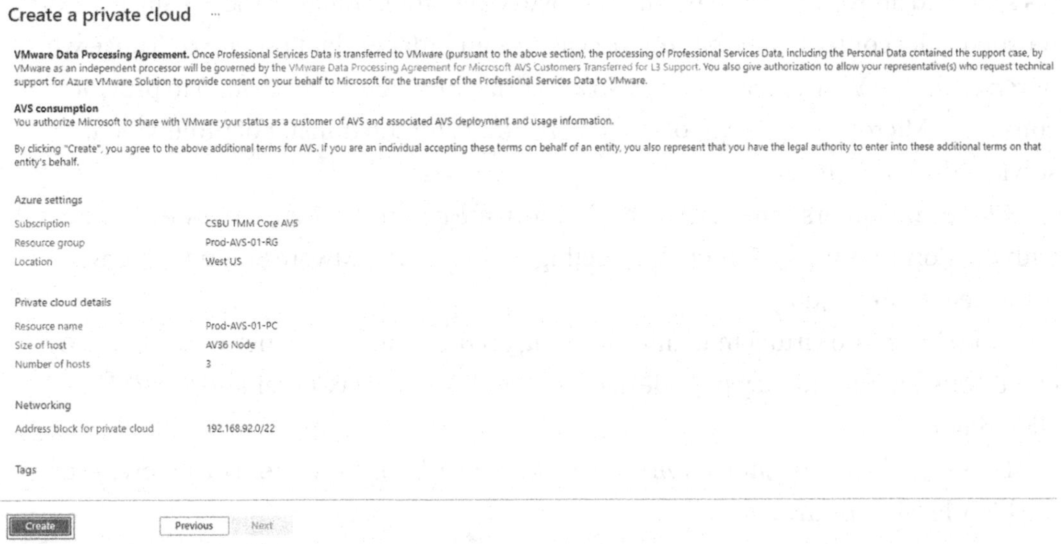

Create a private cloud

VMware Data Processing Agreement. Once Professional Services Data is transferred to VMware (pursuant to the above section), the processing of Professional Services Data, including the Personal Data contained the support case, by VMware as an independent processor will be governed by the VMware Data Processing Agreement for Microsoft AVS Customers Transferred for L3 Support. You also give authorization to allow your representative(s) who request technical support for Azure VMware Solution to provide consent on your behalf to Microsoft for the transfer of the Professional Services Data to VMware.

AVS consumption
You authorize Microsoft to share with VMware your status as a customer of AVS and associated AVS deployment and usage information.

By clicking "Create", you agree to the above additional terms for AVS. If you are an individual accepting these terms on behalf of an entity, you also represent that you have the legal authority to enter into these additional terms on that entity's behalf.

Azure settings

Subscription	CSBU TMM Core AVS
Resource group	Prod-AVS-01-RG
Location	West US

Private cloud details

Resource name	Prod-AVS-01-PC
Size of host	AV36 Node
Number of hosts	3

Networking

Address block for private cloud	192.168.92.0/22

Tags

[Create]   [Previous]   Next

Figure 5-14. *Create a private cloud - deploy*

Check if the deployment was successful. Click on the private cloud in the cloud consumers' resource group. If the deployment has been successfully completed, it will display Succeeded.

Note   Usually, this step takes 3-4 hours, and adding a single node takes between 30-45 minutes in the same cluster.

At the time of writing this book, AVS does not support data retention or extraction from AVS clusters. Once an AVS cluster is deleted, all data and configuration settings are destroyed, including public IP addresses, and all running workloads are terminated.

If a cloud consumer contacts Microsoft for technical support for an Azure VMware Solution and Microsoft is required to engage VMware for assistance with the issue, Microsoft will transfer the professional services data and the personal data contained in the support case to VMware. VMware and Microsoft have signed a Support Transfer Agreement that outlines the terms and conditions of the transfer of professional services data between them. The consent of cloud consumers for the transfer of professional services and data to VMware will be obtained and recorded by Microsoft before the transfer takes place.

The VMware Data Processing Agreement for Microsoft AVS Customers Transferred for L3 Support will apply once the professional services data is transferred to VMware (as specified above). VMware will then process the professional services data, including personal data contained in the support case, as an independent processor. Those who purchase Azure VMware Solutions also authorize their representative(s) to provide consent to Microsoft on behalf of cloud consumers for the transfer of professional services data to VMware.

Cloud consumers cannot manage their private clouds via Azure VMware Solution with their on-premises vCenter. Connecting to the Azure VMware Solution vCenter instance requires a jump box.

Jump boxes are virtual machines running on the same virtual network created by cloud consumers, and they provide access to both VMware vCenter and the VMware NSX Manager.

Let's create a new Windows virtual machine in Microsoft Azure. The following are the high-level steps involved:

> **Step 1:** Log into a personal or business account on the Azure portal at `https://portal.azure.com/`
>
> and select Create a Resource. Figure 5-15 depicts the Azure portal.

Figure 5-15. *Azure portal*

Step 2: Create a VM. You can choose an image from the Azure marketplace or customize your own, as depicted in Figure 5-16.

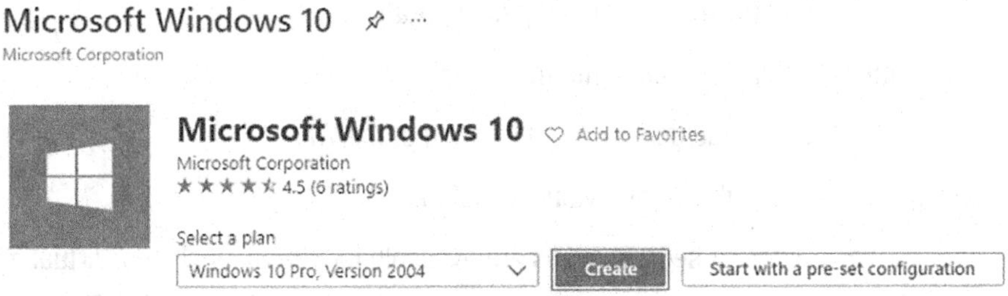

Microsoft Windows 10 📌 ····
Microsoft Corporation

Microsoft Windows 10 ♡ Add to Favorites
Microsoft Corporation
★ ★ ★ ★ ☆ 4.5 (6 ratings)

Select a plan

| Windows 10 Pro, Version 2004 ∨ | **Create** | Start with a pre-set configuration |

Figure 5-16. *Windows 10 – jump box*

To create a virtual machine with default settings, see Figure 5-17.

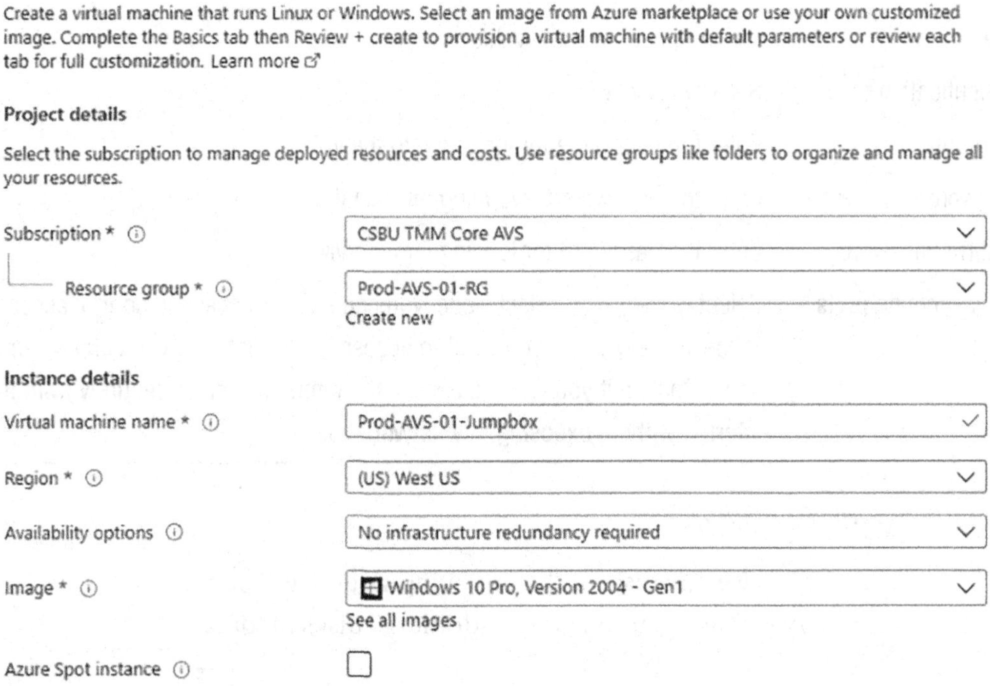

Create a virtual machine that runs Linux or Windows. Select an image from Azure marketplace or use your own customized image. Complete the Basics tab then Review + create to provision a virtual machine with default parameters or review each tab for full customization. Learn more ☐

Project details

Select the subscription to manage deployed resources and costs. Use resource groups like folders to organize and manage all your resources.

Subscription * ⓘ   CSBU TMM Core AVS   ∨

└── Resource group * ⓘ   Prod-AVS-01-RG   ∨
                          Create new

Instance details

Virtual machine name * ⓘ   Prod-AVS-01-Jumpbox   ✓

Region * ⓘ   (US) West US   ∨

Availability options ⓘ   No infrastructure redundancy required ∨

Image * ⓘ   🖼 Windows 10 Pro, Version 2004 - Gen1 ∨
                          See all images

Azure Spot instance ⓘ   ☐

Figure 5-17. *Create a VM - basics*

Complete the Basics tab, then Review + create, as listed in
Table 5-4.

***Table 5-4.** Information to Create a Project*

Field	Value
Subscription	This value is prepopulated with the subscription belonging to the resource group.
Resource group	This value is prepopulated for the current resource group, which you created in the preceding configuration.
Virtual machine name	Enter a unique name for the VM.
Region	Select the geographical location of the VM.
Availability options	Leave the default value selected.
Security	Different security types are available for virtual machines. Virtual machines in Azure generation 2 are more secure due to features like Trusted Launch and Confidential Virtual Machines. Furthermore, additional security features do not support backup, managed disks, or ephemeral OS disks.
Image	Select the VM image.
Size	Leave the default size value.
Authentication type	Select Password.
Username	Enter the username for logging into the VM.
Password	Enter the password for logging into the VM.
Confirm Password	Enter the password for logging into the VM.
Public inbound ports	Select None. If you select None, you can use JIT access to control access to the VM only when you want to access it. Alternatively, you can use an Azure Bastion if you want to access the jump box server securely from the Internet without exposing any network port.

Step 3: Add Disks.

Azure VMs have one disk for the operating system and one for
temporary storage. You can attach additional disks for data
storage.

Step 4: Configure Networking.

By configuring network interface card settings, you can define network connectivity for your virtual machines. You can control ports and inbound and outbound communication with security group rules or place them behind a current load balancing solution. Figure 5-18 depicts the network interface of a VM.

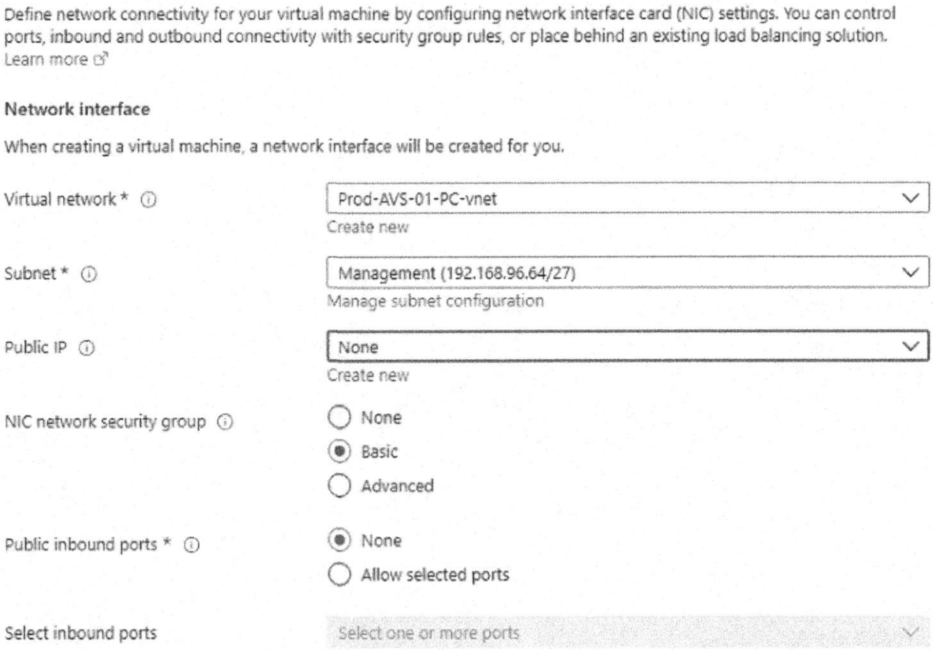

Define network connectivity for your virtual machine by configuring network interface card (NIC) settings. You can control ports, inbound and outbound connectivity with security group rules, or place behind an existing load balancing solution. Learn more ☐

Network interface

When creating a virtual machine, a network interface will be created for you.

Virtual network * ⓘ	Prod-AVS-01-PC-vnet ▽
	Create new
Subnet * ⓘ	Management (192.168.96.64/27) ▽
	Manage subnet configuration
Public IP ⓘ	None ▽
	Create new
NIC network security group ⓘ	◯ None
	◉ Basic
	◯ Advanced
Public inbound ports * ⓘ	◉ None
	◯ Allow selected ports
Select inbound ports	Select one or more ports ▽

Figure 5-18. *Create a VM - networking*

Step 5: Configure Management Settings.

Step 6: Configure Advanced Settings.

Step 7: Configure Tags.

Step 8: Review and create.

Figure 5-19 depicts the created VM.

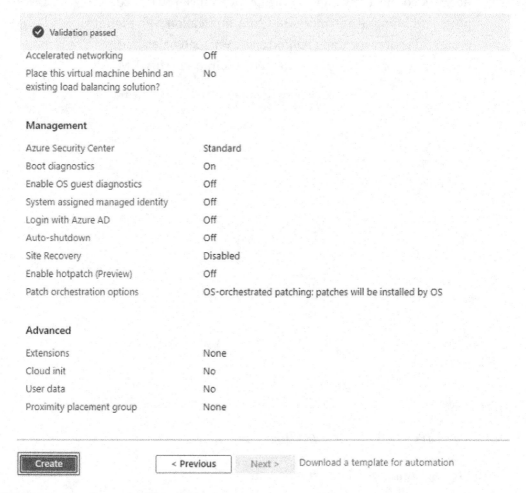

Figure 5-19. *Create a VM - complete*

Step 9: Download a template.

Step 10: Complete deployment.

Step 11: Document the IP address of the new VM.

Step 12: RDP/SSH to the new VM.

The VM will act as jump box; from the jump box, sign into vSphere Client with VMware vCenter SSO using a CloudAdmin username and verify that the user interface displays successfully.

Stage 3: Connect to a New Azure VNet

In this stage, AVS administrators need to determine whether to use an existing or new ExpressRoute virtual network gateway in the planning phase.

You should deploy a VNet close to your hosts with an ExpressRoute virtual network gateway if you plan to scale Azure VMware Solution hosts using Azure disk pools.

You might undergo the following scenarios. If you don't already have a virtual network, then create a virtual network, gateway subnet, and virtual network gateway, and then connect ExpressRoute to the gateway.

If you do already have a virtual network without a gateway subnet, then create a gateway subnet and a virtual network gateway and then connect ExpressRoute to the gateway.

If you do already have a virtual network with a gateway subnet, then create virtual network gateway and connect ExpressRoute to the gateway.

Figure 5-20 depicts the deployment workflow for choosing a deployment pattern.

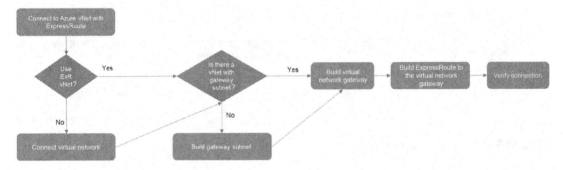

Figure 5-20. *Connect to a New Azure vNET workflow*

Stage 1: Deploy a Virtual Network in Azure via Azure Portal

A VNet in Azure is the fundamental building block for private networks. Azure VMs communicate with one another over VNets. Azure's VNets provide the same benefits as traditional data centers, including scalability, availability, reliability, broad network access, hybrid connectivity, segmentation, isolation, and security.

An Azure VNet represents your own network in the cloud, and an Azure subscription is isolated and logically isolated from the Azure cloud. In Azure, you can create and manage virtual private networks. The VNets can also be linked to other Azure VNets or your on-premises IT infrastructure to create hybrid or hybrid cross-premises solutions. You can link each VNet you make with another VNet and an on-premises network if the CIDR blocks do not overlap. The administrator can also control VNet settings; subnets can also be segmented.

Azure allows resources to securely communicate with each other, the Internet, and on-premises networks. With a virtual network, it's possible to communicate between your own Azure resources, communicate Azure resources with the Internet, communicate with on-premises resources, filter network traffic, route network traffic, and integrate Azure services.

To create a new virtual network using the Azure portal, take the following steps:

> **Step 1:** Log into a personal or business account into Azure portal at `https://portal.azure.com/`. Figure 5-21 depicts the Azure portal.

Figure 5-21. *Azure portal*

> **Step 2:** Click the Create a resource button in the Azure portal, enter the virtual network name in the search box, and click on create Virtual Network. Figure 5-22 depicts the virtual network.

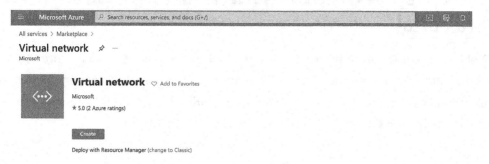

Figure 5-22. *Azure portal- virtual network*

Step 3: In the Basics tab, provide the inputs listed in Table 5-5.

Table 5-5. *Fields and Values for Basics*

Field	Value
Project details	
Subscription	Choose your subscription.
Resource group	Choose a resource group or create a new resource group.
Instance details	
Name	Provide your new VNet as per your defined naming standards.
Region	Choose the region you want to deploy or close to your resource needs.

Once the inputs are provided, click on the Next tab, which takes you to IP addresses.

Step 4: In the IP Addresses tab, provide the inputs depicted in Table 5-6.

Before you get started with IP addresses, you need to determine the first IPv4 address space range of the subnet.

Table 5-6. *Fields and Values for the Networking Configuration*

Field	Value
Project details	
IP addresses space	In CIDR notation, one or more address prefixes define a virtual network's address space. After creating the virtual network, you can add address spaces.
Subnet	Address range in CIDR notation for a subnet. Virtual networks must contain it within their address space. There are no special characters in subnet names except letters, numbers, underscores, periods, or hyphens.

Classless interdomain routing (CIDR) is the format in which you define the internal address space of a virtual network. Any network you connect to must have a unique address space within your subscription.

For this deployment, choose an address space of 10.0.0.0/24 for your first virtual network. The addresses defined in this address space range from 10.0.0.1 - 10.0.0.254.

Next, create a second virtual network and choose an address space of 10.0.0.0/8. The addresses in this address space range from 10.0.0.1 - 10.255.255.254.

Remarkable IP addresses overlap, and as a result, you cannot connect the two virtual networks. Technically it is possible, however, to use 10.0.0.0/16, which ranges from 10.0.0.1 through 10.0.255.254, and 10.1.0.0/16, which ranges from 10.1.0.1 through 10.1.255.254. None of these address spaces overlap with any of your virtual networks.

The virtual network address space can be partitioned into one or more subnets within each address range. If not, you can define custom routes to route traffic between subnets. Alternatively, all virtual networks' address ranges can be combined into one subnet.

In the Add Subnet pane, you must enter the subnet name and the subnet address range. You can include the services you want to connect to the virtual network. Azure service endpoints provide a means of securely connecting to Azure services, thus eliminating the need for a public IP address.

> **Step 5:** On the Security tab, you can choose whether to enable or disable Bastion Host, DDoS protection, and Firewall. If any of these options are allowed, you need to provide additional information for that service.

BastionHost: A new PaaS service inside your virtual network, Azure Bastion is fully platform-managed. RDP/SSH connections are made secure and seamless over SSL directly from the Azure console. You do not need a public IP address for your virtual machines when you connect via Azure Bastion.

Distributed denial of service (DDoS) protection: Standard DDoS protection is available. As part of the standard DDoS protection, the virtual network will be protected against the impacts of a DDoS attack with adaptive tuning, attack notifications, and telemetry. Azure provides essential DDoS protection by default at no additional cost.

Firewall: The Azure Firewall is a managed service from Microsoft that offers network security for Azure VNets.

Step 6: The Tags tab.

Tags are used to organize Azure resources, resource groups, and subscriptions logically. As you apply the same tag to multiple resources and groups, you can categorize them and view consolidated billing.

Step 7: On the Review and Create tab, wait for the validation pass status before you create.

Finalize by clicking on Create to create your virtual network.

Stage 2: Create a Virtual Network Gateway

Now that you've created a virtual network, you'll create a virtual network gateway. Virtual network gateways are added to virtual networks by Azure, which are counted as next hops in routes. A virtual network gateway is listed as a source because it adds routes to the subnet. Consider an on-premises network gateway that exchanges routing information with an Azure virtual network gateway via the border gateway protocol (BGP). As a result, each route propagated from the on-premises network gateway will be added to the routing table. In Azure virtual network gateways, there is a limitation to the number of routes you can propagate; as per Microsoft recommendations, your on-premises network team should translate on-premises routes to the most significant address ranges.

Step 1: In your resource group, select + Add to add a new resource.

Step 2: In the Search the Marketplace text box, type virtual network gateway. Find the Virtual Network resource and select it.

Step 3: On the Virtual Network gateway page, select Create.

Step 4: On the Basics tab of the Create virtual network gateway page, enter values for the fields as listed in Table 5-7, and then select Review + create.

Table 5-7. *Fields and Values for a Network Gateway*

Field	Value
Subscription	This value is prepopulated with the subscription belonging to the resource group
Resource group	This value is prepopulated for the current resource group, which you created in the preceding configuration
Name	Enter a unique name for the virtual network gateway.
Region	Select the geographical location of the VM.
Gateway type	Select ExpressRoute.
SKU	Leave the default value: Standard.
Virtual network	Select the virtual network you created previously. If you don't see the virtual network, make sure the gateway's region matches the region of your virtual network.
Gateway subnet address range	This value is populated when you select the virtual network. Don't change the default value.
Public IP address	Select Create new.

Step 5: Verify that the details are correct and select Build to start the deployment of your virtual network gateway.

Once the deployment finishes, move to the next section to attach your ExpressRoute connection to the virtual network gateway collecting your Azure VMware Solution private cloud.

Stage 3: Connect ExpressRoute to the Virtual Network Gateway

Now that you've configured a virtual network gateway, you'll add a connection with it and your Azure VMware Solution private cloud.

Many cloud consumers also use Azure VPN Gateway to connect Azure VNets to on-premises resources. A VPN may not meet the requirements of every cloud consumer. For example, a VPN is limited to a maximum bandwidth of 1.25 Gbps. Cloud users who require higher speeds should avoid VPNs. In contrast, all traffic is also routed over the public internet, which can be prohibitively expensive for some end users.

In addition to meeting many of the enterprise organization's needs, including security and resiliency, Microsoft Azure ExpressRoute, which uses private connectivity, is an alternative method of connecting cloud consumers' on-premises networks to Microsoft Azure services.

Connectivity providers connect cloud consumers' on-premises infrastructure with Microsoft cloud services via an ExpressRoute circuit. ExpressRoute circuit types are available to cloud consumers. Each circuit can be connected to the premises of cloud consumers through a connectivity provider, either within the same region or in another.

Using ExpressRoute helps cloud consumers connect their on-premises infrastructure to the Azure Cloud. Network service providers offer a wide variety of services according to the cloud consumers' choice of location.

The ExpressRoute connectivity provider's infrastructure is directly connected to Microsoft's network edge, allowing organizations worldwide to gain performance advantages. Since the Internet is typically provided through partnerships and relationships among telecommunication companies, cloud consumers may experience suboptimal connectivity even with ExpressRoute.

When cloud consumers choose a dedicated and private connection with a connectivity provider, it helps ensure that the provider is directly responsible for setting up an optimized connection with the Microsoft network. An optimizing experience is more likely to result from this responsibility.

To connect ExpressRoute to the virtual network gateway using the Azure portal, take the following steps:

Step 1: You can request an ExpressRoute authorization key here:

- In the Azure portal, click on VMware Solution. Choose Manage ➤ Connectivity ➤ ExpressRoute, and then select and request an authorization key.

- Provide a name for it and select Create.

  - The key will take about 30 seconds to generate. A newly created key appears in the list of authorization keys for the private cloud.

  - You will need the authorization key and ExpressRoute ID for peering. The authorization key vanishes after some time, so duplicate it as soon as it appears.

Step 2: Then select Connections > + Add from the virtual
network gateway you plan to use. On the Add connection
wizard, enter the values depicted in Table 5-8 and choose OK.

Figure 5-23 depicts the Azure VMware Solution connectivity.

Figure 5-23. *Azure VMware Solution - connectivity*

Table 5-8. *Fields and Values to Connect to ExpressRoute*

Field	Value
Name	Enter a name for the connection.
Connection type	Select ExpressRoute.
Redeem authorization	Ensure this box is selected.
Virtual network gateway	The virtual network gateway you intend to use
Authorization key	Paste the authorization key you copied earlier.
Peer circuit URI	Paste the ExpressRoute ID you copied earlier.

The connection between the ExpressRoute circuit and the VNet is created.

Stage 4: Connect to On-Premises VMware

This is where you connect your VMware environment on-premises to the Azure VMware Solution. Connect your on-premises domain to the private cloud of Azure VMware Solution with ExpressRoute Global Reach. The ExpressRoute Global Reach connection is made between your private cloud ExpressRoute circuit and an existing ExpressRoute connection to your on-premises environments.

To enable management access to Azure VMware Solution, ensure that additional routes containing your on-premises networks are advertised in addition to the default route to Azure (0.0.0.0/0). To ensure the successful operation of Azure VMware Solution, a 0.0.0.0/0 route will be discarded by the management network. Figure 5-24 depicts the Azure VMware Solution connection to on-premises SDDC.

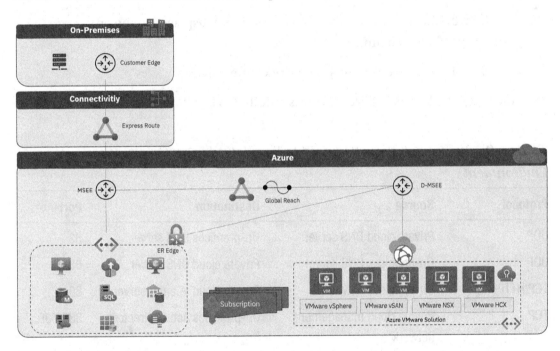

Figure 5-24. *Azure VMware Solution - connecting to an on-premises VMware SDDC*

Phase 1: Build an Azure ExpressRoute auth key in the on-premises ExpressRoute circuit.

Step 1: Log into Azure portal.

Step 2: Click on Authorizations.

Step 3: Provide the name for the authorization key and select Save.

Step 4: Once built, the new key appears in the list of authorization keys for the circuit.

Step 5: Keep a note of the authorization key and the ExpressRoute ID. You need them in phase 2 to complete the peering.

Phase 2: Peer Azure VMware private cloud to on-premises VMware environment.

Step 1: From the AVS private cloud, under Manage, select Connectivity ➤ ExpressRoute Global Reach ➤ Add.

Step 2: Provide the ExpressRoute ID and the authorization key created in phase 1.

Step 3: Choose Create. The new connection is displayed in the on-premises cloud connections list.

Step 4: Validate on-premises network connectivity.

Table 5-9 provides a list of firewall ports required to be allowed.

Table 5-9. *All Firewall Ports Required to Be Allowed in an On-Premises Environment*

Protocol	Source	Destination	Port
UDP	Private cloud DNS server	On-premises DNS server	53
UDP	On-premises DNS server	Private cloud DNS server	53
TCP(HTTP)	On-premises network	Private cloud vCenter server	80
TCP	Private cloud management network	On-premises Active Directory	389/636
TCP	Private cloud management network	On-premises Active Directory Global Catalog	3268/3269
TCP(HTTPS)	On-premises network	Private cloud vCenter server	443
TCP(HTTPS)	On-premises network	HCX Manager	9443
SSH	Admin network	Hybrid Cloud Manager	22

(continued)

Table 5-9. (*continued*)

Protocol	Source	Destination	Port
TCP(HTTPS)	HCX Manager	Cloud gateway	8123
HTTP TCP(HTTPS) ·	HCX Manager	Cloud gateway	9443
TCP(HTTPS)	Cloud gateway	L2C	443
TCP	Cloud gateway	ESXi hosts	80,902
UDP	Cloud gateway (local)	Cloud gateway (remote)	4500
UDP	Cloud gateway (local)	Cloud gateway (remote)	500
TCP	On-premises vCenter server network	Private cloud management network	8000

AVS Essential Post Deployment Information

This section covers post-deployment considerations with Azure VMware Solution. You'll read the entire end-to-end deployment essentials of the private cloud in the last section of this chapter.

To ensure the environment is fully ready to support workloads on the Azure side, you must implement the proper role-based access controls. That private cloud object contains the keys to the CloudAdmin credential, so anyone who has access to that object can log into vCenter.

Your vSphere admins may need access to that object through the Azure portal for administrative purposes, so you don't want to restrict that too much. There are some features in that portal that aren't available elsewhere. Creating placement policies, storage policies, VM configurations, and external identity sources are among them.

To change the DHCP and DNS services on the default UH Tier-one gateway, you must have private cloud access. You will not be able to make those changes if you limit the vSphere admins.

In addition, VMware and Microsoft recommend purchasing reserved instances for your AVS hosts, which are likely to persist. The on-demand pricing for these hosts is usually not justified.

You may also want to create budgets and alerts to track your spending. Because you pay a set price per month for those hosts, you may make a budget that is a little over that cost so you can track if any other resources are being spun up in your environment. Resources consistency controls are also essential.

Azure policies allow you to enforce standards and assess compliance. In addition to defining what services are allowed in which regions, you can force a tagging strategy, force monitoring configuration, set alarms for expired keys, and other things. Tagging is extremely useful in making sense of resources at scale, so I suggest you also look at your tagging policy.

AVS administrators can use tags for resource management, cost management optimization, operations management, security governance, regulatory compliance classification, support automation, and workload optimization.

It is also possible to use resource locks. This is a quick solution to prevent a terrible day. The resource group that holds the AVS private cloud object can be resource-locked.

In addition to Azure considerations, you must also consider AVS- and vSphere-specific considerations. For example, role-based access control must be configured. Ask the following questions:

- How do we configure those identity sources?

- How do we provide different access levels to our domain users and groups next?

- How do we prepare to host your VMs in the private cloud?

DHCP configuration, DNS forwarding, and building network segments are things you need help with. Setting up a content library is also critical, whether you create a new content library, upload ISO images, or subscribe to an on-premises content library and pull in your gold images and standard templates.

The last benefit is that you have almost full admin access through the CloudAdmin account by integrating the vCenter server with management tools such as monitoring, logging, and backup. Unlike the administrative account, this one has fewer privileges. In a managed service, you won't be able to manage the appliances, the vSphere clusters, ESXi hosts, or particular components within vCenter.

Your admin account will not be accessible. CloudAdmin accounts should be used only for initial setup and emergency purposes; they should not be used for daily operations. You can access the CloudAdmin password via the Azure portal once the private cloud has been deployed.

Using the Azure Cloud Shell, you can also change the password of the CloudAdmin. As AVS supports LDAP or Active Directory with or without SSL today, configuring identity sources is critical. Active Directory may be on-premises or within the AVS private cloud, even though Microsoft and VMware highly recommend SSL.

VMware and Microsoft recommend deploying an ad instance in the private cloud if there is a connectivity issue between the cloud and on-premises.

CloudAdmin roles are equal to or less privileged than those created by AVS. Adding domain users and groups to custom roles will grant them access to vCenter once an identity source has been configured.

You access the NSX manager using the local admin account when using NSX-T. Using this account, you can manage t0 and t1 gateway network segments.

NSX manager should limit the admin account as much as possible for all NSX services, like with vCenter. You can add an identity source and use existing roles and create custom roles to assign admin passwords automatically generated during the private cloud deployment to domain users and groups. Still, if you want to change the admin password, it is impossible to do it via the Azure portal. You'll need to create a support request.

Configure NSX-T Data Center Network Components

From the Azure portal or NSX-T Manager, you can configure an NSX-T network segment after deploying Azure VMware Solution. NSX-T Manager, vCenter Server, and Azure VMware Solution display the segments once they are configured. An NSX-T Tier-0 gateway in Active/Active mode is preinstalled by default in NSX-T Data Center and a default NSX-T Tier-1 gateway is in Active/Standby mode. Gateways enable east-west and north-south connectivity among segments (logical switches).

The NSX-T Data Center objects can be configured from the Azure portal after deploying Azure VMware Solution. It presents a simplified view of NSX-T Data Center operations to a VMware administrator who needs daily updates and targets users unfamiliar with NSX-T Manager.

The Azure VMware Solution console offers four options, listed in Table 5-10, for configuring NSX-T Data Center components.

Table 5-10. *Four Options for Configuring NSX-T*

Options	Descriptions
Segments	NSX-T Manager and vCenter Server segments can be created.
DHCP	If you plan to use DHCP, you will need a DHCP server or a DHCP relay.
Port mirroring	Set up port mirroring to troubleshoot network issues.
DNS	Create a DNS forwarder to route DNS requests to a designated DNS server for resolution.

Private clouds powered by Azure VMware Solution, with access to NSX-T Manager and vCenter Server.

Use NSX-T Manager to Add a Network Segment

VMs created in vCenter Server are placed into NSX-T network segments and are visible in vCenter Server.

Step 1: In NSX-T Manager, select Networking ➤ Segments, and then select Add Segment.

Step 2: Enter a name for the segment.

Step 3: Select the Tier-1 Gateway (TNTxx-T1) as the Connected Gateway and leave the Type as Flexible.

Step 4: Select the preconfigured overlay Transport Zone (TNTxx-OVERLAY-TZ) and then select Set Subnets.

Step 5: Enter the gateway IP address and then select Add.

Step 6: Select Apply and then Save.

Step 7: Select No to decline the option to continue configuring the segment.

Verify the New Network Segment

Verify the presence of the new network segment. In this example, ls01 is the new network segment.

> **Step 1:** In NSX-T Manager, select Networking ➤ Segments.

> **Step 2:** In vCenter Server, select Networking ➤ SDDC-Datacenter.

For lookup and IP address assignment, applications and workloads running in the AVS private cloud environment require name resolution and DHCP services. You will need a proper DHCP and DNS infrastructure for these services, and you can configure a virtual machine to provide them in your private cloud environment.

Instead of routing broadcast DHCP traffic over the WAN back to on-premises, use the DHCP service included in NSX or a local DHCP server in the private cloud.

DHCP servers provide DHCP clients with IP addresses, subnet masks, default gateways, DNS, and so on automatically. Common uses of DHCP include:

- Creating DHCP servers on a segment for handling DHCP requests

- Creating a DHCP relay service on a router port

Don't associate a DHCP server and DHCP relay service with the same segment if you want.

DHCP server dynamically distributes network configuration parameters, such as IP addresses. Common DHCP configurations are

- Gateways are always connected to distributed routers (DRs).

- Gateways with routing services, such as NAT or DHCP configured, have one or more service routers (SRs).

- DHCP must be configured on Tier-1 or Tier-0 gateways using an NSX Edge cluster.

- Tier-1 and Tier-0 gateways can be configured with DHCP servers and relay servers.

Create a DHCP Server or Relay

DHCP servers and relays can be created directly from the Azure VMware Solution in the Azure portal. You create a Tier-1 gateway when you deploy Azure VMware Solution so the DHCP server or relay can connect to it. Your segments where you specified DHCP ranges will also be included. Once you have created a DHCP server or DHCP relay, you must define a subnet or range on the segment level to consume it.

Step 1: In an Azure VMware Solution private cloud, under Workload Networking, choose DHCP ➤ Add.

Step 2: Choose either DHCP Server or DHCP Relay and then provide a name for the server or relay and three IP addresses.

Step 3: Finish the DHCP configuration by providing DHCP ranges on the logical segments and selecting OK.

Use NSX-T to Host a DHCP Server

You must create a DHCP server and a relay service if you want to host your DHCP server in the NSX-T Data Center. Then you specify the range of DHCP IP addresses for your network segment.

Step 1: Create a DHCP server.

Step 2: In NSX-T Manager, Choose Networking ➤ DHCP, and then select Add Server.

Step 3: Choose DHCP for the Server Type, provide the server name and IP address, and select Save.

Step 4: Choose Tier 1 Gateways, choose the vertical ellipsis on the Tier-1 gateway, and then select Edit.

Step 5: Choose No IP Allocation Set to add a subnet.

For Type, select DHCP Local Server.

For the DHCP Server, select Default DHCP, and then select Save.

Step 6: Select Save again and then select Close Editing.

Add a Network Segment

Step 1: In NSX-T Manager, select Networking ➤ Segments, and then select Add Segment.

Step 2: Enter a name for the segment.

Step 3: Select the Tier-1 Gateway (TNTxx-T1) as the Connected Gateway and leave the Type as Flexible.

Step 4: Select the preconfigured overlay Transport Zone (TNTxx-OVERLAY-TZ) and then select Set Subnets.

Step 5: Enter the gateway IP address and then select Add.

Step 6: Select Apply and then Save.

Step 7: Select No to decline the option to continue configuring the segment.

Define the DHCP IP Address Range

When you create a relay to a DHCP server, you also specify the DHCP IP address range.

Step 1: In NSX-T Manager, select Networking ➤ Segments.

Step 2: Select the vertical ellipsis on the segment name and select Edit.

Step 3: Select Set Subnets to specify the DHCP IP address for the subnet.

Modify the gateway IP address if needed and enter the DHCP range IP.

Step 4: Select Apply and then Save. The segment is assigned a DHCP server pool.

Build a DHCP Relay Service

Any non-NSX-based DHCP service should utilize a DHCP relay. DHCP is available in VMware Solution in Azure, in Azure IaaS, or on-premises.

Step 1: In NSX-T Manager, select Networking ➤ DHCP, and then select Add Server.

Step 2: Select DHCP Relay for the Server Type, provide the server's name and IP address, and select Save.

Step 3: Select Tier 1 Gateways, select the vertical ellipsis on the Tier-1 gateway, and then select Edit.

Step 4: Select No IP Allocation Set to define the IP address allocation, or type select DHCP Server.

Step 5: For the DHCP Server, select DHCP Relay, and then select Save.

Step 6: Select Save again and then select Close Editing.

Specify the DHCP IP Address Range

Step 1: In NSX-T Manager, choose Networking ➤ Segments.

Step 2: Choose the vertical ellipsis on the segment name and Choose Edit.

Step 3: Choose Set Subnets to specify the DHCP IP address for the subnet.

Step 4: Modify the gateway IP address if required and provide the DHCP range IP.

Step 5: Choose Apply and then Save.

The segment is assigned a DHCP server pool.

DNS is a computer application that implements a service for resolving a computer name to an IP address. Tier-1 and Tier-0 gateways can be configured as DNS forwarders in the DNS relay mode using NSX-T Data Center.

NSX-T Data Center can forward DNS client requests to external DNS servers through the DNS forwarder feature:

- DNS forwarders are servers that forward requests for DNS records to upstream DNS servers.

- DNS forwarders cache responses received from upstream DNS servers.

- Unless the cached entry (TTL) expires, the DNS forwarder can respond to the subsequent request without contacting the upstream DNS server.

- DNS forwarding can be configured on Tier-1 and Tier-0 gateways.

- On Tier-1 and Tier-0 gateways, the DNS forwarder acts as a DNS relay, forwarding client requests to external DNS servers.

As a result of using the local cache for DNS queries, the DNS forwarder reduces the load on upstream name servers and improves system performance.

By delegating the internal DNS resolution to the internal DNS servers, you can also hide internal DNS information from external networks.

Create a DNS Forwarder

Step 1: In NSX-T Manager, Choose ➤ IP Address Management ➤ DNS.

Step 2: Click the DNS Services tab and configure details.

The following details must be configured:

- Provide a name.

- Choose the Tier0/Tier1 gateway.

- DNS service IP: This IP address is used to listen for DNS requests.

- Default zone: DNS client requests are forwarded to the default zone unless the conditional zone is configured to relay them.

- Below are the parameters of the default zone:
  - **Zone name:** Name for the DNS forwarder.
  - **Domain:** The default value is ANY and it is the default DNS forwarder for all domains except for the ones listed in the fully qualified domain name (FQDN) zone.
  - **DNS servers:** IP addresses of upstream DNS servers
  - **Source IP:** The IP address that the DNS forwarder utilizes as the source IP address to transmit the DNS query to outward DNS servers and obtain the DNS reply from outward DNS servers.
  - **Description:** Provide a description for the DNS forwarder.
  - **Tags:** Optional tags for the DNS forwarder

Configure the DNS Services and DNS Zones

Step 1: In NSX-T Manager, choose IP Address Management ➤ DNS.

Step 2: Click the DNS Services tab and configure details.

Step 3: Click the vertical ellipsis icon next to the FQDN Zones box.

Step 4: Configure the FQDN zones and enter the details.

- **Zone name:** Name for the DNS forwarder.
- **Domain:** The default value is ANY and it is the default DNS forwarder for all domains except for the ones listed in the FQDN zone.
- **DNS servers:** IP addresses of upstream DNS servers
- **Source IP:** The IP address that the DNS forwarder utilizes as the source IP address to transmit the DNS query to outward DNS servers and obtain the DNS reply from outward DNS servers
- **Description:** Provide a description for the DNS forwarder.
- **Tags:** Optional tags for the DNS forwarder

Any client request for the vclass.local domain name is forwarded to the DNS server specified in the FQDN zone if the FQDN zone is configured with the domain name.

Table 5-11 lists firewall ports required to be allowed.

Table 5-11. *All Firewall Ports Required Between the Source and the Destination for NSX-T*

Protocol	Source	Destination	Port
TCP	Management clients	NSX Autonomous Edge Nodes	443
TCP	NSX Manager	External LDAP server	389,636
TCP	NSX Manager	NSX Manager	9000, 5671, 1234, 443, 8080
TCP	NSX Managers, vCenter server	NSX Manager	8080
TCP	NSX Managers,	NSX Manager	5671, 1234, 1235, 443
TCP	ESXi host	NSX Manager	1234
UDP	NSX-T Data Center transport node	NSX-T Data Center transport node	3784, 3785
TCP	NSX Manager	KVM host	443
TCP	NSX Manager	ESXi host	443
TCP	Bare metal server host	NSX Manager	5671, 1235, 1234, 8080
TCP	ESXi host	NSX Manager	443
TCP	ESXi host	NSX Manager	443
TCP	ESXi host	NSX Manager	8080
TCP	ESXi host	NSX Manager	1235
UDP	SNMP servers	NSX Manager	161
TCP	Management clients	NSX Manager	443
TCP	Management clients	NSX Manager	22
UDP	NTP servers	NSX Manager	123
TCP	NSX Manager	vCenter server	443
TCP	NSX Manager	vCenter server	80
UDP	NSX Manager	Traceroute destination	33434-33523
TCP	NSX Manager	Intermediate and root CA servers	80

(continued)

Table 5-11. (*continued*)

Protocol	Source	Destination	Port
UDP	NSX Manager	Syslog servers	6514
TCP	NSX Manager	Syslog servers	6514
UDP	NSX Manager	Syslog servers	514
TCP	NSX Manager	Syslog servers	514
UDP	NSX Manager	SNMP servers	161, 162
TCP	NSX Manager	SNMP servers	161, 162
UDP	NSX Manager	NTP servers	123
TCP	NSX Manager	Management SCP servers	22
UDP	NSX Manager	DNS servers	53
TCP	NSX Manager	DNS servers	53

Deploy a Disaster Recovery Solution Using VMware HCX

There is no longer a predeployment of VMware HCX Advanced and Cloud Manager in Azure VMware Solution. You can install HCX Connector as an Azure portal add-on, but you will still have to download and deploy the OVA on your on-premises vCenter Server.

With VMware HCX, you can pair up to 25 sites (on-premises-to-cloud or cloud-to-cloud). You can open a support request if you want HCX Enterprise Edition enabled. You will have 30 days to decide how to proceed after the service is generally available. HCX Enterprise Edition can be turned off or opted out, but HCX Advanced remains part of the node cost.

Without redeploying, HCX Enterprise Edition can be downgraded to HCX Advanced. Ensure you have reverted to an HCX Advanced configuration and are not using the Enterprise features. If you plan to downgrade, ensure there are no scheduled migrations, that RAV and HCX Mobility Optimized Networking (MON) aren't running, and that there are no more than three site pairings.

To enable HCX in Azure VMware Solution, the following is the workflow:

Stage 1: Deploy HCX Advanced through the Azure portal.

Stage 2: Download and deploy the VMware HCX Connector OVA.

Stage 3: Activate HCX Advanced with a license key.

Stage 4: Configure the on-premises HCX Connector.

Stage 1: Deploy HCX Advanced Through the Azure Portal

Step 1: In an Azure VMware Solution private cloud, choose Manage ➤ Add-ons.

Step 2: Choose Get started for HCX Workload Mobility.

Step 3: Choose the I agree with terms and conditions checkbox and then choose Install.

Installing HCX Advanced and configuring Cloud Manager takes approximately 35 minutes. On the Migration using HCX tab, you'll see the URL and HCX keys for the HCX Manager and the on-premises connector site pairing.

After installing the software, click the ADD button if you do not see the HCX key. This will generate the key that can be used for site pairing.

Stage 2: Download and Deploy the VMware HCX Connector OVA

In this step, you will download the VMware HCX Connector OVA file and deploy it on the on-premises vCenter Server.

Step 1: Open a browser window and log into the Azure VMware Solution HCX Manager on https://x.x.x.9 port 443 with the cloudadmin@vsphere.local user credentials. See Figure 5-25.

Note   The HCX Cloud Manager IP (https://x.x.x.9)can be obtained via Connectivity from a private cloud.

Figure 5-25. *Azure VMware Solution - connectivity*

Step 2: Under Administration ➤ System Updates, choose Request Download Link.

Figure 5-26 depicts the Azure VMware Solution HCX.

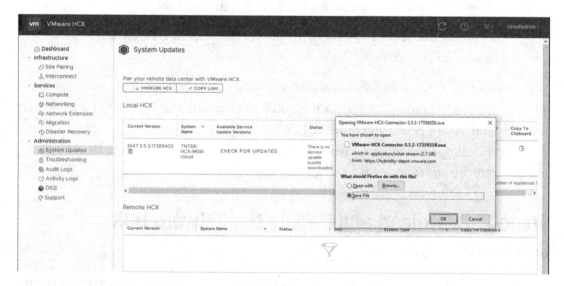

Figure 5-26. *Azure VMware Solution - HCX*

Step 3: Either download or receive a link for the VMware HCX Connector OVA file you deploy on your local vCenter Server.

Step 4: In your on-premises vCenter Server, choose an OVF template to deploy the VMware HCX Connector to your on-premises vSphere cluster.

Step 5: Navigate to and select the OVA file that you downloaded and then select Open.

Step 6: Choose a name and location and choose the resource or cluster where you're deploying the VMware HCX Connector. Then review the details and required resources and select Next.

Step 7: Review license terms, choose the required storage and network and then select Next.

Step 8: Select the VMware HCX management network segment that you defined in the planning stage. Then choose Next.

Step 9: In Customize template, provide all required information and then choose Next.

Step 10: Validate and then choose Finish to deploy the VMware HCX Connector OVA.

Figure 5-27 depicts the Azure VMware Solution HCX deploy OVA.

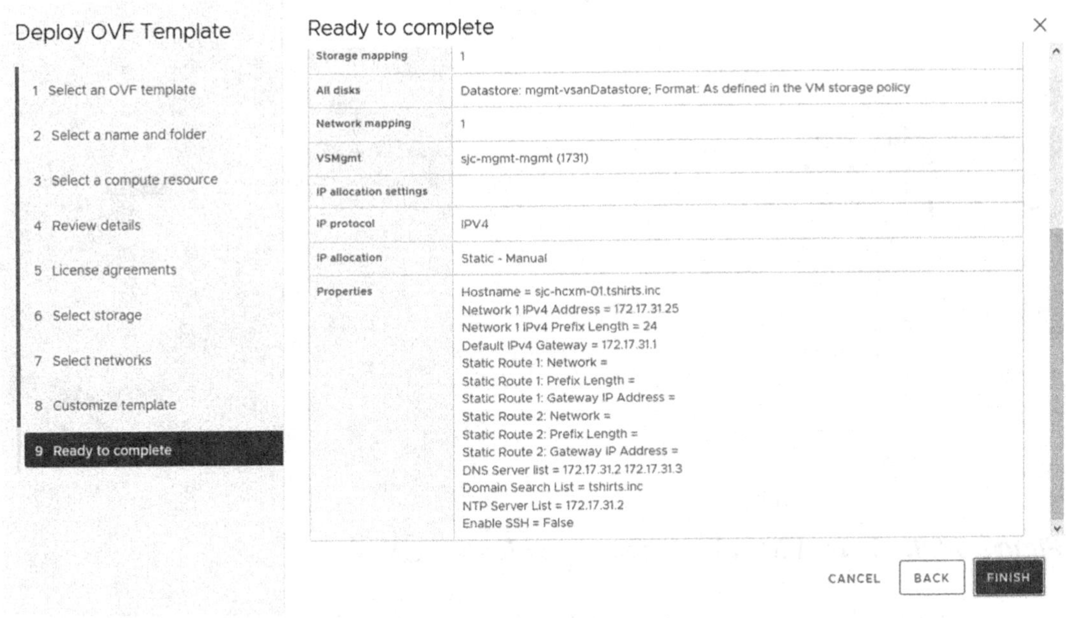

Figure 5-27. *Azure VMware Solution - HCX deploy OVA*

Stage 3: Activate HCX Advanced with a License Key

The VMware HCX Connector OVA is ready to activate after being deployed on-premises and started. A license key can be obtained from the Azure VMware Solution portal, and then it can be activated in VMware HCX Manager. You'll also need a key for every HCX connector you deploy on-premises.

> **Step 1:** In your Azure VMware Solution private cloud, select Manage ➤ Add-ons ➤ Migration using HCX. Then copy the activation key.

> **Step 2:** Log into the on-premises VMware HCX Manager at `https://HCXManagerIP:9443` with the admin credentials. Accommodate the 9443 port number with the VMware HCX Manager IP address.

> **Step 3:** In Licensing, type your key for HCX Advanced Key and choose Activate.

Figure 5-28 depicts Activate HCX page.

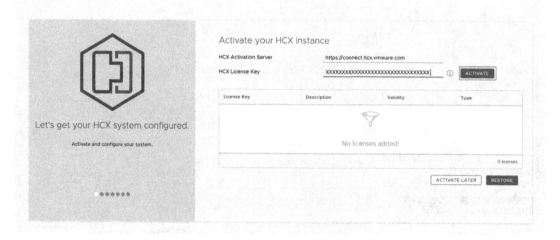

Figure 5-28. *Azure VMware Solution - activate HCX*

> **Step 4:** For Datacenter Location, enter the nearest location for deploying the VMware HCX Manager on-premises. Then choose Continue.

> **Step 5:** In System Name, modify the name or accept the default and choose Continue. Select Yes, Continue.

Step 6: In Connect your vCenter, enter the FQDN or IP address of your vCenter server and the enter credentials and then choose Continue.

Step 7: In Configure SSO/PSC, enter your Platform Services Controller's FQDN or IP address, and choose Continue.

Step 8: Validate that the information entered is correct and choose Restart.

The screen that appears will show vCenter Server as green after restarting. Both vCenter Server and SSO must have the correct configuration parameters, which should be the same as the previous screen.

Stage 4: Configure the On-Premises HCX Connector

After HCX is deployed, you're ready to configure the private cloud VMware HCX Connector for your Azure VMware Solution. Here's how:

Phase 1: Connect your Azure VMware Solution HCX Cloud Manager with your on-premises VMware HCX Connector.

Phase 2: Define the network profile, the compute profile, and the service mesh.

Once you've completed these steps, you'll have a production-ready environment for creating and migrating VMs.

Phase 1: Connect your Azure VMware Solution HCX Cloud Manager with your on-premises VMware HCX Connector

VMware HCX Cloud Manager can be paired with VMware HCX Connector in Azure VMware Solution.

Step 1: Log into your on-premises vCenter Server, and underneath Home, choose HCX.

Step 2: Beneath Infrastructure, choose Site Pairing and choose the Connect To Remote Site.

Figure 5-29 depicts the method to connect to a remote site.

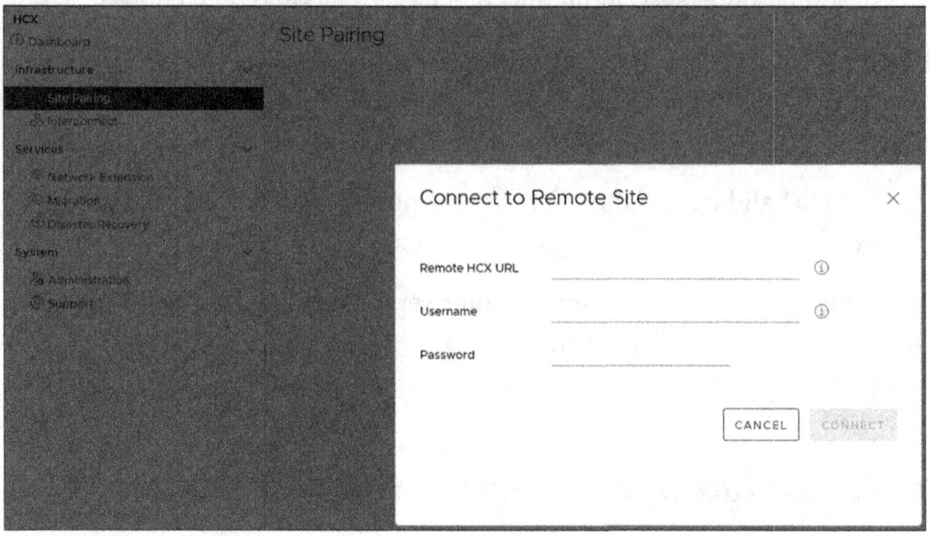

Figure 5-29. *Azure VMware Solution - HCX connect to a remote site*

> **Step 3:** Join the Azure VMware Solution HCX Cloud Manager
> URL or IP address that you copied earlier, `https://x.x.x.9`, and
> the credentials for a user who holds the CloudAdmin role in the
> private cloud. Then choose Connect.

You'll see a screen that shows that your VMware HCX Cloud Manager in Azure
VMware Solution and your on-premises VMware HCX Connector are connected
(paired).

Phase 2: Define the network profile, the compute profile, and the service mesh.

To deploy network profiles

HCX Connector deploys a subset of virtual appliances (automatically) that require
multiple IP segments. During the planning phase, you identify IP segments for your
network profiles. There are four profiles to complete such as Management, vMotion,
Replication and Uplink.

> **Step 1:** Under Infrastructure, choose Interconnect ➤ Multi-Site
> Service Mesh ➤ Network Profiles ➤ Deploy Network Profile.

> **Step 2:** For each network profile, choose the network and port
> group, enter a name, and build the segment's IP pool. Then
> choose Create.

To deploy compute profiles

Step 1: Under Infrastructure, choose Interconnect ➤ Compute Profiles ➤ Build Compute Profile.

Step 2: Provide a name for the profile and choose Continue.

Step 3: Choose the services to enable, such as migration, network extension, or disaster recovery, and then choose Continue.

Step 4: In Choose Service Resources, choose one or more service resources (clusters) to enable the selected VMware HCX services.

Choose the Continue button when you see your on-premises datacenter's clusters.

Step 5: From Select Datastore, choose the datastore storage resource for deploying the VMware HCX Interconnect appliances. Then choose Continue.

The first resource selected in multiple resource selections will be used until its capacity is exhausted by VMware HCX.

Step 6: From the Management Network Profile, choose the management network profile you created in earlier steps. Then choose Continue.

Step 7: From Choose Uplink Network Profile, choose the uplink network profile you deployed in the earlier procedure. Then choose Continue.

Step 8: From Choose vMotion Network Profile, choose the vMotion network profile you deployed in earlier steps. Then choose Continue.

Step 9: From Choose vSphere Replication Network Profile, select the replication network profile you deployed in earlier steps. Then select Continue.

Step 10: From Select Distributed Switches for Network Extensions, choose the switches containing the virtual machines to be migrated to Azure VMware Solution on a layer-2 extended network. Then choose to Continue.

Step 11: Review the connection rules and choose Continue.

Step 12: When done, click on Finish to build the compute profile.

To deploy a service mesh

Step 1: Under Infrastructure, choose Interconnect ➤ Service Mesh ➤ Create Service Mesh.

Step 2: Review the prepopulated sites and then choose Continue.

Step 3: Choose the source and remote compute profiles from the drop-down lists and then choose Continue.

The selections define the resources that VMs can use to consume VMware HCX services.

Step 4: Review the services that will be enabled and then choose Continue.

Step 5: In Advanced Configuration - Override Uplink Network profiles, choose Continue.

Uplink network profiles connect to the network via which the remote site's interconnect appliances can be accessible.

Step 6: In Advanced Configuration - Network Extension Appliance Scale Out, review and choose Continue.

Step 7: In Advanced Configuration - Traffic Engineering, review and perform any modifications that you require and then choose Continue.

Step 8: Review the topology preview and choose Continue.

Step 9: Provide a user-friendly name for this service mesh and choose Finish to complete.

Step 10: Choose View Tasks to monitor the deployment.

Step 11: Validate the service mesh's health by verifying the appliance status.

Step 12: Choose Interconnect ➤ Appliances.

Green indicates that the HCX interconnect tunnel is up. VMware HCX can be used to migrate and protect VMware Azure VMware Solution VMs. Azure VMware Solution supports workload migrations (with or without a network extension). You can still migrate workloads in your vSphere environment, create on-premises networks, and deploy VMs to those networks

As the next step in HCX, let's explore various operations possibilities.

Using VMware HCX disaster recovery solution, you can restore your VMs to an Azure VMware Solution private cloud as a target site for recovery or disaster recovery.

VMware HCX allows replication policies to be configured granularly and finely. The available operations are illustrated in Table 5-12.

Table 5-12. *Operations and Descriptions of Various Functions*

Operations	Description
Reverse	Site B becomes the new source site after a disaster, while Site A becomes the new location of the protected VM.
Pause	Stops replication of the selected VM
Resume	Resumes the replication policy for the selected VM
Remove	Deletes the replication policy associated with the selected virtual machine
Sync Now	Sync source VMs out of bounds

The following scenarios are covered in this section:

- Protecting a virtual machine or a group of virtual machines

- Performing a test recovery of a virtual machine or group of virtual machines

- Recovering one or more virtual machines

- Reverse protection of a virtual machine or a group of virtual machines

Protect a Virtual Machine or a Group of Virtual Machines

Step 1: Log into the VMware vCenter and access the HCX plugin.

Step 2: Select PROTECT VMS under Disaster Recovery.

Step 3: Click on the source site and the remote site. The remote site in this case would be the Azure VMware Solution private cloud.

Step 4: If necessary, choose the Default replication option as listed in Table 5-13

Table 5-13. *Fields and Values to Protect VMs*

Field	Value
Enable compression	Suitable for low-throughput scenarios
Enable quiescence	Stops the VM to ensure that a consistent copy is synced
Destination storage	In an Azure VMware Solution private cloud, which should be a vSAN datastore for the protected VMs
Compute container	A virtual cluster or resource pool
Destination folder	This is an optional destination folder; if no folder is selected, the VMs will be placed directly under the selected cluster.
RPO	There is an interval of synchronization between the source VM and the protected VM, and the interval can range from five minutes to 24 hours.
Snapshot interval	Snapshot interval
Number of snapshots	Number of snapshots within the configured interval

Step 5: Select one or more VMs from the list and configure the replication options as required.

In the default replication options, the Global Settings Policy is automatically applied to the VMs. Select Finish to begin the protection process for each network interface in the selected VM.

Step 6: Monitor the process for each of the selected VMs in the same disaster recovery site.

Step 7: The Snapshots tab lets you view different snapshots after the VM has been protected.

Yellow triangles indicate that the snapshots and virtual machines have not been tested.

When a VM is powered off, it has critical differences from when it is powered on. An image of a virtual machine powered on shows a syncing process. The syncing process begins with the first snapshot, a full copy of the VM, and continues until the next one is completed in the time interval. It synchronizes a copy for a powered-off VM, and then the VM appears inactive, and the protection operation completes. When the VM is powered on, it begins the syncing procedure to the remote site.

Perform a Test Recovery of a Virtual Machine or Group of Virtual Machines

Step 1: Log into VMware vCenter on the remote site that is an ASV private cloud.

Step 2: Within the HCX plugin, in the Disaster Recovery site, choose the vertical ellipses on any VM to display the operations menu and then choose Test Recover VM.

Step 3: Choose the options for the test and the snapshot you want to use to validate different states of the VM.

Step 4: After choosing Test, the recovery operation starts.

Step 5: When completed, you can check the new virtual machine in the AVS private cloud vCenter.

Step 6: After testing has been completed on the virtual machine and applications deployed on it, do a cleanup to remove the test instance.

Recover a VM

Step 1: Log into VMware vCenter on the remote site that is the AVS private cloud and access the HCX plugin.

Step 2: Choose the VM to be recovered from the list, open the ACTIONS menu, and select Recover Virtual machine.

Step 3: Configure the recovery options for each instance and choose Recover to start the recovery operation.

Step 4: Once the recovery operation is finished, the new VM will appear in the remote vCenter Server.

Reverse Protection of a Virtual Machine or a Group of Virtual Machines

Step 1: Log into VMware vCenter on the remote site that is the AVS private cloud and access the HCX plugin.

Step 2: From the list, choose the VM to be replicated back to the primary site, open the ACTIONS menu, and select Reverse.

Step 3: Choose Reverse to begin the replication.

Step 4: Monitor the details section of each virtual machine.

VMware HCX does not include a built-in way to create and automate a disaster recovery plan. VMware HCX provides REST APIs, including those for the Disaster Recovery function, and API specifications are available in VMware HCX Manager via the URL.

These APIs cover operations such as Protect, Recover, Test Recover, Planned Recover, Reverse, Query, Test Cleanup, Pause, Resume, Remove Protection, and Reconfigure in Disaster Recovery.

Table 5-14 lists the firewall ports required to be allowed.

Table 5-14. *All Firewall Ports Required Between the Source and the Destination for HCX*

Protocol	Source	Destination	Port
UDP	HCX-NE in HA Group	HCX NE in HA Group (same site)	3784
TCP	HCX-NE in HA Group	HCX NE in HA Group (same site)	8182
TCP	ESXi Management or Replication Network	Interconnect (HCX-IX)	31031
TCP	vCenter server	Interconnect (HCX-IX)	902
TCP	Interconnect (HCX-IX)	vCenter server	443
TCP	HCX Admin	HCX Manager	22
TCP	HCX Admin	HCX Manager	443
TCP	HCX Admin	HCX Manager	9443
TCP	HCX Manager	Interconnect (HCX-IX)	443
TCP	HCX Manager	Interconnect (HCX-IX)	8123
TCP	HCX Manager	Interconnect (HCX-IX), Network Extension (HCX-NE)	9443
TCP	HCX Manager	ESXi Management Network	80
TCP	HCX Manager	ESXi Management Network	902
TCP/UDP	Interconnect (HCX-IX)	Syslog server	514
TCP	vCenter server	Interconnect (HCX-IX)	443
UDP	Interconnect (HCX-IX)	vCenter server	902
TCP	Interconnect (HCX-IX)	ESXi Management Network	80, 443
TCP	Interconnect (HCX-IX)	ESXi vMotion Network	8000
TCP	ESXi vMotion Network	Interconnect (HCX-IX)	8000
TCP	Interconnect (HCX-IX)	ESXi Management Network	902
TCP	ESXi Management Network	Interconnect (HCX-IX)	902
TCP	HCX Manager (cloud)	vCloud Director	443
TCP	HCX Manager (cloud)	AMQP/RabbitMQ Broker	5672

(continued)

Table 5-14. (*continued*)

Protocol	Source	Destination	Port
TCP	vRealize Operations Manager	HCX Manager	443
TCP	HCX Sentinel agent on a VM	Sentinel Gateway (HCX-SGW)	443
TCP	HCX Manager (cloud/destination)	Sentinel Data Receiver (HCX-SDR	9443
TCP	HCX Manager (connector/source)	Sentinel Gateway (HCX-SGW)	9443
TCP	vCenter server	HCX Manager	443
TCP/UDP	HCX Manager	Syslog server	514
TCP	HCX Manager	NTP server	123
TCP/UDP	HCX Manager	DNS server	53
TCP	HCX Manager	NSX Manager	443
TCP	HCX Manager	vCenter server	7444
TCP	HCX Manager	vCenter server	9443
TCP	HCX Manager	vCenter server	443
TCP	HCX Manager (connector)	HCX Manager (cloud)	443
UDP	Network Extension (HCX-NE at source)	Network Extension (HCX-NE at destination)	4500
UDP	Interconnect (HCX-IX at source)	Interconnect (HCX-IX at destination)	4500
TCP	Interconnect (HCX-IX)	ESXi NFC Network	902
TCP	HCX Manager	ESXi Management Network	443
TCP	HCX Manager (connector and cloud)	hybridity-depot.vmware.com	443
TCP	HCX Manager (connector and cloud)	connect.hcx.vmware.com	443
TCP	Interconnect (HCX-IX at destination)	Sentinel Data Receiver (HCX-SDR at destination)	44500 to 44502

(*continued*)

Table 5-14. (*continued*)

Protocol	Source	Destination	Port
TCP	Sentinel Gateway (HCX-SGW at source)	Interconnect (HCX-IX at source)	44500 to 44600
TCP	HCX-IX-I (initiator at the source)	HCX-IX-R (receiver at the destination)	4500
TCP	HCX-NE-I (initiator at the source)	HCX-NE-R (receiver at the destination)	4500

Deploy a Disaster Recovery Solution Using VMware SRM

This section covers implementing disaster recovery for on-premises and Azure VMware Solution-based VMs. VMware Site Recovery Manager (SRM) and vSphere Replication with Azure VMware Solution are used in this section. SRM and replication servers are installed at the protected and recovery sites.

VMware's SRM is the disaster recovery orchestration solution. In a virtualized environment, it automates the recovery of mission-critical workloads and simplifies the management of recovery and migration plans.

AVS is a Microsoft Azure service that puts VMware compute, networking, and storage on dedicated, bare-metal hosts. AVS delivers a VMware SDDC as a service that is managed and operated by Microsoft, integrated with the Azure portal and Resource Manager, and works with familiar VMware interfaces.

Because vSphere runs on bare metal, customers get the same performance and resilience they're used to on-premises, without performance penalties associated with nested virtualization. To increase performance and reliability of AVS storage, vSAN all-flash and hybrid storage are used. Within AVS clusters, NSX-T enables software-defined networking for easy connectivity to Azure backbone networks and compatibility with on-premises networks. vCenter running in the AVS SDDC cluster manages the VMware components.

Microsoft and VMware jointly developed AVS, with Microsoft acting as the operator. Microsoft provides the initial environment and periodic software updates and fixes; resolves failures of the hypervisor, the server, or the network; and provides support. Azure native services are also fully integrated into the service.

An Azure VMware Solution environment uses SRM to minimize downtime if a disaster occurs. By automating and orchestrating failover and failback, SRM ensures minimal downtime in a disaster. Furthermore, non-disruptive testing ensures that your recovery time objectives are met. Overall, SRM simplifies management through automation and provides fast and highly predictable recovery times.

In VMware's hypervisor, vSphere Replication is the replication technology for VMs. It protects against site failures. Additionally, it simplifies disaster recovery through storage-independent, VM-centric replication. vSphere Replication can be configured per VM, allowing you to choose which virtual machines to replicate.

vCenter Server Recovery Manager allows you to plan, test, and run VM recovery between protected vCenter Server sites and recovery vCenter Server sites. SRM can handle the following two DR scenarios with Azure VMware Solution:

- **Scenario 1:** Private cloud disaster recovery using VMware to Azure

- **Scenario 2:** Disaster recovery using a primary Azure VMware Solution and a secondary Azure VMware Solution

A variety of recovery methods can be implemented with SRM, including the following. A planned migration starts when primary and secondary Azure VMware Solution sites are fully operational. The migration of virtual machines from the protected site to the recovery site is done orderly so that no data loss occurs during the process.

An Azure VMware Solution site that is protected can be brought back online using SRM when it becomes unavailable. The site Recovery Manager minimizes data loss and system downtime by orchestrating the recovery process with replication mechanisms.

By combining SRM with vSphere Replication, Azure VMware Solution only protects individual virtual machines.

In bidirectional protection, VMs are protected in both directions using a pair of SRM sites. VMs on each site can be protected and recovered simultaneously, but for different sets of VMs.

AVS private cloud deployment requires a few prerequisites to be in place:

- On-premises ExpressRoute connectivity to Azure VMware Solution

- Make sure that appropriate network ports are open between on-premises and Azure VMware Solution for SRM and vSphere Replication.

- For DNS resolution between on-premises SRM and the virtual cloud appliances

- As a minimum, running Site Recovery Manager 8.3.1

The installation can start once all prerequisites are met. Table 5-15 lists all firewall ports required to be allowed.

Table 5-15. *All Firewall Ports Required Between the Source and the Destination for SRM*

Protocol	Source	Destination	Port
	ESXi host	vSphere Replication appliance on the recovery site	31031
HTTPS	Site Recovery Manager server	Site Recovery Manager server on target site	9086
HTTPS	vCenter server	Site Recovery Manager server	9086
HTTPS	vSphere web client	Site Recovery Manager	9086
HTTPS	Site Recovery Manager	vSphere Replication appliance on the recovery and protected sites	8043
HTTPS	Web browser	Site Recovery Manager appliance	5480
TCP	Site Recovery Manager	Oracle Database Server	1526
TCP	Site Recovery Manager	Oracle Database Server	1521
TCP	Site Recovery Manager	Microsoft SQL Server	1433
TCP and UDP	Site Recovery Manager server on the recovery site.	Recovery site ESXi host	902
HTTPS	vSphere web client	Site Recovery Manager appliance	443

(*continued*)

Table 5-15. (*continued*)

Protocol	Source	Destination	Port
HTTPS	Site Recovery Manager HTML 5 user interface	Site Recovery Manager	443
HTTPS	Site Recovery Manager on the recovery site	Recovery site ESXi host	443
HTTPS	Site Recovery Manager	Platform Services Controller and vCenter Server	443
HTTPS	Site Recovery Manager	Platform Services Controller	443
HTTPS	Site Recovery Manager	vCenter server	443
HTTPS	Site Recovery Manager	vCenter server	443
HTTPS	Site Recovery Manager Server appliance	Site Recovery Manager server appliance on target site	443
HTTPS	vCenter server	Site Recovery Manager server appliance	443
TCP	ESXi host on the source site	vSphere Replication server at the target site	32032
HTTPS	vCenter server	Remote Platform Services Controller	443
HTTPS	Site Recovery Manager server	Site Recovery Manager server on the target site	9086
	ESXi host	vSphere Replication appliance on the recovery site	44046

Deploy a Monitoring Solution Using VMware vROPS

Monitoring system resources is possible with VMware vRealize Operations Manager, a platform for operations management. Applications or infrastructure objects (physical and virtual) can make up these system resources. Monitoring and managing VMware private cloud components such as vCenter, ESXi, NSX-T, vSAN, and VMware HCX is typically done with vRealize Operations. Each Azure VMware Solution private cloud includes dedicated deployments of vCenter, NSX-T, vSAN, and HCX.

The following prerequisites should be meet:

- Installation of the vRealize Operations Manager

- A VPN or Azure ExpressRoute configured between the on-premises VMware Solution SDDC and Azure

- A private cloud deployed in Azure for VMware Solution

Deployment Model 1: On-premises vRealize Operations managing Azure VMware solutions

Customers typically use vRealize Operations to manage one or more vCenters domains on-premises. To provision an Azure VMware Solution private cloud, they connect their on-premises environment with the private cloud using an Azure ExpressRoute or Layer 3 VPN.

You create an adapter instance for the Azure VMware Solution private cloud resources to extend the vRealize Operations capabilities. The data is collected from the Azure VMware Solution private cloud and brought into vRealize Operations. On-premises vRealize Operations Manager can be directly connected to vCenter and NSX-T Manager on Azure VMware Solution. The Azure VMware Solution private cloud can also be used to deploy vRealize Operations remote collectors. Data collected from the private cloud is compressed and encrypted before sending it to the vRealize Operations Manager running on-premises over the ExpressRoute or VPN network.

Azure VMware Solution cloud accounts must be added to vRealize Operations to monitor Azure VMware Solution instances from On-Premises vROPS.

To add, perform the following steps:

> **Step 1:** In the left menu of vROPS Manager, click Data Sources ➤ Integrations.

> **Step 2:** In the Accounts tab, choose Add Account ➤ Azure VMware Solution.

> **Step 3:** Provide the Azure VMware Solution configuration as per Table 5-16.

Table 5-16. *Fields and Values to Connect vROPS*

Field	Value
Subscription ID	Enter the Subscription IDs for Microsoft Azure.
Directory ID	Enter the Azure Active Directory tenant ID here.
Credential	Click the plug-in sign to enter the credentials used to access the Azure VMware Solution.
Collector/Group	Select the collector or collector group that manages the cloud account.

Step 4: Click Validate Connection to validate the connection and click Save.

Additionally, you can configure desired AVS private cloud vCenter, vSAN, and NSX-T adapter.

Adapters for Service Discovery are optional. Configuring the Azure VMware Solution Service Discovery adapter is similar to setting up vCenter Service Discovery.

Deployment Model 2: vRealize Operations deployed on Azure VMware Solution.

A vSphere cluster in a private cloud is another option for deploying vRealize Operations Manager. The vRealize Operations instance can be configured to collect data from vCenter, ESXi, NSX-T, vSAN, and HCX once it is deployed.

Through specialized analytic algorithms, VMware vRealize Operations Manager tracks and analyzes multiple data sources in the SDDC virtual infrastructure. vRealize Operations Manager uses these algorithms to learn and predict the behavior of every object it monitors. vRealize Operations Manager provides views, reports, and dashboards accessible to VMware Administrators and system consumers.

The Operations Management layer is the management component of a virtual infrastructure. This component enables the following use cases.

Continuous performance optimization:

- Intelligent remediation

- Automated workload balancing

- Unified operations

- Continuous and automated workload placement throughout a VM's lifecycle

- 360-degree troubleshooting

- Automated host-based placement, driven by business intent
- Native SDDC integrations
- Predictive Distributed Resource Scheduler (DRS)

Efficient capacity management and planning:

- Global operations view within vCenter
- Reclaim and right-size virtual resources
- Integration with Wavefront by VMware for application-level monitoring
- Correlate business and operational insights
- Configuration and compliance monitoring
- Capacity planning
- Open and extensible platform

Figure 5-30 provides an overview of on-premises deployment.

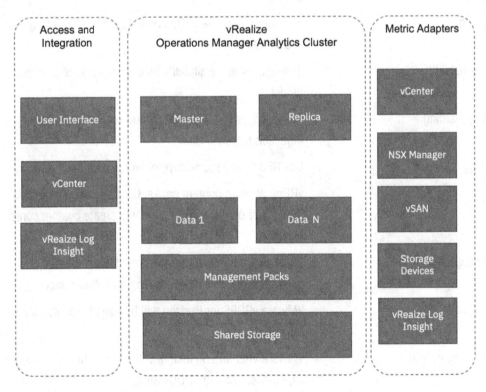

Figure 5-30. *VMware vROPS*

Table 5-17 illustrates the key features associated with vROPS.

Table 5-17. *Firewall Features and Descriptions of Various Services of vROPS*

Feature	Description
Performance monitoring and analytics	Collection of key performance metrics for analysis and troubleshooting
Capacity management and planning	Visibility on-demand and allocated capacity
vSphere security and compliance	Customize compliance policies to find non-compliant objects
Remediation and troubleshooting Metric correlation	Correlation between metrics to find trends during troubleshooting
Dashboards and reporting	vROps provides a new automation tool to create new dashboards.
Log integration	Integration with vRealize Log Insight
vRO workflows	Improved management and action workflows based on triggered alerts
Clustering	Join more than one vROps node to increase capacity and availability
High availability	Increase vROps availability with a clustered deployment model.
Event forwarding	Forward logs to a different Syslog server or another ingestion target.
Archiving	Use NFS storage to archive older log data.
Content packs	vROps VMware content packs, Content Pack Marketplace for third-party packs, and the ability to create custom content packs
vSAN integration	vSAN aware for performance optimization on vSAN operations like resync operations and slack space
VDI integration	VMware vROPS for Horizon will be used to monitor VDI Environment.
vRealize Log Insight	VMware vRLI for Log Insight will be used to monitor logging capabilities withing SDDC stack.

Table 5-18 provides a list of firewall ports required to be allowed.

Table 5-18. *All Firewall Ports Required Between the Source and the Destination for SRM*

Protocol	Source	Destination	Port
TCP	Analytics nodes and remote collectors	vCenter server	443
TCP	Analytics nodes and remote collectors	External resources	5989
TCP	vRealize Operations Manager	vSphere 5.x	10433
REST	vCenter server	vRealize Operations Manager	443
TCP	Analytics nodes and remote collectors	External resources	22
TCP	Analytics nodes and remote collectors	External resources	
TCP, UDP	Witness node	External resources	53
UDP	Data node	Witness node	443
UDP	Witness node	External resources	123
TCP	Witness node	Data node	443
TCP	Witness node	Data node	80
UDP	Witness node	Master node	123
UDP	Witness node	Replica node	123
HTTPS	Application Remote Collector	VCenter	443
TCP	Endpoint VM	Application Remote Collector	8999
TCP	Endpoint VM	Application Remote Collector	5480
HTTPS	Master node	Application Remote Collector	9000
TCP/SSL	Master node	Application Remote Collector	8883
TCP	Data node	Remote Collector	80
TCP	Data node	Data node	80
TCP	Remote Collector	Data node	80
TCP	Data node	Remote Collector	443
TCP	Data node	Data node	443

(*continued*)

Table 5-18. (*continued*)

Protocol	Source	Destination	Port
TCP	Data node	Master node	6061
TCP	Data node	Replica node	6061
TCP	Data node	Data node	10000
TCP	Data node	Data node	10002-10010
UDP	Data node	Data node	10002-10010
TCP	Data node	Master node	20002-20010
UDP	Data node	Master node	20002-20010
TCP	Data node	Master node	5433
TCP	Data node	Replica node	5433
TCP	Data node	Localhost	5432
TCP	Data node	Data node	7001
TCP	Data node	Data node	9042
UDP	Data node	Master node	123
UDP	Data node	Replica node	123
TCP	End Point Operations Management Agent	Analytics node	443
TCP	End Point Operations Management Agent	Remote Collector	443
TCP	Analytics nodes and Remote Collectors	External resources	443
TCP, UDP	Analytics nodes and Remote Collectors	External resources	53
TCP	Analytics nodes and Remote Collectors	External resources	389
TCP	Analytics nodes and Remote Collectors	External resources	636
TCP	Analytics nodes and Remote Collectors	External resources	3268, 3269
UDP	Analytics nodes and Remote Collectors	External resources	123
TCP	Analytics nodes and Remote Collectors	External resources	25
UDP	Analytics nodes and Remote Collectors	External resources	161
TCP/SSL	Endpoint VM	Application Remote Collector	4505

(*continued*)

Table 5-18. (*continued*)

Protocol	Source	Destination	Port
TCP/SSL	Endpoint VM	Application Remote Collector	4506
TCP	Endpoint VM	Application Remote Collector	8883
TCP	Witness node	External resources	22
UDP	Data node	Replica node	20002-20010
TCP	Data node	Replica node	20002-20010

There are several VMware vROPS features that cannot be used with Azure VMware Solution.

- The CPU and memory utilization of management VMs are hidden from end users, so their usage is not included in the utilization of hosts, clusters, and upper-level objects. As a result, the utilization of hosts and clusters might appear lower than expected, while the remaining capacity might appear higher than expected.

- Azure VMware Solution supports cost calculations based on a reference database.

- The end user has limited privileges on the vCenter Server on Azure VMware Solution. The collection of in-guest memory using VMware tools is not supported in virtual machines. Active and consumed memory utilization continue to work in this case.

- Logging into vRealize Operations with the credentials of the vCenter Server on Azure VMware Solution is not possible.

- Azure VMware Solution's cloudadmin@vsphere.local user has limited permissions. VMware tools do not support in-guest memory collection on Azure VMware Solution.

- It is not possible to install the vRealize Operations plugin on the vCenter Server on Azure VMware Solution.

- The end user does not have appropriate privileges to manage cluster configurations, so workload optimization, including DRS, is not supported.

Deploy a Virtual Desktop Infrastructure Solution Using VMware Horizon

VMware Horizon is a virtual desktop and application platform that runs in the data center and provides simple and centralized management. It provides desktop and application virtualization on any device. Horizon allows you to create and broker connections to local computers, virtual desktops, and Remote Desktop Server-hosted applications and desktops.

VMware Horizon is a desktop virtualization solution that gives IT control of virtual machines, applications, licensing, and security while providing access from a thin client.

VMware Horizon is a unified solution that fulfills requirements such as multi-user virtualization, application, and desktop virtualization and will provide the best ROI by consolidating desktops and reducing PC refresh exercises.

Figure 5-31 provides the logical architecture of Horizon.

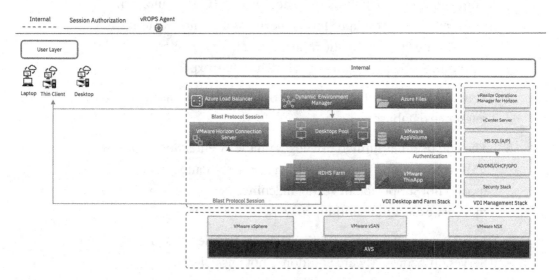

Figure 5-31. *Azure VMware Solution - Horizon*

VMware Horizon allows

- End-users to run applications and desktops independently of the device's operating system and interface.

- Administrators to manage the user and control their access from selected devices or restrict from all devices.

Let's focus on the deployment of Horizon on the Azure VMware Solution. Now that Horizon has been introduced on the Azure VMware Solution, there are two VDI solutions on the Azure platform.

VMware Horizon 2006 and later versions of Horizon 8 support both on-premises and cloud deployments. On-premises Horizon features are not supported by Azure VMware Solution but are available on-premises. Other Horizon products are supported as well.

Horizon can be deployed in a hybrid cloud environment using Horizon Cloud Pod Architecture (CPA) to connect on-premises and Azure datacenters. Your deployment scales up, and a hybrid cloud is built for business continuity and disaster recovery.

The Horizon pods are not stretched in CPA; they are each a separate deployment. From a network perspective, all connection servers for each pod must be located simultaneously and run on the same broadcast domain.

Horizon can be deployed in an Azure VMware Solution private cloud, such as on-premises or a private data center. The following sections describe how Horizon on-premises and Azure VMware Solution differ.

Private clouds in Azure are conceptually like VMware SDDCs, a term commonly used in documentation regarding Horizon. In the following text, both terms are used interchangeably.

To manage subscription licenses for Horizon on Azure VMware Solution, the Horizon Cloud Connector is needed. Azure Virtual Network can be used to deploy Cloud Connector alongside Horizon Connection Servers.

Horizon Management Deployment Considerations

The following are the Horizon Management deployment considerations that need to be considered during the installation and configuration of Horizon on Azure VMware Solution:

- Horizon in Azure VMware Solution, recommended for scaling beyond a single SDDC, places the management components in Azure and not within the SDDCs. The unified access gateways, located outside of the SDDC, ensure that only the network traffic intended for that SDDC is routed to that SDDC. There are several components involved in managing that SDDC.

  - VMware Horizon Connection Servers

  - VMware Unified Access Gateway appliances

- VMware App Volumes Managers

- Azure Load Balancer (ALB) for external/internal load balancing

- VMware Horizon Cloud Connector

- VMware Dynamic Environment Manager configuration data

- File shares for user data, profiles, and DEM shares

- Database server for App Volumes and Horizon events

- Azure Traffic Manager (ATM) for global load balancing

- VNet and subnets for internal and external networks

- Express Route Gateway for connecting the private AVS cloud to VNET

- VMware Horizon on Azure can be used with Dynamic Environment Manager

- With Horizon on Azure VMware Solution, you can use App Volumes, version 4 or later with a known storage replication limitation. Azure VMware Solution vCenter cannot automatically replicate application packages from storage groups with "not attachable" storage. Package replication is currently required manually. No support is available for App Volumes 2.x.

- Unified Access Gateway can be used instead. In Azure VMware Solution, UAG High Availability is supported, but requires multicasting between Unified Access Gateways.

- The Horizon Cloud Connector can be used to enable Horizon universal subscriptions and subscription licenses for Horizon VMware Solution. You will need to download the appropriate version. If you are running the Horizon Connection Server in a native Azure VNet, please download the VHD version of the Cloud Connector.

- With Horizon on Azure VMware Solution, Horizon Control Plane services such as Universal Broker, JMP Assignment, Helpdesk, and Cloud Monitoring Service (CMS) are supported. Horizon on Azure VMware Solution does not support Image Management Service (IMS) and Horizon Lifecycle Management (HLCM).

- Workspace ONE Access SaaS edition supports desktops that are deployed using Azure VMware Solution.

- Microsoft and VMware recommend running the Horizon Connection Servers and VMware Unified Access Gateways within the Azure Virtual Network due to the limits of the Azure private cloud and SDDC. These virtual clouds and SDDCs are effectively isolated. As a result, Horizon running on Azure VMware Solution is scalable.

- Horizon 7.x does not work on VMware Azure Solution and is not supported. When customers are deploying Windows 8.1 and therefore need Horizon 7.x, Azure VMware Solution supports Horizon 7.13 Agent combined with Horizon 2006 (and later) Connection Server. Once you move off of Windows 8.1, VMware recommends upgrading to Horizon 8.x for both Agents and Connection Servers.

- Horizon can now be deployed on Azure VMware Solution (AVS), starting with Horizon 2006 on the Horizon 8 release.

- The overall costs of running Horizon on Azure VMware Solution are broken down into four components: Azure VMware Solution capacity cost, Horizon licensing cost (Horizon subscription licenses and Horizon universal subscription licenses), and Azure instance types.

Horizon Network Considerations

The following are the Horizon network deployment considerations that need to be considered during the installation and configuration of Horizon on Azure VMware Solution:

- Fast Path uses Azure ExpressRoutes between the on-premises (or the Exchange provider facility), customer VNet, and the Azure VMware Solution private cloud (SDDC).

- For routing between ExpressRoute circuits, such as on-premises to SDDCs or between SDDCs, Global Reach is also required.

- The Horizon Cloud Pod Architecture works between on-premises environments, Active Directory, file servers, and Azure VNet Horizon PODs.

- Each NIC should reside in a different DMZ using dual NIC configurations, acting as a gateway between them. The login page should be the only page accessible after authentication.

- AVI, F5 LTM, or Azure Load Balancer can be considered for deployment to allow multiple Unified Access Gateway appliances and Connection Servers to be implemented in a highly available configuration. Load balancing with Azure Load Balancer can be performed on UAG and Connection Servers.

- Configure a public IP address with Network Address Translation towards the load balancer's virtual IP address if direct external access for virtual desktops and published apps is required.

- Creating an ExpressRoute to the tier 0 router is required for external management or access to external resources.

- With Azure Express Route, you can easily set up a dedicated network connection between your on-premises resources and Azure. You can use ExpressRoute to establish a private connection between Azure and your data center, office, or colocation environment, which, in many cases, can reduce your network costs, increase bandwidth, and provide a more consistent network experience than Internet-based connections.

- Azure ExpressRoute allows you to establish a dedicated connection between your network and one of the connectivity providers. These reliable connections can be separated into multiple virtual interfaces by using industry-standard 802.1q VLANs.

- Depending on your deployment use case, you may incur costs for all or some of the following types of data egress traffic:

  - **End-user traffic via the Internet:** You have configured an environment so your end users can access their virtual desktops remotely via the Internet through Azure VMware Solution. There will be egress charges for any data leaving the Azure VMware

Solution data center. Data egress consists of outbound data from Horizon protocols and outbound data from remote experience features (for instance, remote printing). While the former is usually predictable, the latter has more variance and depends on the user's exact activity.

- **End-user traffic via the on-premises data center:** By configuring your Azure VMware Solution environment, your end users will be able to access their virtual desktops from your on-premises data center. The Azure VMware Solution data center will be linked to your data center using ExpressRoute. You will be charged for egress charges for data that leaves the Azure VMware Solution data center and travels back to your data center. Consider an on-premises VMware Solution environment and an Azure VMware Solution environment configured with Cloud Pod Architecture. If that is the case, you will be charged for any CPA traffic between the two pods (although typically, CPA traffic is not too heavy).

- **External application traffic:** You have configured your Azure VMware Solution environment so that your virtual desktops can access applications hosted either on-premises or in another cloud environment. These other data centers will charge egress fees for data traffic leaving the Azure VMware Solution data center.

- You will not be charged for data traffic within your Azure VMware Solution organization or between the organization and Azure services within the same region. The organization will have to pay egress charges for any traffic to another AVS region or availability zone.

- There is no charge for data ingress (data that flows into the Azure VMware Solution data center).

- Since the data egress cost is priced per GB, the best way to estimate your data egress cost is by evaluating the expected data egress traffic in your existing on-premises environment (whether it is already virtualized or not). Estimate the various data egress traffic types separately as applicable. An example is SysTrack from Lakeside Software.

Table 5-19 list the firewall ports required to be allowed.

Table 5-19. *All Firewall Ports Required Between the Source and the Destination for a Horizon Stack*

Protocol	Source	Destination	Port
TCP	Horizon Agent	Horizon Connection Server	4001
TCP	Administrative console in browser	vCenter Server	443
TCP	Administrative console in browser	Horizon Connection Server	443
TCP	App Volumes Manager	Database	1433
TCP	App Volumes Manager	ESXi	443
TCP	Horizon client	Unified Access Gateway	443
TCP	Horizon client	Horizon Connection Server	443
TCP	Horizon client	Horizon Connection Server	8443
TCP	Horizon client	Horizon Connection Server	4172
UDP	Horizon client	Horizon Connection Server	4172
TCP	Horizon agent	Horizon Connection Server	4002
TCP	Horizon agent	Horizon Connection Server	389
TCP	Enrollment server	AD Certificate Services	135
TCP	Administrative console in browser	Unified Access Gateway	9443
TCP	Administrative console in browser	App Volumes Manager	443
TCP	Horizon client	Horizon agent	32111
TCP	Horizon client	Unified Access Gateway	443
TCP	Horizon client	Unified Access Gateway	4172

(continued)

Table 5-19. (*continued*)

Protocol	Source	Destination	Port
UDP	Horizon client	Unified Access Gateway	4172
UDP	Horizon client	Unified Access Gateway	443
TCP	Horizon client	Unified Access Gateway	8443
UDP	Horizon client	Unified Access Gateway	8443
TCP	Horizon client	Horizon agent	9427
TCP	Horizon client	Horizon agent	3389
TCP	Horizon client	Horizon agent	4172
UDP	Horizon client	Horizon agent	22443
TCP	Horizon client	Horizon agent	22443
TCP	Horizon client	Horizon Connection Server	443
TCP	Horizon Cloud Connector	VMware Cloud Service	443
TCP	Horizon Cloud Connector	Horizon Connection Server	443
UDP	Horizon Connection Server	RSA SecurID Authentication Manager	5500
TCP	App Volumes Manager	vCenter Server	443
TCP	Browser	Horizon Connection Server	8443
TCP	Browser	Unified Access Gateway	8443 or 443
TCP	Browser	Horizon Connection Server	8443
TCP	Dynamic Environment Manager FlexEngine	File shares	445
	Enrollment server	AD Domain Controllers	
UDP	Unified Access Gateway	RADIUS	5500
TCP	Unified Access Gateway	Horizon agent	32111
TCP	Unified Access Gateway	Horizon agent	9427
TCP	Unified Access Gateway	Horizon agent	3389
UDP	Unified Access Gateway	Horizon agent	4172

(*continued*)

Table 5-19. (*continued*)

Protocol	Source	Destination	Port
TCP	Unified Access Gateway	Horizon agent	4172
UDP	Unified Access Gateway	Horizon agent	22443
TCP	Unified Access Gateway	Horizon agent	22443
TCP	Unified Access Gateway	Horizon Connection Server	443
TCP	vCenter Server	ESXi	902
TCP	App Volumes Agent	App Volumes Manager	443
TCP	Administrative console in browser	Horizon Cloud Connector	443
TCP	App Volumes Agent	App Volumes Manager	5985
TCP	Administrative console in browser	Horizon Cloud Connector	443
TCP	Horizon Connection Server	Enrollment server	32111
TCP	Horizon Connection Server	Database	1521
TCP	Horizon Connection Server	Database	1433
TCP	Horizon Connection Server	Horizon Connection Server	49152–65535
TCP	Horizon Connection Server	Horizon Connection Server	135
TCP	Horizon Connection Server	Horizon Connection Server	8472
TCP	Horizon Connection Server	Horizon Connection Server	22636
TCP	Horizon Connection Server	Horizon Connection Server	22389
TCP	Horizon Connection Server	Horizon Connection Server	389
TCP	Horizon Connection Server	Horizon Connection Server	32111
TCP	Horizon Connection Server	Horizon Connection Server	4101
TCP	Horizon Connection Server	Horizon Connection Server	4100
TCP	Horizon Connection Server	vCenter Server	443
TCP	Horizon Connection Server	Horizon agent	32111
TCP	Horizon Connection Server	Horizon agent	32111

(*continued*)

Table 5-19. (*continued*)

Protocol	Source	Destination	Port
TCP	Horizon Connection Server	Horizon agent	9427
TCP	Horizon Connection Server	Horizon agent	3389
TCP	Horizon Connection Server	Unified Access Gateway	9443
TCP	Horizon Connection Server	App Volumes Manager	443
TCP	Horizon Connection Server	Horizon agent	22443
TCP	Horizon Connection Server	Horizon agent	4172
UDP	Horizon Connection Server	Horizon agent	4172
TCP	Web console in browser	Horizon Recording Server	9443
TCP	Horizon Recording Server	Horizon Recording Server	9443
TCP	Horizon Recording Server	Active Directory	636
TCP	Horizon Recording Server	Microsoft SQL Server database	1443
TCP	Horizon Recording Server	PostgreSQL database	5432
TCP	Horizon Recording Agent	Horizon Recording Server	9443
TCP	Horizon Connection Server	View Composer	18443
TCP	View Composer	ESXi	902
TCP	View Composer	vCenter Server	443

Summary

In this chapter, you read about the deployment methodology for AVS Solution, such as a deployment overview, deployment and connectivity details, post deployment information, how to configure NSX-T Data Center network components, how to deploy a disaster recovery solution using VMware HCX, how to deploy a disaster recovery solution using VMware SRM, how to deploy a monitoring solution using VMware vROPS, and how to deploy a virtual desktop infrastructure solution using VMware Horizon.

In the next chapter of the book, you will read about the management and security methodology of AVS Solution.

CHAPTER 6

Manage and Secure AVS

The manage part focuses on running and monitoring AVS to deliver client business value and continually improve processes and procedures. It's the capability to manage and monitor AVS services to provide business value and continuously improve supporting processes and procedures. It includes managing and automating changes, responding to events, defining standards to manage daily operations successfully, and achieving ITOps with code.

The security part focuses on protecting the AVS systems. Security is the ability to protect the information, procedures, and assets while delivering business value through risk assessments and mitigation strategies. It involves confidentiality, integrity, and availability of apps, data, and infrastructure.

This chapter provides the management and security essentials. By the end of this chapter, you should understand the following:

- AVS management and security essentials overview
- Day 2 operation on managing
- Day 2 operation on securing

AVS Management and Security Overview

Managing Azure VMware Solution based on the Microsoft Azure platform and VMware Products in SRE way. Let's get started by apprehending what SRE (site reliability engineering) is.

A VMware Azure Solution can operate under undefined conditions during a specified period. AVS reliability engineering maintains the ability to run without a crash by incorporating a subprocess of systems engineering. As reliability and availability are closely related, AVS's ability to run at a specific moment or time interval defined by a service provider and consumer is typically reliable.

© Puthiyavan Udayakumar 2022
P. Udayakumar, *Design and Deploy Azure VMware Solutions*, https://doi.org/10.1007/978-1-4842-8312-7_6

On-premises virtualization environments are operated by system and security administrators in compliance with security standards and compliance requirements. Cloud-based infrastructure evolved from on-premises infrastructure. Because public and private clouds are current, hybrid clouds are the future of digital transformation. Companies need to adopt agile approaches to work. Agile methodologies require features that reduce waste and eliminate unnecessary costs. Now is the time for VMware administrators to develop the skills of site reliability engineers to meet the demands of digital transformation.

Reliability engineering fundamentally changes the way infrastructure and security operations teams work. IT administrators are being piled on to replace manual, repetitive tasks with automation by using Infrastructure as Code (IaC) skills. AVS-specialized SREs require various critical skills, including software engineering, design thinking, analysis, business needs, functional and non-functional requirements gathering, design, deployment, testing, implementation, changes, and maintenance of well-engineered AVS systems.

Figure 6-1 depicts the traditional system administrators vs. site reliability engineering, which is a key change in the digital era approach.

Traditional System Administrators

- Repeat and Redo
- Manage the workload
- Console operations
- Configuration management
- Evolution of infrastructure, applications, and data
- Work on incident, change and problem tickets

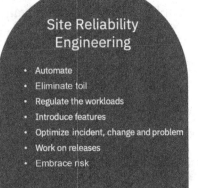

Site Reliability Engineering

- Automate
- Eliminate toil
- Regulate the workloads
- Introduce features
- Optimize incident, change and problem
- Work on releases
- Embrace risk

Figure 6-1. *View of SRE*

The goal of the SRE process is to advance efficiently, secure, and deliver a flawless AVS system of services for AVS users. The SRE AVS team works to ensure automation, reliability, availability, latency, performance, efficiency, change management, monitoring, emergency response, capacity planning, compliance, and security of services. SRE is a solution that combines software engineering, automation, and orchestration tools to ensure that applications run efficiently and reliably. A key concept in engineering includes a scientific approach to operations, an emphasis on automation to increase efficiency and reduce toil, and a data-driven approach to incident, performance, and capacity management.

SRE is in a solid position to become much more than that because it focuses more on the people and processes involved in improving AVS functions than on the technologies and software components. However, SREs on an organizations' staff may have a different description of SRE. As the next step, let's learn why SREs are demanding a modern digital transformation. To manage a complex VMware environment, companies have traditionally employed L1-L4 administrators.

The continuous shift in IT digital services to meet business needs is causing constant change. It is essential to change business strategies and develop a new set of principles and guidelines that support the best practices for achieving the desired outcomes for cloud consumers. With the hybrid cloud solution from SRE, modern businesses can achieve reliability, availability, velocity, flexibility, quality, recoverability, and performance.

When enterprises migrate to hybrid cloud-native, they must deliver more fantastic speed and excellent system and site reliability. VMware systems were traditionally managed and controlled via numerous processes, methodologies, and tools. Many applications, products, and infrastructure components are designed with reliability, but crucial non-functional requirements are not prioritized at the operational level.

The global markets expect this essential list of characteristics from every SRE:

- SREs are software engineers who specialize in reliability and resiliency.

- The skills of SREs should be centered around DevOps, DevSecOps, and AI-Ops.

- SREs should focus on delivering IT services without disruptions regardless of location and connectivity.

- IT Services should remain available from a user's perspective, but SREs should focus on service availability that should not fail.

- Developers should develop, deploy, upgrade, and maintain software engineering methodologies to create, modify, and update code, and write code on demand for better visibility into IT functions.

- SREs should handle operations like system engineering issues and Infrastructure as Code should be used to simplify deployments and configurations.

- SREs must work with the core product and development teams for production outages.

- As per agile methodologies, SREs should actively participate in releasing new features.

- Whenever possible, SREs should reduce tasks that are human-dependent, repetitive, automatable, tactical, without lasting value, and scale linearly as a service grows through automation.

- SREs should use data to find facts and reach conclusions about driving factors.

SSRE ensures that features are regularly delivered and services run efficiently with reliability by using system thinking, software engineering, automation, and artificial intelligence capabilities.

AVS SREs should always write code following automation principles for building, provisioning, updating, upgrading, decommissioning, rolling back, and rebuilding using the desired state configuration. AVS SREs should write code, apply policies per context, and integrate/reuse the existing code from GitHub with an automation environment. Figure 6-2 depicts the automation environment.

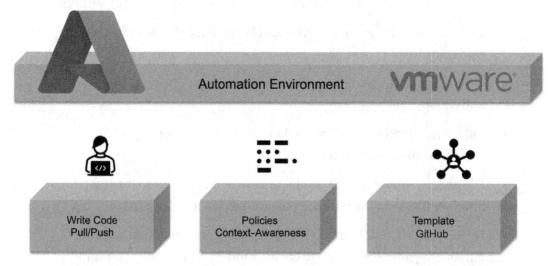

Figure 6-2. *Foundation for automation environment with respect to site reliability engineering*

Automated deployments allow AVS administrators to deploy Azure VMware Solution environments repeatedly, and AVS administrators can then design and deploy the environments as needed. With an automated method, multiple domains and regions can be deployed at scale efficiently. Additionally, they offer an on-demand, repeatable deployment process that is low-risk.

The Azure VMware Solution private cloud is a resource within the ARM, providing interaction with several automation tools. ARM specifications are typically supported by first-party Microsoft tools soon after their release.

Automation Management Considerations: Take the following information into consideration.

- Implementing an Azure VMware Solution private cloud could take several hours. ARM deployment status or the status property of the private cloud can be used to monitor this process. Appropriate timeout values are selected to accommodate the personal cloud provisioning process, whether you use a pipeline or programmatically deploy using PowerShell or the Azure CLI.

- According to the network topology and connectivity recommendations, you can preallocate address ranges for private clouds and workload networks. Include them in the environment configurations or parameter files. Address range overlap is not verified during deployment. A private cloud with the same address range can cause issues due to this lack of validation. When the field overlaps with existing networks within Azure or on-premises, there can also be problems.

- To provide the least amount of privilege, use service principles for deployment. The deployment process can also be limited using Azure role-based access control (RBAC).

- DevOps can be used for private cloud deployment, using pipelines for automated and repeatable deployments without depending on local tools.

- Scaling out automatically can increase capacity on demand, but consider the cost of adding more hosts. The price is limited to the quota assigned to the subscription, but manual limits should be implemented.

- Consider the impact of automating scale-in on running workloads and storage policies before automating it. RAID 5 workloads, for example, cannot be scalably distributed among three machines. The use of memory and storage may hinder scale-up operations.

- Scale operations can only be performed in one cluster at a time, so it's essential to consider orchestrating them across multiple groups.

- Consider the time it takes to add another node to an existing cluster when scaling an Azure VMware Solution.

- Some third-party solutions and integrations may not be able to cope with the continuous removal and addition of hosts. Make sure all third-party products are functioning correctly. When hosts are added or removed, this validation ensures there aren't more steps to refresh or reconfigure the product.

- To define configuration as a single artifact, use declarative toolings like ARM and Bicep templates. Azure CLI and PowerShell are command-line and script-based tools requiring a step-by-step execution similar to manual deployment.

- Azure VMware Solution and Azure native services can be deployed with third-party automation tools such as Terraform. When working with Azure VMware Solution, you must ensure that the features you intend to use are currently available.

- Consider the consequences of failure to deploy and monitor appropriately when taking a script-based deployment approach. Specifically for Azure VMware Solution, monitor both deployment and private cloud status.

- AVS administrators may also opt to automate resource creation within vCenter and NSX-T Manager within an Azure VMware Solution private cloud using vCenter automation, PowerCLI.

- In Azure VMware Solution, you can automate virtual machine provisioning using vRealize automation just as you would in an on-premises environment.

- However, Azure VMware Solution supports deployment models to a limited extent. Consider deploying vRealize Cloud Management or hosting the vRealize automation appliances on-premises.

- Terraform provides vSphere and NSX-T providers for the deployment of resources. A declarative approach is used to deploy these resources in the private cloud.

- Terraform must have private connections to the private cloud management network to talk to the API endpoints in vCenter and NSX-T Manager. If you want to deploy from Azure, consider routing the traffic to a private cloud.

Microsoft and VMware recommended best practices: Take the following recommendations into consideration.

- Set up a minimal private cloud and then scale as needed.

- A successful deployment depends on requesting host quota or capacity ahead of time.

- Before deploying subresources, monitor both the deployment process and the status of the private cloud. Once the private cloud has been marked as Successful, further configuration updates can be made. VMware and Microsoft recommend that you stop any additional operations if your private cloud is in a Failed status and open a support ticket.

- Make sure the appropriate resource locks are included in the automated deployment or have them applied via a policy.

- Scale-in and scale-out operations should have hard limits outside of quotas.

- Don't let quotas impact scale operations by requesting them ahead of time. Capacity isn't guaranteed by a percentage but rather the ability to deploy up to a specific limit. Maintain a regular review of the quota limit to ensure there is always headroom.

- If you use an automated scaling system, make sure it is monitored and alerts you when a scale operation has occurred. That way, you won't be surprised by an unexpected scaling event.

- Confirm cluster capacity using Azure Monitor Metrics before scaling
  operations to ensure adequate headroom. Before, during, and after
  any scaling process, pay attention to CPU, memory, and storage.
  Keeping an eye on capacity will ensure that it won't impact the
  service-level agreement (SLA).

Infrastructure as Code is used to manage automation environments for infrastructure in the digital transformation. This approach uses software development practices for infrastructure automation, and it emphasizes consistent, repeatable routines for provisioning and changing AVS solution and their configuration. Using automation, you test and apply changes to your plans after changing your code.

This book shows example code to perform Day 2 operations using IaC. IaC refers to managing and provisioning VMs, containers, and serverless platforms, either on-premises or in the cloud, via machine-readable definition files rather than interaction tools. SREs should distinguish between "configuration orchestration" and "configuration management" tools, both of which are considered tools. The deployment of infrastructure components can be automated using configuration orchestration systems, such as Terraform and Azure Resource Manager (ARM templates).

First, let's set up the display and look at how Infrastructure as Code works for those just beginning the journey. Recognizing this is key to the glory of Terraform.

New doors can be opened by refactoring a physical data center into an AVS private cloud one. By defining an infrastructure architecture based on lines of code, it established the concept of Infrastructure as Code.

What is Terraform? Terraform is an open-source tool invented by HashiCorp that permits AVS administrators to provide Infrastructure as Code.

Infrastructure as a Service at AVS SRE evolved from maintaining VMs to full engineering stacks. Let's review the foundation. Infrastructure volume and complexity are continuing to grow in AVS services. With inadequate time and engineers, the AVS SRE team is often unable to maintain this increase, resulting in slow provisioning, release, updates, patching, and resource commitment. Automation is used for daily SRE management tasks such as provisioning, adding, removing, configuring, deploying, and deprovisioning. It allows AVS SREs to reacquire limitations and clarity into infrastructure by elucidating AVS SRE at scale.

Infrastructure and networks are becoming more complex and extensive, making it increasingly difficult to manually manage risk, security, and compliance. A manual process can result in slower exposure and remediation of effects, resource configuration failures, and inconsistent policy application, leaving end users and downstream systems vulnerable to compliance concerns, threats, and attacks. Automating processes, apps, and infrastructure/cloud can streamline a SRE's daily work and integrate security from Day 1.

In the digital transformation, automation environments for infrastructure are managed via IaC. It is the process of collecting and provisioning VMs, containers, and serverless platforms, either on-premises or in the cloud, via machine-readable definition files rather than via interaction tools.

The difference between "configuration orchestration" and "configuration management" tools, both of which are considered tools, must be clarified by an AVS SRE. A configuration orchestration system, such as Terraform or VMware vRealize Automation Manager, automates the deployment of infrastructure components. Software and services running on-premises or in the cloud already that have been provisioned can be configured using configuration management systems such as Chef, Puppet, and others.

Here are the differences between provisioning and configuration tools. A provisioning tool is Terraform. It provisions the infrastructure such as virtual machines, networks, and storage where you would host an application; strictly speaking, it does not deploy the application. It is just semantics, as Terraform facilitates the deployment of custom server images with preinstalled applications. A configuration management tool like Chef, Puppet, or Ansible deploys and manages software on existing servers but does not provide the infrastructure components themselves. AVS architects often combine provisioning tools such as Terraform with configuration management tools such as Chef, Puppet, and Ansible to gain complete control over their infrastructure and application stacks.

If you're new to IaC as a theory, it is the method of maintaining IT functions through regulation instead of configuring IT resources in a console. Resources are any part of the infrastructure, whether on-premises or in the cloud, such as bare metal, virtual machines, containers, storage, backup, security groups, and network interfaces. As a whole, IaC enables SREs to execute automated tasks that include scoping, authoring, planning, bootstrapping, initializing, releasing, restoring, and destroying infrastructure components using CLI.

Many of the current tools for IAC can be found in the AVS world of digital transformation. However, as an AVS SRE, you have to make sure it is fit for the purpose, aligns with your AVS environment, and is both vendor and platform agnostic., wants state management and SRE, gains confidence in the tool, ensure you can orchestrate, manage configuration, deploy the software, implement continuous delivery, and control security and compliance via automation.

The method of building IAC works with the workflow depicted in Figure 6-3.

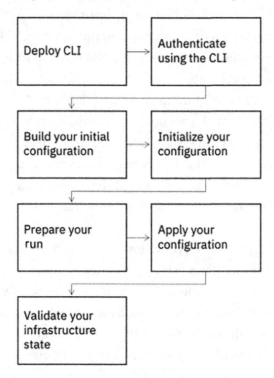

Figure 6-3. *Method of technical enablement*

This area is silently automatable and is not limited to the list below. As you learn more about different use cases, the site will grow. The following focuses on the getting-started area.

First responders should receive automatic alert notifications: When you are an SRE, you can visualize the best way to communicate with first responders: by combining alert notification solutions with SRE monitoring solutions to create alerts when an issue is identified automatically.

The notification solution can send notifications via various channels, including email, SMS, and messages, and integrate with enterprise collaboration platforms, such as Slack and MS Teams. Also, you can choose how each responder accepts information.

Controlling security centrally reduces sprawl: The problem is that both infrastructure and applications require security to be centralized. Additionally, static IP-based solutions do not scale with ever-changing applications and platforms in the hybrid cloud. Using the solution, SREs can manage, control, and enforce access to security based on trusted applications, user identities, and context awareness.

Protect sensitive information in transit and at rest: Data in transit and at rest should be encrypted in AVS; however, deploying cryptography and key management infrastructure is expensive.

IAC is based on the principle of idempotence. Idempotency means SREs run IAC code no matter what the situation is. No matter what the current state of the business is, you will still end up with the same agreed-upon and defined business state. This method simplifies provisioning the infrastructure and reduces the uncertainty of variable results. Stateful tools with declarative languages can achieve immutability.

IaC is characterized by immutability. SREs can implement an immutable infrastructure by replacing an existing infrastructure with new components. As an SRE, you must ensure that the new infrastructure is reproducible and doesn't allow configuration drift over time when provisioning it in a hybrid cloud. An immutable infrastructure empowers scalability.

Defining, previewing, and deploying a Terraform cloud infrastructure is attainable. The HCL syntax is used to create configuration files in Terraform.

The HCL syntax can be used to describe AVS SRE and the components of the AVS solution. Before deploying their changes, AVS SREs create AVS configuration files and make an execution plan. Following the verification of the changes, AVS can be deployed.

Azure VMware solution resources are built and operated using the Azure command-line interface. Using the Azure CLI, you can automate all parts of Azure. As a result, Terraform requires the Azure CLI. Using an Azure Cloud Shell environment is the most comfortable way to learn how to use the Azure CLI. Now let's examine various Microsoft Azure PowerShell VMware command lines.

With the VMware vSphere provider, Terraform can work with VMware vSphere products, including vCenter Server and ESXi. Virtual machines, standard and distributed networks, datastores, and other aspects of a VMware vSphere environment can be managed by this provider. See Table 6-1.

Table 6-1. *The Command-Line Syntax and General Descriptions*

Command-Line Syntax	General Description
vsphere_license	VMware vSphere license
vsphere_entity_permissions	For creating and managing entity permissions
vsphere_role	For creating and managing roles
vsphere_compute_cluster	For creating and managing clusters of hosts allowing for resource control of compute resources, load balancing through DRS, and high availability through vSphere HA
vsphere_compute_cluster_host_group	For managing groups of hosts in a cluster
vsphere_host	A data source to discover the ID of a vSphere host
vsphere_datastore	For naming the vSAN datastore
vsphere_storage_policy	For naming the storage policy
vsphere_datacenter	For naming the data center
vsphere_user	For naming the vSphere administrator level user
vsphere_password	Password of the vSphere administrator level user
vsphere_server	Managing the IP address or, preferably, the fully qualified domain name (FQDN) of vCenter server
vsphere_network	Managing the data source that can be used to discover the ID of a network in vSphere
vsphere_virtual_machine	Managing the data source that can be used to find the UUID of an existing virtual machine or template

Terraform provides the NSX administrator a way to automate NSX for providing virtualized networking and security services, using both ESXi and KVM hypervisors and container networking and security.

You can use the following federation resources:

- Tier-0 Gateway

  - nsxt_policy_tier0_gateway

- Tier-0 Gateway Interface

    - `nsxt_policy_tier0_interface`

- Tier-1 Gateway

    - `nsxt_policy_tier1_gateway`

- Tier-1 Gateway

    - `Interface nsxt_policy_tier1_interface`

- Segment

    - `nsxt_policy_segment`

- VLAN Segment

    - `nsxt_policy_vlan_segment`

- Group

    - `nsxt_policy_group`

- Service

    - `nsxt_policy_service`

- DFW Security Policy

    - `nsxt_policy_security_policy`

- Gateway Policy

    - `nsxt_policy_gateway_policy`

- NAT Rule

    - `nsxt_policy_nat_rule`

You can use the following data sources with federation:

- Content Profile

    - `nsxt_policy_context_profile`

- Service

    - `nsxt_policy_service`

- IP Discovery Profile

  - `nsxt_policy_ip_discovery_profile`

- QOS Profile

  - `nsxt_policy_qos_profile`

- Segment Security Profile

  - `nsxt_policy_segment_security_profile`

- MAC Discovery Profile

  - `nsxt_policy_mac_discovery_profile`

- Federation Site

  - `nsxt_policy_site`

- Transport Zone

  - `nsxt_policy_transport_zone`

- Edge Cluster

  - `nsxt_policy_edge_cluster`

- Gateway QoS Profile

  - `nsxt_policy_gateway_qos_profile`

- Edge Node

  - `nsxt_policy_edge_node`

- Tier-0 Gateway

  - `nsxt_policy_tier0_gateway`

- Realization Info

  - `nsxt_policy_realization_info`

Terraform's validation can be seen below. Terraform can be deployed through the Azure Cloud Shell. Whenever Terraforms releases a new version, Cloud Shell updates automatically. Nonetheless, if you wish to install Terraform immediately, you can follow these steps.

Test Terraform using the following code:

```
terraform version
```

Day 2 Operations for Managing

All right! You've built the backbone of the AVS solution in previous chapters, but how do you make it work? This section will discuss these and other topics of interest, focusing on the hands-on administration and delivery of the AVS to serve AVS end users. The AVS Cloud hosted solution provides you with the main methods of delivering this private cloud to AVS.

In this section, you'll explore the top six Day 2 tasks required to be performed on your Azure VMware Solution.

- Task 1: Change the CloudAdmin password on AVS and change the NSX-T password on AVS

- Task 2: Alerts and monitoring of AVS

- Task 3: Scale the AVS private cloud

- Task 4: Backup with Azure Backup Server

- Task 5: Configure VMware Syslog

- Task 6: Deploy a VM

Task 1: Change the CloudAdmin credentials on AVS and change the NSXT Admin credentials on AVS

In this Day 2 operations task, the AVS administrator needs to rotate the CloudAdmin credentials for Azure VMware Solution components.

Step 1: Open an Azure Cloud Shell session from the Azure portal.

Step 2: Revise your vCenter CloudAdmin password.

Step 3: On the Azure CLI, provide the following command:

```
az resource invoke-action --action rotateVcenterPassword --ids "/
subscriptions/{SubscriptionID}/resourceGroups/{ResourceGroup}/
providers/Microsoft.AVS/privateClouds/{PrivateCloudName}" --API-
version "2020-07-17-preview"
```

In this Day 2 operations task, the AVS administrator must rotate the NSXT admin credentials for Azure VMware Solution components.

Step 1: From the Azure portal, open an Azure Cloud Shell session.

Step 2: Revise your vCenter NSXT Admin password.

Step 3: On the Azure CLI, provide the following command:

```
az resource invoke-action --action rotateNSXTPassword --ids
    "/subscriptions/{SubscriptionID}/resourceGroups/{ResourceGroup}/
    providers/Microsoft.AVS/privateClouds/{PrivateCloudName}"
    --api-version "2020-07-17-preview"
```

Task 2: Alerts and monitoring AVS

Azure Monitor collects, analyzes, and acts upon telemetry from your cloud and on-premises environments. It does not require any installation. For Azure VMware Solution or on-premises VMs, you can monitor guest operating system performance to discover and map application dependencies. Log Analytics workspaces in Azure Monitor enable log collection and performance counter collection using the Log Analytics agent or extensions.

With Azure Monitor, you can collect data from multiple sources to monitor, visualize, and alert various data types. As well as creating alert rules, you can use your environment to identify issues, such as high resource utilization, missing patches, low disk space, and the heartbeat of your virtual machines. By sending an alert to ITSM tools, you can set an automated response to events detected. Alert detection notifications can also be mailed via email.

The software and underlay hardware components are continuously monitored with Azure VMware Solution. The following conditions are observed on the host by Azure VMware Solution:

- Processor status

- Memory status

- Connection and power state

- Hardware fan status

- Network connectivity loss

- Hardware system board status

- Errors occurred on the disk(s) of a vSAN host

- Hardware voltage

- Hardware temperature status

- Hardware power status

- Storage status

- Connection failure

Through Azure Monitor Metrics, you can see the list of metrics in Table 6-2.

Table 6-2. *Metrics, Service, and Type*

Name	Monitor Service	Signal Type
Datastore disk total capacity	Platform	Metric
Percentage datastore disk used	Platform	Metric
Percentage CPU	Platform	Metric
Average effective memory	Platform	Metric
Average memory overhead	Platform	Metric
Average total memory	Platform	Metric
Average memory usage	Platform	Metric
Datastore disk used	Platform	Metric
All administrative operations	Administrative	Activity Log
Register Microsoft.AVS resource provider (Microsoft.AVS/privateClouds)	Administrative	Activity Log
Create or update a private cloud (Microsoft.AVS/ privateClouds)	Administrative	Activity Log
Delete a private cloud (Microsoft.AVS/privateClouds)	Administrative	Activity Log

The following step-by-step walkthrough shows how to configure an alert rule.

Step 1: Log into your personal or business account on the Azure portal at `https://portal.azure.com/`.

Step 2: On the overview page of an AVS private cloud, under Monitoring, choose Alerts. Next, Nthe ew alert rule.

Step 3: Under Scope, choose the target resource you want to monitor. The AVS private cloud from where you opened the Alerts menu has been defined by default.

Step 4: Under Condition, choose Add condition, and in the window that opens, select the signal you want to deploy for the alert rule.

Step 5: Define the logic to start the alert and choose Done.

Step 6: To add an action group, select Actions. The action group determines how and who will receive the notification. Azure Mobile App push notifications, email, SMS, and voice messages can all be used to receive notifications.

Step 7: Create a new action group by selecting Create action group or selecting an existing one.

Step 8: Name the action group and provide a display name on the Basics tab in the opening window.

Step 9: You can choose Notification Types and names from the Notification tab. Then choose OK.

Step 10: If you want to receive notifications of events and take proactive actions, configure the Actions. From the available Action types, choose Review + Create.

Bicep is a domain-specific language (DSL) for deploying Azure resources using the declarative syntax. Bicep files are used to define the Azure infrastructure you want to deploy and repeatedly deploy it throughout the development lifecycle. Consistent deployment is achieved.

The following code enables AVS monitoring:

```
cd Bicep

az deployment group create -g AVS-Step-By-Step-RG -n AVS-Monitoring-
Deployment -c -f "AVSMonitor.bicep" -p "@AVSMonitor.parameters.json"
```

The Azure Resource Manager (ARM) is a service that lets you manage and deploy resources using the IaC paradigm. Access controls, tags, and locks enable you to provision, modify, and delete resources.

The following code enables AVS monitoring:

```
cd ARM
az deployment group create -g AVS-Step-By-Step-RG -n AVS-Monitoring-
Deployment -c -f "AVSMonitor.deploy.json" -p "@AVSMonitor.
parameters.json"
```

Task 3: Scale an AVS private cloud.

Scale the clusters and hosts to reflect the workloads you plan to run on Azure VMware Solution for best results. Hosts and groups can be scaled according to your application workload in a private cloud. It's best to address specific services' performance and availability limitations on a case-by-case basis.

An AVS private cloud allows you to scale clusters and hosts for your application workload. Specific service limitations should be addressed on a case-by-case basis.

The following step-by-step walkthrough shows how to scale an AVS private cloud.

> **Step 1:** Log into your personal or business account on the Azure portal at https://portal.azure.com/.

> **Step 2:** On the overview page of an AVS private cloud, under Manage, choose Scale private cloud. Next, select + Add a cluster.

> **Step 3:** In the Add cluster page, use the slider to increase or decrease the number of hosts to a minimum. Choose Save.

> In the above step, the deployment of the cluster will start.

> **Step 5:** On the Azure portal, go to the existing private cloud, choose Scale AVS private cloud, and choose to edit the cluster.

> **Step 6:** In the Edit Cluster wizard, choose the number of hosts, add a number like 1 or 3, and click Save.

Task 4: Backup with Azure Backup Server

With Azure Backup Server, you can implement a business continuity and disaster recovery strategy. Only Azure Backup Server allows you to configure VM-level backups with Azure VMware Solution.

Azure Backup Server stores backup data in the following places:

- **Disk:** Azure Backup Server uses disk pools to store data short-term.

- **Azure cloud:** Azure Backup Server data stored in disk pools can be backed up to the Microsoft Azure cloud for short-term and long-term storage.

Data can be restored to an alternate location or source using Azure Backup Server. The original data can be converted to an alternate location if unavailable due to planned or unexpected issues.

- For Azure Backup Server to back up VMs, no agent needs to be installed on the vCenter Server or ESXi server. Instead, use the VMware vCenter Server IP address or FQDN and the Azure Backup Server sign-in credentials.

- Workloads can be protected on disk and in the cloud with Azure Backup Server. You can manage offsite backup and long-term retention with Azure Backup Server's backup and recovery workflow.

- VMs deployed on a vCenter Server or an ESXi host can be protected using Azure Backup Server. VMs managed by vCenter Server are also detected by Azure Backup Server so that large deployments can be protected.

- VM folders in vCenter Server are detected by Azure Backup Server, which helps you organize your virtual machines. This allows you to protect VMs on a folder level, including all subfolders. In addition to protecting VMs in folders, Azure Backup Server protects any VMs added later.

- Azure Backup Server automatically detects new VMs daily. By organizing your VMs in recursive folders, Azure Backup Server automatically detects and protects new VMs deployed in the recursive folders.

- Azure Backup Server detects and continues VM protection when VMs are vMotioned for load balancing within a cluster.

- A Windows VM can be recovered from Azure Backup Server without restoring the entire VM.

Virtual machines can also be backed up using Data Protection Manager (DPM) or Microsoft Azure Backup Server (MABS). You can use this method for specialized workloads, virtual machines, files, folders, and volumes. For example, you can use this method for SharePoint, Exchange, or SQL Server.

The following step-by-step walkthrough shows how to back up an AVS private cloud.

> **Step 1:** Deploy the DPM or MABS protection agent on the machines you want to protect. AVS administrators then add the devices to a DPM protection group.

> **Step 2:** The DPM or MABS server must be located on-premises to protect on-premises machines.

> **Step 3:** For Azure VMs to be protected, the MABS server must reside within Azure, running as an Azure VM.

> **Step 4:** A backup volume, share, or file can be protected with DPM/MABS. Additionally, administrators of AVS can back up the bare metal state of a machine and protect specific apps with app-aware backup settings.

> **Step 5:** For online protection, AVS administrators can choose to back up to the MABS/DPM local disk for short-term storage and Azure for long-term storage. The backup to local DPM/MABS storage as well as the online backup to Azure is also specified by AVS administrators.

> **Step 6:** As per the AVS administrator's schedule, MABS/DPM backs up the disk of the protected workload.

> **Step 7:** On the DPM/MABS server, the MARS agent backs up the disks to the vault.

Task 5: Configure VMware Syslog

Diagnostic settings enable a streaming export of platform logs and metrics for a resource to a destination of your choice. To send catalogs and metrics to independent destinations, you can create up to five diagnostic settings.

You configure a diagnostic setting to collect VMware Syslog for your Azure VMware Solution private cloud. To analyze vCenter Server logs for diagnostic purposes, you store the Syslog in a storage account.

The following step-by-step walkthrough shows how to configure VMware Syslogs in an AVS private cloud.

> **Step 1:** From an Azure VMware Solution private cloud, choose Diagnostic settings, and then Add diagnostic settings.

> **Step 2:** Choose the VMware Syslog, all metrics, and choose one of the following options presented.

> a) In the Diagnostic setting, choose the storage account where the AVS administrators want to keep the logs and select Save.

> b) Go to the cloud consumer's storage accounts, validate that the insight logs vmwarelog has been deployed, and choose it.

> c) Go to Insight logs vmwarelog and locate and download the JSON file to read the records.

Task 6: Deploy a VM AVS private cloud

Azure uses virtual networks (VNets) to provide private connectivity between VMs and other Azure services. Services and VMs on the same virtual network can communicate with one another. Services cannot access a virtual network outside of it by default. However, it is possible to configure the network to allow access to the external service and your on-premises servers.

Spend some time thinking about your network configuration because of this last point. When using Azure services, you must consider the topology before putting any virtual machines into place. Network addresses and subnets are not trivial to change once configured.

In vCenter, click Hosts and Clusters, select the datacenter where you want to create the virtual machine and click the ESXi host. Once you have chosen an ESXi host, ensure that you have enough CPU, memory, and storage. You can use VMware vSphere Client to create a new virtual machine on the selected ESXi host by clicking Actions ➤ New virtual machine.

The following step-by-step walkthrough shows how to configure a VM in an AVS private cloud.

Step 1: Login to your personal or business account on the Azure portal at `https://portal.azure.com/`.

Step 2: On the overview page of an AVS private cloud, connect the jump box and browse to vCenter.

Step 3: From the vSphere client, choose Menu ➤ Hosts and Clusters.

Step 4: In the left panel, extend the tree and choose a cluster.

Step 5: Choose Actions ➤ New Virtual Machine.

Step 6: Go through the wizard and adjust the configuration you want.

Step 7: Choose New CD/DVD Drive ➤ Client Device ➤ Content Library ISO File.

Step 8: Choose the ISO uploaded in the prior section and select OK.

Step 9: Choose the Connect check box, so the ISO is mounted at power-on time.

Step 10: Choose New Network ➤ Select dropdown ➤ Browse.

Step 11: Choose the logical switch (segment) and choose OK.

Step 12: Update any other hardware settings and choose Next.

Step 13: Validate the configuration and choose Finish.

Day 2 Operations on Securing

Microsoft manages the AVS physical infrastructure components, while enterprise customers manage their VMs. This approach allows an enterprise to focus on what's essential to them, such as application modernization and end user experiences.

Azure VMware Solution adheres to the Microsoft security baseline, and the Microsoft Azure Security Benchmark offers recommendations for securing and using compliance. Table 6-3 shows how Microsoft Azure Security Benchmark groups security controls.

Azure VMware Solution differs significantly from traditional on-premises VMware environments in security management. In an on-premises VMware environment, the customer is typically responsible for all security aspects.

SDDC, virtual machines, and data in the cloud must be deployed and configured by cloud consumers. In addition to configuring the network firewall, ExpressRoute, and VPN, customers are responsible for managing virtual machines (including guest security and encryption) and implementing appropriate user controls via Azure role-based access control (or Azure Active Directory) and vCenter Roles and Permissions.

Microsoft's responsibility is to protect the software and systems that make up Azure VMware Solution. Azure VMware Solution is comprised of the compute, storage, and networking software that makes up this software infrastructure.

Microsoft is responsible for the physical facilities, security, infrastructure, and hardware supporting the service. Table 6-3 provides details on the shared responsibility model employed by Azure VMware Solution. As you can see, Microsoft handles much of the low-level operational work, leaving the customer free to focus on managing their workloads.

Table 6-3. *Solutions and Responsibilities of AVS Components*

Azure VMware Solution Components	Responsibility
Physical datacenter inclusive of host, storage, and networks	Microsoft managed
Azure regions	Microsoft managed
Azure availability zone	Microsoft managed
Azure edge locations	Microsoft managed
vSphere lifecycle	Microsoft managed
vSAN lifecycle	Microsoft managed
NSX lifecycle	Microsoft managed

Table 6-4 illustrates the AVS cloud consumer's responsibilities.

Table 6-4. *Solutions and Responsibilities of AVS Components*

Azure VMware Solution Components	Responsibility
Virtual machine	AVS cloud consumer
User apps, OS, data, device, and identity	AVS cloud consumer
AVS networking configuration and connectivity	AVS cloud consumer
AVS authentication, backup, firewall, and VPN	AVS cloud consumer
AVS end point protection	AVS cloud consumer
AVS threat and vulnerability assessment	AVS cloud consumer
AVS patch management	AVS cloud consumer

Azure security benchmarks provide recommendations for securing Azure cloud solutions.

A new feature or service is added to Microsoft Azure every day. New cloud applications are built using these services, and attackers are always looking for new ways to exploit misconfigured resources. Cloud computing moves quickly, developers are always on the move, and attackers are always on the move. What can you do to maintain the security of your cloud deployments? What security practices are different for cloud systems than on-premises systems? Is it possible to monitor for consistency across multiple independent development teams?

According to Microsoft, using security benchmarks can help you quickly secure cloud deployments. With standard recommendations from your cloud service provider, you can soon choose specific security configuration settings in your environment and reduce organizational risk.

Azure Security Benchmark includes a set of high-impact security recommendations you can use to help secure the services you use in Azure.

Security controls: These recommendations apply to all Azure tenants and Azure services. There is a list of stakeholders typically involved in planning, approving, and implementing each benchmark.

The controls are applied to individual Azure services in service baselines to recommend their security configuration.

Each building block is based on the Azure Security Benchmark; the components shown in Figure 6-4 are essential to security as per the Azure security benchmark.

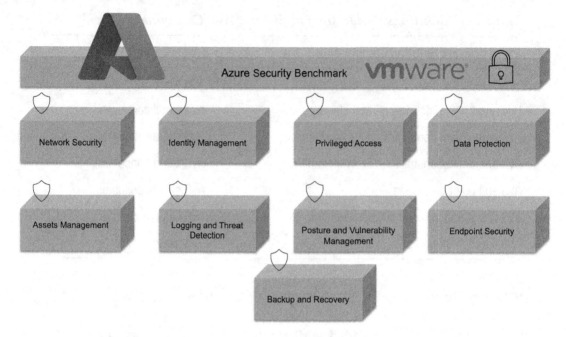

Figure 6-4. Foundation for Azure Security baseline

Network Security

As a result of applying controls to network traffic, network security could be defined as protecting resources from an unauthorized access or attack. This involves ensuring that only legitimate traffic is allowed to flow. With Azure, you can access a robust networking infrastructure that supports your application and service needs. Connections can be made between resources located in Azure, between on-premises and Azure-hosted resources, and between Azure and the Internet.

The following are very high-level guidelines offered by Microsoft:

- Deploy security for internal traffic.

- Connect private networks.

- Access Azure services via a private network.

- Apps and services should be protected from external attacks.

- Deploy intrusion detection/intrusion prevention systems (IDS/IPS).

- Security rules should be simplified.

- DNS security

Table 6-5 lists the AVS network security controls.

Table 6-5. *Network Security Controls*

Azure VMware Solution Components	Responsibility
Deploy security for internal traffic.	AVS cloud consumer
Connect private networks together.	AVS cloud consumer
Access Azure services via a private network.	AVS cloud consumer
Apps and services should be protected from external attacks.	AVS cloud consumer
Security rules should be simplified.	AVS cloud consumer
DNS security	AVS cloud consumer and Microsoft

Deploy security for internal traffic: Microsoft recommends creating or using an existing virtual network when deploying VMware Solution resources. Ensure that Azure virtual networks are segmented. Business risks should be taken into consideration. Any system that poses a higher risk for the organization should be isolated within its virtual network. Secure the system sufficiently with either a network security group (NSG) or Azure Firewall.

Using Microsoft Defender for Cloud Adaptive Network Hardening, configure NSG to limit ports and source IPs based on external network traffic rules.

Configure your NSG rules to restrict or allow traffic between internal resources based on your applications and enterprise segmentation strategy. For specific, well-defined applications like a three-tier application, this can provide highly secure deny-by-default protection.

Connect private networks: Microsoft recommends using Azure ExpressRoute or an Azure VPN to establish private connections between Azure datacenters and on-premises infrastructure in a colocation environment.

ExpressRoute connections are more reliable, faster, and have lower latency than a typical Internet connection. A VPN can be used to connect on-premises devices or networks to a virtual network, and VPN options can be combined with Azure ExpressRoute.

Use virtual network peering to connect two or more Azure virtual networks. The traffic between peer virtual networks is private and remains on the Azure backbone network.

Access Azure services via a private network: The Azure VMware Solution resources use virtual network injection, and they are deployed directly into a virtual network by Microsoft. There is no support for a private link for establishing private network connectivity.

You must create or use an existing virtual network when deploying Azure VMware Solution resources. Ensure that your application's trusted ports and sources are listed in the network security group assigned to your virtual network. A virtual network allows users to configure resources that aren't publicly addressable and can only be accessed within the virtual network.

Create, enforce, and log your organization's application and network connectivity policies using Azure Firewall based on your organization's needs.

Apps and services should be protected from external attacks: According to Microsoft, Azure VMware Solution resources should be protected against attacks from external networks. These include

- Attacks tailored to a specific application

- Unsolicited Internet traffic, such as DDoS

You can use Azure Firewall to protect applications and services from potentially malicious traffic coming from the internet. Azure virtual networks enable the DDoS Protection Standard to protect assets against DDoS attacks. To detect network-related misconfiguration risks, use Microsoft Defender for Cloud.

Protect your applications running on the Azure VMware solution against application-layer attacks using the Web Application Firewall (WAF) capabilities of Azure Application Gateway, Azure Front Door, and Azure Content Delivery Network (CDN).

Security rules should be simplified: The Azure Virtual Network Service Tags or Azure Firewall can be used to control network access on NSGs. When creating security rules, service tags can be used to alternative specific IP addresses. The name of the service tag must be specified in the source or destination field of the rule to allow or deny traffic to the service. Address prefixes are managed by the Microsoft service tag, which updates itself as addresses change.

The Azure VMware Solution service does not have a specific service tag. It is still possible to simplify network rules on networks in which VMware Solution resources are deployed using service tags.

DNS security: Microsoft recommends following the best practices for DNS security to mitigate against attacks such as

- Dangling DNS

- DNS amplification attacks

- DNS poisoning

- DNS spoofing

Ensure your DNS zones and records are protected against accidental or malicious changes by using Azure RBAC and resource locks.

Identity Management

Identity management in Azure Active Directory covers controls for securing identity and access control. It includes single sign-on, strong authentications, managed identities (and service principles) for applications, conditional access, and account anomaly monitoring.

Table 6-6 illustrates the AVS identity management security controls.

Table 6-6. *Identity Management Security Controls*

Azure VMware Solution Components	Responsibility
Provide a central authentication and identification system based on Azure Active Directory.	AVS cloud consumer
Secure and manage application identities.	AVS cloud consumer
SSO using Azure Active Directory for application access.	AVS cloud consumer
Prevent unauthorized access to credentials.	AVS cloud consumer

Provide a central authentication and identification system based on Azure Active Directory: As the default identity and access management service for Azure VMware Solution, Microsoft recommends Azure Active Directory. Your organization's identity and access management can be standardized by using Azure AD resources provided by Microsoft. Examples include the following:

- Azure Portal, Azure Storage, and so on

- Windows and Linux VMs in Azure

- Azure Key Vault

- PaaS

- SaaS

The resources of your organization, such as Azure applications and corporate networks.

Securing Azure AD should be a high priority for your organization. Azure AD provides a secure identity score By comparing your identity security posture with Microsoft's best practices. You can use the score to determine how closely your configuration matches recommended best practices and improve your security posture.

Azure AD allows external identities. Access to applications and resources can had by using external identities of users who do not have a Microsoft account.

You can integrate Azure VMware Solution into Azure Active Director using the CloudAdmin group. Credentials are provided for a CloudAdmin user in vCenter and NSX-T manager admin access.

Securing and managing application identities: Microsoft recommends that Azure VMware Solution not support assigning identities managed by Azure AD to its resources. Private clouds powered by Azure VMware Solution use vSphere role-based access control to enhance security.

Whenever you need to configure application permissions for Azure VMware Solution, you should use Azure AD to create a service principal with restricted permissions for the resource level to configure service principals with certificate credentials and fallback to client secrets. You can use this service principal to perform actions in Azure through scripts or applications that run on the service. Using Azure Key Vault with Azure AD-managed identities will allow a runtime environment like an Azure function to retrieve credentials from the key vault.

SSO using Azure Active Directory for application access: Microsoft recommends that Azure VMware Solution use Azure AD as an identity provider to manage Azure resources.

Azure VMware Solution private clouds use vSphere role-based access control to enhance security internally. With vSphere SSO LDAP capabilities, you can integrate your organization's data and resources on-premises and in the cloud using SSO. Azure AD provides seamless, secure access to all your users, applications, and devices and greater visibility and control.

Preventing unauthorized access to credentials: Customers can deploy Microsoft's Azure VMware Solution via IaC deployments, which may contain embedded secrets. Identify credentials contained within any infrastructure templates for your Azure VMware Solution resources with Credential Scanner. Credential Scanner will also encourage you to store discovered credentials in a more secure location such as Azure Key Vault.

Utilize the native secret scanning feature of GitHub to look for credentials and other secret information.

Privileged Access

Azure Privilege Access protects privileged access for your tenants and resources. The controls included here protect your administrative model, administrative accounts, and privileged access workstations against deliberate and unintentional risks. The following are very high-level guidelines offered by Microsoft:

- Limit the access of highly privileged users by limiting their access to business-critical systems.

- Reconcile access of users regularly through Azure AD using automated entitlement management on privileged access workstations.

- Implement the least privilege principle (just enough administration).

- Decide how Microsoft support is approved.

Table 6-7 illustrates the AVS Privilege Access Management security controls.

Table 6-7. *AVS Privilege Access Management Security Controls*

Azure VMware Solution Components	Responsibility
Limit the access of highly privileged users.	AVS cloud consumer
Reconcile access of users regularly on privileged access workstations.	AVS cloud consumer
Implement the least privilege principle (just enough administration).	AVS cloud consumer
Decide how Microsoft support is approved.	AVS cloud consumer

Limit the access of highly privileged users: Microsoft recommends that the Global Administrator and Privileged Role Administrator are the two most critical built-in Azure AD roles. Those with these two roles can delegate administrator roles to others.

- The Global Administrator or Company Administrator has access to all Azure AD administrative features and services using Azure AD identities.

- Privileged Role Administrators can manage role assignments in Azure AD and Azure AD Privileged Identity Management (PIM). This role contains PIM and administrative units.

As part of Azure VMware Solution, vCenter has a built-in local user named CloudAdmin assigned the role of CloudAdmin. As a local user, CloudAdmin sets up users in AD, and as a role, CloudAdmin creates and manages workloads in your private cloud. CloudAdmin privileges differ from other VMware cloud solutions in Azure VMware Solution.

Establish a limit on the number of highly privileged accounts or roles and protect these accounts at an elevated level. All Azure resources can be accessed and modified by highly privileged users directly or indirectly.

You can enable just-in-time (JIT) privileged access to Azure resources and Azure AD using Azure AD PIM. JIT grants temporary permissions to do privileged tasks only when needed. PIM can also generate Azure AD security alerts for suspicious or unsafe activity.

Reconcile access of users regularly: Azure VMware Solution uses Azure AD accounts to manage its resources, as recommended by Microsoft. Maintain user accounts and access assignments regularly to ensure they are valid. With Azure AD and access reviews, reviewing group memberships, access to enterprise applications, and roles is possible. Logs from Azure AD can be used to uncover stale accounts. Azure

AD PIM allows you to create access review report workflows to streamline the review process.

Azure AD PIM can be configured to alert you when there are too many administrator accounts. It can identify stale or incorrectly configured administrator accounts.

Azure VMware Solution private clouds are provisioned with vCenter Servers and NSX-T Manager. NSX-T Manager manages and extends the private cloud with vCenter and VM workloads. CloudAdmin and restricted administrator rights are used for access and identity management in vCenter and NSX-T Manager.

On privileged access workstations: It is critical to secure sensitive roles such as administrators, developers, and service operators with secured, isolated workstations. As an administrator, use Azure Bastion to secure user workstations.

You can deploy a secure and managed user workstation using Azure AD, Microsoft Defender ATP, or Microsoft Intune. Managed workstations can be enforced with a security configuration that includes

- Robust authentication

- Based on both software and hardware baselines

- Limited logical and network access

Implement the least privilege principle (just enough administration): For resource management, Microsoft recommends integrating Azure VMware Solution with Azure RBAC. RBAC allows you to assign roles to resources in Azure. A role can be allocated to an individual, a group, a service principal, or a managed identity. There are predefined, built-in roles for specific resources. Azure CLI, Azure PowerShell, or the Azure portal can be used to inventory or query these roles.

Through Azure RBAC, limit the permissions you grant to resources to what the roles require. Review roles and assignments periodically. This practice complements the JIT approach of Azure AD PIM. Permissions can be granted using built-in roles instead of creating custom roles.

NSX-T Manager and vCenter Server are provisioned on Azure VMware Solutions private clouds. NSX-T Manager for managing and extending the private cloud is used with vCenter to manage VM workloads. In vCenter, access and identity management are handled by the CloudAdmin role, while restricted administrator rights manage NSX-T Manager.

The CloudAdmin role is assigned to a built-in local user in Azure VMware Solution called CloudAdmin. The CloudAdmin user creates and manages workloads in your private cloud, and the CloudAdmin role creates and manages users in Azure AD. The CloudAdmin role in the Azure VMware Solution differs from other VMware cloud solutions in that it has vCenter privileges.

Azure VMware Solution also supports custom roles with the same or fewer privileges as CloudAdmin. Using the CloudAdmin role, you can create, modify, or delete custom roles with fewer privileges than or equal to those of their current roles. Roles with privileges greater than CloudAdmin cannot be assigned to users or groups and cannot be deleted.

Decide how Microsoft support is approved: Azure VMware Solution does not support customer lockbox, according to Microsoft. Microsoft may use the method of non-lockbox access to customer data to work with customers.

Data Protection

Data protection covers data protection control at rest, in transit, and via authorized access mechanisms. This includes discovering, classifying, protecting, and monitoring sensitive data assets using access control, encryption, and logging in Azure. The following are very high-level guidelines offered by Microsoft:

- Discover, classify, and label sensitive data.

- Protect sensitive data.

- Monitor for unauthorized transfer of sensitive data.

- Encrypt sensitive information in transit.

- Encrypt sensitive data at rest.

Table 6-8 illustrates the AVS data protection security controls.

Table 6-8. *AVS Data Protection Security Controls*

Azure VMware Solution Components	Responsibility
Protect sensitive data.	Microsoft and AVS cloud consumer
Encrypt sensitive information in transit.	Microsoft and AVS cloud consumer
Encrypt sensitive data at rest.	AVS cloud consumer

Protect sensitive data: Microsoft recommends using Azure RBAC, network-based access controls, and specific controls in Azure services to protect sensitive data. Encrypting SQL databases is an example of this.

Align all types of access control with your enterprise segmentation strategy. You can inform your enterprise segmentation strategy by locating sensitive or business-critical data and systems.

Microsoft considers all customer content in the underlying Microsoft-managed platform sensitively, and the company guards against data loss and exposure. Azure customers' data is protected by Microsoft's default data protection controls and capabilities.

Encrypt sensitive information in transit: Microsoft recommends complementing access controls with out-of-band protection against attacks such as traffic capture. Encrypt the data so that attackers cannot easily read or modify it. Azure VMware Solution supports TLS v1.2 encryption for data in transit.

Traffic on public and external networks must meet this requirement, while traffic on private networks is optional. Ensure clients connecting to your Azure resources can use TLS v1.2 or higher.

Avoid using unencrypted protocols for remote management. SSL and TLS versions that are outdated or use weak ciphers should be disabled.

By default, Azure encrypts traffic between Azure datacenters.

Encrypt sensitive data at rest: The Azure VMware Solution encrypts data at rest to protect against out-of-band attacks, such as accessing underlying storage through encryption. Microsoft recommends complementing access controls. By encrypting data, attackers are prevented from quickly reading or modifying it.

All data in Azure is encrypted by default, and there are options to encrypt sensitive data at rest on all Azure resources where available. As part of Azure VMware Solution, Azure manages your encryption keys by default, and it does not provide a way for you to manage your customer-managed keys.

The data at rest in vSAN datastores is encrypted by default using Azure Key Vault encryption keys. Key management is handled by vCenter operations using a KMS-based encryption solution. If you remove a host from a cluster, the data on SSDs is immediately invalidated.

Asset Management

Security visibility and governance of Azure resources are covered under asset management. Permissions for security personnel, security access to asset inventories, and managing service approvals (inventory, track, and correct) are included. The following are very high-level guidelines offered by Microsoft:

- Ensure that the security team is aware of asset risks.

- Give them access to asset inventories and metadata.

- Only use Azure services approved by the security team.

- Secure asset lifecycle management.

- Do not allow users to interact with Azure Resource Manager.

- Use only approved applications for computing.

Table 6-9 illustrates the AVS asset management security controls.

Table 6-9. *AVS Asset Management Security Controls*

Azure VMware Solution Components	Responsibility
Ensure the security team is aware of asset risks.	AVS cloud consumer
Give them access to asset inventories and metadata.	AVS cloud consumer
Only use Azure services approved by the security team.	AVS cloud consumer
Use only approved applications for computing.	AVS cloud consumer

Ensure the security team is aware of asset risks: In your Azure tenant and subscriptions, Microsoft recommends granting security teams Security Reader permissions so that they can monitor for security risks using Microsoft Defender for Cloud.

Depending on how you structure responsibilities, security monitoring could be the responsibility of a central or local security team. Make sure insights about security and risks are aggregated centrally within an organization.

Access permissions can be granted broadly to the Root Management Group or to specific management groups or subscriptions.

Give them access to asset inventories and metadata: Microsoft recommends that security teams have access to a continuously updated inventory of assets on Azure, such as Azure VMware Solution. Security teams often use the inventory to evaluate their organization's exposure to emerging risks and provide input for continuous security improvement. Provide your organization's security team with reading access to each Azure VMware Solution resource by creating an Azure AD group. Utilizing a single high-level role assignment within your subscription can simplify the process.

Use tags to logically organize your Azure resources, resource groups, and subscriptions. You can have up to three tags per resource. To all of the resources used in production, you can apply the name "Environment" and the value "Production."

You can automate the collection of information about software on VMs by using Azure VM Inventory. The Azure portal provides information about a software's name, version, publisher, and refresh time. Log Analytics Workspaces can be used to access installation dates and other information in Windows Event Logs.

You can specify which file types a rule applies or does not apply to by using Microsoft Defender for Cloud Adaptive Application Controls.

Only use Azure services approved by the security team: Microsoft recommends auditing and restricting which services users can provide in your environment using Azure Policy. Discover resources in your subscription using the Azure Resource Graph. A rule can also be created to trigger alerts when Azure Monitor detects an unapproved service.

Use only approved applications for computing: To automate collecting information about all software installed on VMs related to Azure VMware Solution, Microsoft recommends Azure VM inventory. You can view the software name, version, publisher, and refresh time for an application from the Azure portal. The install date and other information can be retrieved by enabling guest-level diagnostics and bringing Windows Event Logs into a Log Analytics Workspace.

Logging and Threat Detection

Logging and threat detection enables you to enable, collect, and store audit logs for Azure services and detect threats on Azure. By enabling detection, investigation, and remediation processes with controls within Azure services, high-quality alerts can be generated. Azure Monitor can collect logs and Azure Sentinel can be used to perform security analysis and retain logs. The following are very high-level guidelines offered by Microsoft:

- Enable Azure threat detection.

- Through Azure identity and access management

- By enabling Azure network logging

- To log Azure resources

- Use security logs.

- Set log retention.

- Use time synchronization sources that are approved.

Table 6-10 illustrates the AVS Assets Management Security Controls.

Table 6-10. *AVS Asset Managemnt Security Controls*

Azure VMware Solution Components	Responsibility
Enable Azure threat detection	AVS cloud consumer
Through Azure identity and access management	AVS cloud consumer
By enabling Azure network logging	AVS cloud consumer
To log Azure resources.	AVS cloud consumer
Use security logs.	AVS cloud consumer
Set log retention.	AVS cloud consumer
Use time synchronization sources that are approved.	AVS cloud consumer

Enable Azure threat detection: Microsoft recommends that any logs from Azure VMware Solution that can be used to set up custom threat detections should be forwarded to your SIEM. Ensure that all Azure assets are monitored for potential threats and anomalies. To reduce false positives for analysts, concentrate on getting high-quality alerts. Log data, agents, or other sources of alerts can be used to generate them.

Through Azure identity and access management: Microsoft recommends the following user logs for Azure AD. The logs can be viewed in Azure AD reporting. You can integrate the logs with Azure Monitor, Microsoft Sentinel, or other monitoring and SIEM tools for more sophisticated monitoring and analytics.

- **Login logs:** Information about how managed applications are used and how users log in

- **Audit logs:** Tracking of all changes made by Azure AD features through logs. Any change made to Azure AD resources, including users, apps, groups, roles, and policies, is recorded in audit logs.

- **Risky sign-ins:** Signs that someone is trying to log in to an account that isn't theirs.

- **Users flagged for risk:** An indication that a user account may have been compromised.

You can also receive notifications from Microsoft Defender for Cloud if you experience an excessive number of failed authentication attempts. You can also receive alerts if any accounts in the subscription are deprecated.

Besides monitoring basic security hygiene, Microsoft Defender for Cloud's Threat Protection module can collect more detailed security alerts from

- Azure compute resources such as virtual machines, containers, and app services

- Azure data resources such as Azure SQL Database and Azure Storage

- Service layers in Azure

This enables you to see any anomalies within an account.

By enabling Azure network logging: Microsoft recommends that you enable and collect NSG resource logs, NSG flow logs, Azure Firewall logs, and Web Application Firewall (WAF) logs. For incident investigation, threat hunting, and generating security alerts, analyze the logs to support security analysis. Flow logs can be sent to an Azure Monitor Log Analytics workspace for traffic analytics analysis.

Additionally, DNS query logs can be collected to help correlate network data. You can implement a DNS logging solution from Azure Marketplace to satisfy your organization's needs.

To log Azure resources: Microsoft recommends enabling automatic access to activity logs. PUT, POST, and DELETE operations are logged for your Azure VMware Solution resources logs (except read operations such as GET). Activity logs can help you identify errors during troubleshooting and monitor how users in your organization modify resources.

The Azure VMware Solution should enable Azure resource logs. Resource logs and log data collection can be enabled using Microsoft Defender for Cloud and Azure Policy. These logs can be vital for investigations of security incidents and forensic exercises.

In Azure VMware Solution, audit logs are also created for local administrators. Enable audit logs for local administrators.

Security logs: Microsoft recommends centralized log storage and analysis to enable correlation. Check that you have

- Data owners assigned

- Permissions

- Based on the storage location

- The tools you use to access and process the data

- Retention periods for data

- It's best to integrate Azure activity logs into your central logging.

Logs from endpoint devices, network resources, and other security systems are gathered and aggregated via Azure Monitor. To query and analyze them, use Log Analytics workspaces. Archived data can be stored in Azure Storage accounts.

If you use the Azure VMware Solution, forward all security-related logs to your SIEM for centralized management.

Organizations typically use Microsoft Sentinel to store "hot" or frequently used data and Azure Storage to store "cold" or less frequently used data.

Set log retention: Be sure to set log retention periods in any storage accounts or Log Analytics workspaces you use to store Azure VMware Solution logs. If you haven't done so already, set the log retention periods according to your organization's compliance regulations.

Time synchronization sources that are approved: Microsoft maintains time sources for most PaaS and SaaS services its Azure platform offers. If you want your VMs to be time-synchronized, use a Microsoft network time protocol server (NTP). You should secure UDP service port 123 if you are setting up your own NTP server. Azure logs generate timestamps based on the default time zone.

To ensure the host's time and date are synchronized with other components in the vSphere network, you can synchronize the host with an NTP server.

NTP and PTP can't be used at the same time. Disable the PTP service and enable NTP synchronization. Furthermore, the manual time configuration is inactive when the NTP service is enabled.

Posture and Vulnerability Management

Controls for assessing and improving Azure security posture are included in posture and vulnerability management. Security configuration tracking, reporting, and correction in Azure resources include vulnerability scanning, penetration testing, and remediation. The following are very high-level guidelines offered by Microsoft:

- Ensure that Azure resources are configured securely.

- Keep Azure services configured securely.

- Maintain secure compute resource configurations.

- Make sure compute resources are configured securely.

- Ensure that custom operating system and container images are stored securely.

- Conduct software vulnerability assessments.

- Address software vulnerabilities quickly and automatically.

- Run regular attack simulations.

Table 6-11 illustrates the AVS posture and vulnerability security controls.

Table 6-11. *AVS Posture and Vulnerabilty Controls*

Azure VMware Solution Components	Responsibility
Ensure that Azure resources are configured securely.	AVS cloud consumer
Keep Azure services configured securely.	AVS cloud consumer
Maintain secure compute resource configurations.	AVS cloud consumer
Make sure compute resources are configured securely.	Microsoft and AVS cloud consumer
Ensure that custom operating system and container images are stored securely.	AVS cloud consumer
Conduct software vulnerability assessments.	AVS cloud consumer
Address software vulnerabilities quickly and automatically.	AVS cloud consumer
Run regular attack simulations.	Microsoft and AVS cloud consumer

Ensure that Azure resources are configured securely: Automate deployment and configuration of services and application environments with Azure Blueprints. Azure Resource Manager templates, RBAC controls, and policies can all be included in a blueprint definition.

Keep Azure services configured securely: Monitor your configuration baseline using Microsoft Defender for Cloud. For Azure compute resources, including VMs and containers, use Azure policies [deny] and [deploy if not already present].

Maintain secure compute resource configurations: Create secure configurations for all compute resources, including VMs and containers, by using Microsoft Defender for Cloud and Azure Policy.

Custom operating system images or an Azure Automation State Configuration can be used to configure the security configuration of the operating system needed by your organization.

Make sure compute resources are configured securely: To assess and remediate configuration risks on Azure computing resources, including VMs and containers, use Microsoft Defender for Cloud and Azure Policy. To maintain your organization's operating system security configurations, you can also use Azure Resource Manager (ARM) templates, custom operating system images, or Azure Automation state configuration.

Azure Automation State Configuration combined with Microsoft VM templates can help maintain security requirements.

Azure Marketplace VM images are managed and maintained by Microsoft.

CIS Docker Benchmarks can be used with Microsoft Defender for Cloud to scan container images for vulnerabilities. You can view and fix issues using the Microsoft Defender for Cloud Recommendations page.

Ensure that custom operating system and container images are stored securely: Customers can manage container images with Azure VMware Solution. Make sure only authorized users can access your custom images with Azure RBAC. Using an Azure Shared Image Gallery, you can share images with different users, service principals, or Azure AD groups in your organization. Secure access to container images in Azure Container Registry using RBAC.

Conduct software vulnerability assessments: VMs from customers make up part of the Azure VMware Solution. Perform a vulnerability assessment on your Azure VMs by Microsoft Defender for Cloud recommendations. Ensure that vulnerabilities have been fixed by exporting scan results regularly and comparing them with previous scan results. You can view historical scan data in the chosen solution's portal using Microsoft Defender for Cloud's vulnerability management recommendations.

The Azure VMware Solution can use a third-party solution for conducting vulnerability assessments on network devices and web applications. Don't use a perpetual administrative account when running remote scans, and make the scan account JIT provisionable. Scanning credentials should be protected, monitored, and used only for vulnerability scanning.

Verify vulnerabilities have been remedied by exporting scan results at regular intervals and comparing them with previous scans.

Address software vulnerabilities quickly and automatically: Customers can deploy Azure VMware solutions on their virtual machines. Implement software updates quickly to address software vulnerabilities in operating systems and applications.

Consider using a standard scoring program like the Common Vulnerability Scoring System or the default ratings provided by a third-party scanning tool. Use context to determine which applications pose a high-security risk and which ones require a high degree of uptime.

Ensure that your Windows and Linux virtual machines have the latest security updates by using Azure Automation Update Management or a third-party solution. Make sure Windows Update is enabled and set to update automatically for Windows VMs.

Run regular attack simulations: Penetration testing and red team activities on Azure resources should be conducted as needed, and all critical security issues should be resolved.

Ensure your penetration tests do not violate Microsoft policies by following the Microsoft Cloud Penetration Testing Rules of Engagement. Follow the Red Teaming strategy provided by Microsoft. Perform live penetration tests against cloud infrastructure, services, and applications managed by Microsoft.

Endpoint Security

This is a set of controls for detecting and responding to threats at the endpoint. In Azure environments, these services include endpoint detection and response (EDR) and anti-malware. The following are very high-level guidelines offered by Microsoft:

- EDR is used to detect and respond to vulnerabilities at the endpoints.

- Make use of centrally managed antimalware software.

- Make sure antimalware software and signatures are up to date.

Table 6-12 illustrates the AVS endpoint security controls.

Table 6-12. *AVS Endpoint Security Controls*

Azure VMware Solution Components	Responsibility
EDR is used to detect and respond to vulnerabilities at the endpoints.	AVS cloud consumer
Make use of centrally managed antimalware software	AVS cloud consumer
Make sure antimalware software and signatures are up to date.	Microsoft and AVS cloud consumer

EDR is used to detect and respond to vulnerabilities at the endpoints: Servers and clients should be able to detect and respond to endpoint threats (EDR). SIEM and security operations processes should be integrated.

With Microsoft Defender Advanced Threat Protection, you can prevent, detect, investigate, and respond to advanced threats using an endpoint security platform.

Make use of centrally managed antimalware software: Using modern antimalware software, you can protect Azure ML and its resources. Antimalware solutions that can do real-time and periodic scanning should be managed centrally.

- Default antimalware for Windows VMs is Microsoft Antimalware for Azure Cloud Services.

- Third-party anti-malware software is recommended for Linux VMs.

- When malware is uploaded to Azure Storage accounts, Microsoft Defender for Cloud threat detection can be used to detect it.

- Using Microsoft Defender for Cloud, you can automatically

  - Find popular antimalware solutions for your virtual machines.

  - Report the status of endpoint protection based on the latest findings.

Make sure antimalware software and signatures are up to date: Ensure that antimalware signatures are updated quickly and consistently. In the Microsoft Defender for Cloud Compute & Apps tab, follow the recommendations to ensure that all virtual machines and containers have the latest signatures.

Microsoft Antimalware automatically installs the latest signatures and engine updates on Windows. Consider using a third-party antimalware solution if you're working in a Linux environment.

Backup and Recovery

Backup and recovery protects controls that make sure VMs, apps, data, and configuration backups are performed, validated, and rescued at different service tiers. The following are very high-level guidelines offered by Microsoft:

- Regularly backup VMs, apps, and data.

- Make sure backups are encrypted.

- Check that customer-managed keys are included in backups.

- Mitigate the risk of misplaced or lost keys.

Table 6-13 illustrates the backup and recovery tasks.

Table 6-13. *AVS Backup and Recovery*

Azure VMware Solution Components	Responsibility
Regularly back up VMs, apps, and data.	Microsoft and AVS cloud consumer
Make sure backups are encrypted.	Microsoft and AVS cloud consumer
Check that customer-managed keys are included in backups.	AVS cloud consumer
Mitigate the risk of misplaced or lost keys.	AVS cloud consumer

Regularly back up VMs, apps, and data: Microsoft backing up your data and systems to maintain business continuity in the case of an unexpected event. Use guidance if you have recovery time objectives (RTOs) or recovery point objectives (RPOs).

Make Azure Backup available. You can use Azure VMs, SQL Servers, HANA databases, or file shares as backup sources. You can choose how frequently and for how long the backups should be retained.

For more increased redundancy, allow geo-redundant storage options to replicate backup data to a secondary region and rescue using cross-region restore.

Make sure backups are encrypted: Microsoft recommends protecting your backups against attacks, and backup protection should include encryption to protect against loss of confidentiality.

Using Azure Backup, you can encrypt your data at rest using a passphrase. Azure platform keys are used to encrypt backup data using regular Azure service backup automatically.

Using a customer-managed key, you can encrypt the backup. Ensure that the client-managed key is also included in the backup scope in the key vault.

Use RBAC to protect backups and customer-managed keys in Azure Backup and Azure Key Vault. You can also allow state-of-the-art security elements to demand MFA before backups can be altered or deleted.

Check that customer-managed keys are included in backups: Data restoration from Azure VMware Solution backups is recommended by Microsoft periodically.

Mitigate the risk of misplaced or lost keys: Microsoft recommends that you have measures in place to prevent key loss and recover from it. Protect your keys against accidental or malicious deletion by enabling soft delete and purge protection in Azure Key Vault.

Summary

In the final chapter of the book, you read about managing and securing the essentials of each building block of the AVS solution and a list of best practices to consider in managing and securing from Day 2 operations.

Thank you for choosing to read this book.

Index

A

© Puthiyavan Udayakumar 2022
P. Udayakumar, *Design and Deploy Azure VMware Solutions*, https://doi.org/10.1007/978-1-4842-8312-7

I, J, K, L

M

O

W, X, Y, Z

Printed in the United States
by Baker & Taylor Publisher Services